A

GLOUCESTER

BOY

A story of life in the 50's and 60's

A Gloucester Boy

By

Cliff Ballinger

With best wishes to
my very good friend.
Tina
from
Cliff Ballinger

Date of Publication
October 1999
2nd Edition February 2000

Published by:
Eastnor Publishing,
36 Tuffley Crescent
Gloucester
GL1 5NE

Printed and Bound by:
ProPrint
Riverside Cottage
Great North Road
Stibbington
Peterborough PE8 6LR

ISBN 0 9536268 0 6

First published 1999

CONTENTS:

Foreword

Cliff Ballinger was born in Gloucester in 1950, in the area known as Clapham. He Lived in Sweetbriar Street until its demolition when he moved to Matson, as did many of his neighbours.

This story is an autobiographical account of his formative years, giving a rare and varied insight into the lives of the people of Gloucester during the 1950's and 60's.

Cliff, a married man, still living in Gloucester, has written articles and provided photographs for magazines. He now presents a book about what he considers to be the best hometown anyone could have.

ACKNOWLEDGEMENTS

Special thanks to Roy Cambridge who encouraged me to write this book, without him I may never have started it.

Thanks to all of the following for their help in many different ways. Suresh Karadia, Mike Johns, Dido and Sheila Vance, Charlie and Molly Markwick, Carol MacPherson and Pete Lee.

Martin Kirby of The Citizen, for help and encouragement.

Last but not least, thanks to Cath for not complaining about the months she spent alone while I shut myself in the attic to write this book.

CB
1999

Dedication

I dedicate this book to all of my friends, new and old, and some that I have sadly lost touch with. I value them all. They are not many, as I can be difficult to get along with. Those who have made the effort, and have become my friends, have become friends indeed. I would like to name them all but they will know who they are. Anyway, they may be mentioned by name elsewhere in this book. If I have mentioned you and we have not seen each other for a long time, please get in touch. If I haven't mentioned you, get in touch anyway.

Cliff Ballinger

Chapter 1
Clapham

I was born in the early hours of the 25th January 1950, the second child of Cliff and Etta Ballinger, in a time so different to now that you would think it to be a different world. My mother who was Scottish, from the small village of Tranent in East Lothian, a few miles east of Edinburgh, told me she had just managed to hold on long enough so that I was born on Robbie Burns Day. My father was a Gloucester man, the Ballinger family originating from Upton St Leonards.

My mother and father had both served in the armed forces during the Second World War and were married just after its end. Their first child died soon after she was born, health care was very poor and living conditions for the 'nations heroes' even poorer. I was their second child born in 1950, my brother Gordon followed two years later. Both of us were born in Sweetbriar Street in the Kingsholm area of Gloucester, known as Clapham. It was classed as a slum with houses that had been built cheaply for manual workers and their families around 120 years earlier and had suffered from years of lack of maintenance by the landlords. They were terraced houses, two up and two down. My earliest memories are of the mouse holes that I am always reminded of when I see a Tom and Jerry cartoon. The mice seemed to have no fear, they sat in the small black tiled fireplace in the living room, looking around without a care in the world. I can still see the scullery at the back of the house, where a large belfast sink and one cold tap serviced two houses. This was where we had to wash ourselves and Mum had to wash our clothes, scrubbing them with an old corrugated tin washboard and wash the dishes after our meals. There was a clothesline across the back yard and a tin bath hanging on the wall, next to the outside lavatory, which was also shared. It always amuses me when I hear people discussing the softness of different brands of toilet paper, this one's a bit rough, that one's not as soft as the other one. All newspaper feels pretty much the same and that's all we ever had then.

One of my earliest memories outside of our house in Sweetbriar Street was when the Coal man came by, on his horse and cart, making slow and gentle progress, his horse going clip clop, clip clop, up the street. His cart was fully laden with sacks of coal. As he passed our door, a full sack fell off the back of the cart. The coal man didn't hear it fall, so there it lay with it's contents spilled out all over the road. Almost instantly, many doors opened and the women came out with buckets. In a few moments there was no trace of any coal ever having been there. That coal was a great help to people who had to watch every penny.

Many businesses used horses and carts and people cleared up any mess they made while it was still steaming. There was always a rush to get to it before someone else got there first. I was told me it was for use on their rhubarb. I thought it was a bit unsavoury, but it didn't put me off stewed rhubarb and custard.

Clapham wasn't a slum to me though, it was just home, the only place I had known. It was a place of wonder, the place that formed my attitudes and a playground that was safe for small boys to explore and act out the sort of fantasies all boys of my era grew up with. We had no television but could take our inspiration from comics such as The Eagle, The Beano and The Dandy. Dan Dare was always a favourite of mine, my friends and I imagined ourselves to be protecting the universe from the evil Mekon. We all wanted a raygun, though none of us had toy guns of any kind, we pretended that the piece of wood we ran around with was any kind of gun we imagined it to be. One minute we could be Flash Gordon, the next minute, Billy the kid and the next, a paratrooper fighting the Nazis. All with the same piece of wood as the main prop. I could wander all around Clapham and nobody ever worried where I was, one of my favourite places to go was the rec (recreation field) in Sebert Street, where there were swings to play on. I used to walk or ride my tricycle through the old foundry to my Aunt Ethel and Uncle Dick's house a few streets away in Counsel Street. They were old age pensioners and were really my great aunt and uncle. They had brought my father up as their own son when his parents had both died not long after he was born. My grandmother died from tuberculosis and my grandfather died from the effects of exposure to mustard gas while serving in the trenches in World War One. They left two brothers, Charles and Clifford. They were split up, Charlie going to other relations and Cliff going to Ethel and Dick Riley. Ethel was my Dad's natural aunt. They looked after him until he joined the 9th Lancers in 1937.

When I got to Counsel Street, I would run into the house, shouting 'hello Aunty, hello Uncle' and launch myself onto the old rocking chair in the corner of the front room and start rocking it so violently that it would move around the room. I imagined it to be a horse and I was a cowboy chasing Indians. There was no carpet to stop it moving, just linoleum which was very slippery.
Uncle would shout, 'stop that you little bugger.'
But Aunty would chastise him saying 'leave him alone Dick, he's only playing.'

Aunty Ethel left me that rocking chair in her will when she died in 1980 aged 94, it is now a valuable antique, I shudder when I think of the abuse I gave it then.

I was riding my tricycle to Aunt Ethels taking a shortcut through the old foundry one day when one of the back wheels went down a hole and threw me off onto a piece of corrugated iron which severely gashed my leg. A lady on hearing my screams came running to my aid, she knew who I was and took me home, I don't know who she was but I am eternally grateful for her help. The cut was quite serious and I was taken to the casualty unit at the Royal hospital in Southgate Street. The wound was stitched up and I don't remember much about it. What I do remember vividly is when the stitches were removed, the pain was so excruciating that I remember every detail of it and carry the scar to this day, but I soon got over it as small boys do and didn't lose any of my youthful recklessness.

I had friend called Paul Thorpe in Counsel Street, which gave me another reason to regularly make the short journey round to Aunty Ethel's. I found the biggest torch I had ever seen standing in the corner of Aunty's front room. It was made of tin plate and would have taken four large D cell batteries, alas there weren't any batteries in it so it had no life, but that didn't matter to me, it was still the best raygun I had ever had in my hands. I asked Aunty if I could take it to show Paul and she said I could but only if I was very careful with it as it belonged to Uncle Dick. I ran across the road to call for Paul to show him my prize raygun. A game soon started and we were running up and down the street zapping each other, using the lamp posts for cover, I was running to take advantage of this cover when I misjudged it and ran straight into a lamp post, banging my head and nearly knocking me senseless. During this collision my raygun suffered a serious dent about half way along the shaft, but worse still, I had to tell Aunty what had happened, but I needn't have worried, she was so concerned with the bump on my head that she hadn't the heart to tell me off. She said she would sort it out with Uncle Dick. What she told him, I never knew. I was a bit sheepish the next time I saw him but he never mentioned it.

Uncle Dick died not long after this incident and even though I was only five or six years old I can still see his face whenever I think of him, he had been a small slim man, who always wore a cloth cap. He had been a regular soldier who served with the Duke of Cornwall's Light Infantry from1911 to 1918. When the great war broke out in 1914, he was recalled from his posting in Bermuda to go to France as part of the British Expeditionary Force intended to hold the German army until more troops could be made ready for war. He was one of the brave men known as

3

'The Old Contemptibles' so called by the Kaiser when he derided them as a contemptible little army with no chance against the might of the German war machine. How wrong he was, he soon learned that men like my Uncle Dick should never be underestimated.

I spent even more time at Aunty Ethel's after Uncle Dick died. Mum and Dad were happy for me to be there, so it was like having two homes, but at Aunty Ethel's I got undivided attention not divided two ways, as it had to be at home, between me and my brother Gordon. I had another set of toys there that I didn't have to share, I was quite happy to play on my own for hours with tanks I would make out of matchboxes and empty cotton reels, powered by elastic bands. I got a stamp album which I kept there, I started my collection by taking stamps off some of the postcards Uncle Dick had sent to Aunty Ethel during his time in the army. I now have those cards kept in an album and wish I had left the stamps on them, they are wonderful to browse through occasionally.

I had a scrapbook too, with cuttings of the comic strip 'Bruin the Bear', that I cut from 'The Citizen', sadly lost now.

We had no pets at home, Aunty Ethel had a dog called Rufus, he was a mongrel who stood about 15 inches to the shoulder, I thought he was huge and compared to me, he was. Rufus was a gentle, friendly soul with a long brown shaggy coat. I would often take him, or he would take me to the rec, where we would run after each other and play together, throwing sticks, or rough and tumbling on the grass.

I didn't know it but Rufus was old too and when he died. I was inconsolable, he had been my best friend and in its way his death brought me greater sorrow than when Uncle Dick had died.

After a few weeks I asked Aunty Ethel if she would get another dog but she said she would take me to the pet shop and buy me something small. I chose two white mice, ironic really when I think of it, seeing as my own house was overrun with wild mice. My white mice lived in a metal cage, painted green and had the usual exercise wheel, I would visit them every day and take them out of the cage so that they could run around little obstacle courses I would make for them. They were the first pets I ever had and I loved them dearly.

I went to nursery school at St Marks, then to Kingsholm infants. I remember playing for part of the day and lying in a canvas cot along with all the other children and being told to go to sleep.

When it was time for me to go to junior school, I went to Widden Street, an old red brick building with large classrooms, high ceilings and windows so high up you couldn't see out of them. They had to be opened with a hook on the end of a long pole. I went to school each day wearing the same as everyone else, the school uniform being very important then. Grey shirt that was hairy and itchy, grey short trousers, grey woollen socks and black shoes, finished off with blazer and cap. These clothes weren't very much different to those that I wore out of school time, there were no fashion statements for children then, There was no such thing as a T shirt or sweatshirt, no trainers, just grey or white shirts, grey or black short trousers and black shoes. I only had one pair of shoes, so they had to do for school and for everything else.

Dad worked as a driver for the Bristol Omnibus Company who were the operators of the local buses then, he also worked part time driving coaches taking people on daytrips to the seaside and other places of interest. He was a hard working man who always had more than one job all of his life. Even with two jobs, money was always tight, but he provided for us and we never went short of lifes essentials. From my earliest memories, he had a car, it was the only one in the street. Most working men having only a bicycle, or a motorcycle.

One day, amid great excitement, the car was loaded with our luggage, we were going on holiday, to stay with Mums sister, for two weeks. The journey was a very long one, taking around twelve hours driving to travel the 350 mile journey, we went up the A38, through Tewkesbury, on through Birmingham, up Shap fel to Carlisle, right through the centre of the towns, there were no by passes. Over the border through Gretna Green and on through the southern uplands of Scotland to Edinburgh and finally to our final destination, Tranent.

Aunty May and Uncle Bill Langlands still lived in Tranent where Mum was born . This was the first of many trips we would make to Tranent over the years I was growing up. I had two cousins there, Victor, who is the same age as me and Jennifer, the same age as my brother, Gordon. They lived in a small flat, with only two bedrooms, which made it a bit of a squeeze when another family of four moved in, but it was all part of the adventure and nobody seemed to mind. In the mornings we would all sit at the table for breakfast and Aunty May would serve home made soup and morning rolls. They were soft fresh rolls that are a speciality in Scotland. Some mornings we would have porridge floating on a pool of milk, it was wonderful.

Tranent, being on the east of Edinburgh, not far from the coast, had lots of beaches near to it. We could choose any beach for the day and there would be hardly anybody there, our favourite was Gullane. The two families would usually go together so the four children could play together, running in and out of the sea, hiding in the dunes, or digging in the sand and making sand castles.

We also went to Portobello, a small fishing village. It was fascinating to watch the small boats come in with their catches of mackerel and crabs. I saw some people lying on their bellies on the jetty, curious as to what they were doing. I asked Mum, she told me they were poor people who were hoping for a free fish from a generous fisherman. Sure enough when the boats got close to the jetty a few fish were thrown up for the people to catch. We went on to the beach at Portobello and gathered mussels from the rocks and watched crabs in the rockpools. Altogether an idyllic scene far removed from the streets of Clapham.

I was always pleased to see home though. It's nice to go on holiday, but it's nice to come home too. I went straight round to see how Aunty Ethel was, I ran into the house shouting 'hello Aunty, how are the mice'? She laughed and gave me a big hug and told me she had missed me. She gave me some money to go to Tartaglia's ice cream factory, which was in Sweetbriar Street, across the road from my own house, to buy a small box of ice cream. They would assemble the box then scoop the Ice cream into it, Vanilla was the only flavour available. Then it was off to Mrs Redburns shop for a bottle of Tizer. I would run all the way, as soon as I got the ice cream so that it wouldn't melt before I got back with it. I sat at the table with my Tizer and ice cream and made a Tizer float. I would pour the Tizer into a glass, filling it only to about half full, then drop a spoonful of ice cream into it, it would froth right up to the top of the glass. I ate the ice cream from the glass with a spoon, then drank the Tizer, I repeated this procedure until I couldn't drink any more and then finished the ice cream on it's own.

Later that day, we all walked up Kingsholm Road, through the old cattle market, into Whitfield Street, where my Aunty Ina, Uncle Den and Cousin Hugh lived. Aunty Ina was my Mum's sister who had also moved to Gloucester from Scotland, so we had lots of things to tell them about our holiday in Tranent.

Their flat in Whitfield Street was in the basement of a solicitor's office that had been crudely converted into living accommodation the worst thing about it was that it regularly flooded when it rained. If the rain was heavy, the doors had to be sandbagged, sometimes that didn't work and things had to be stacked on top of the table to save them from being ruined by the flood water.

I stayed overnight there in Whitfield Street with Hugh, quite often. Hugh is two years older than me so I liked to play with him because there was always something I could learn from him. One thing I didn't enjoy learning from him though was how to count from one to ten. We were in the dark, damp coal cellar one day when Hugh decided he would teach me to count. His method was somewhat unorthodox. He had just got a Gat air pistol and he told me he would shoot me if I didn't quickly learn to count from one to ten. I remember the blackness of the place, the quietness, the cold and the fear I felt. It was a fear that I don't think I have ever felt since. He held the gun to my head and taunted me, to get it right or die. I did learn quickly and he never did shoot me, but he had me worried for a while. I soon got over it though and when Aunty Ina called us for tea there was a rush for the table and everything else was forgotten. We had egg and chips which was my favourite. At home Mum made us put our tomato ketchup on the side of the plate and dip our chips into it, but here we could pour it all over. Pouring the ketchup all over seemed to make the meal taste so much better. After tea we would play games of all sorts. Hugh had a magic robot game that answered questions you put to it. It was called 'The ingenious, amazing, mystical, infallible Magic Robot.' There was a selection of questions on overlays, world events, realm of nature, sports and games and countries and cities. The layout of the questions and answers, being in two circles. One for questions and one for answers. You pointed the robot to the question, then moved him to the answer circle, where he quickly spun round from any position to point at the correct answer. I still don't know how it worked. it certainly was a mystery to a young mind. Hugh also had a bagatelle with marbles we had to get into different holes. Uncle Den came in one night with a large luminous skeleton that danced on strings. He turned the lights out and gave us a show and told jokes and funny ghost stories. We laughed till our sides ached. I thought Uncle Den was a very funny man

7

When it was time for bed we had to get washed and brush our teeth then Aunty Ina would inspect us to make sure we had washed behind our ears. We could get incredibly dirty in the course of one day. When we got to bed we would fight with pillows and roll about on the bed we shared, jumping up and down and getting louder and louder until Aunty Ina would come in and threaten to 'scelp our asses' if we didn't settle down. It always worked, we knew it was time to go to sleep, after a little more muffled giggling.

I cannot remember my Dad ever making me laugh or playing with me at any time throughout my childhood, he was a serious type, who showed very little emotion of any kind, while Mum was an outgoing, very loving person. Dad never seemed to be around that much. I assumed he was working all the time, or playing cricket, which was his sporting passion.

Mum was with us all the time and was real good fun, she gave us all the love and attention anyone could ever want. She always wanted the best for us and tried her hardest to give us everything she could. She was a great cook and would make cakes and biscuits for us to eat. Everyone loved coming to our house, Mum made everyone welcome and would always give them something nice to eat. Her meringues were a legend, we couldn't get enough of them. She also made toffee, fudge and tablet (a kind of sweet favoured in Scotland). It always smelled wonderful in our house when Mum was baking. She was very talented and would make birthday and Christmas cakes for other people, she would ice them beautifully. Her talents were always in great demand. She always seemed to be busy, but never too busy for Gordon and me. We had been reading in our comics about Davy Crocket, so Mum cut up her old fur coat and made Gordon and me a coonskin Davy Crocket hat each. They were our prized possessions, nobody else had anything like it.

Even so, I spent as much time at Aunty Ethel's as I did at home. When I was there, it was just me and her and I enjoyed the love and attention she gave me.

Aunty Ethel took me with her every opportunity she had, she often took me shopping in town and I always enjoyed going with her. We went into the Co-op in Eastgate Street, where they had large mechanical cash registers with a row of levers on the front. When you made a purchase they asked for your dividend number, then they would line up the levers to correspond with your number. This was a way of collecting a form of discount that you could cash in when you had enough. I still remember Aunty's number, 13497.

She also regularly took me with her to visit her brother Ben Ballinger and his wife Gertie. My great Uncle Ben and great Aunty Gertie lived in Painswick in a stone cottage in Tibbiwell, overlooking a beautiful valley. It was quite a day out, we walked to the bus station and boarded an old green country bus. Then off we'd go, up the Painswick Road through Upton St Leonards, where Aunty Ethel and Uncle Ben had been born, up the hill, over Painswick beacon and into Painswick village. It takes only about fifteen minutes by car now, but it took an hour by bus as it struggled up the hills, just about making it over the top.

Uncle Ben's cottage was at the end of a row of Cotswold stone cottages, with a garden at the front, so steep that I had difficulty getting up and down it. I used to roll down it, over and over, then struggle back to the top. I don't know how Uncle Ben did it but the garden was well kept, with rows of flowers and vegetables. He often gave Aunty Ethel some rhubarb or gooseberries to take home. In the summer he always had a strawberry patch and would pick some to serve with cream for our tea.

We had our tea in the mid afternoon, it would be fruit and cream with bread and butter. Uncle Ben would stand the loaf of bread on its end and butter it, then cut the slice off the top, repeating this procedure until enough was cut. After this we had cakes and a pot of tea. Uncle Ben had the old fashioned habit of pouring his tea from the cup into his saucer, before slurping down. He insisted that it tasted better that way. In the winter when the fire was lit, the kettle would be set to boil on the black leaded coal range in the living room. In the summer Aunty Gertie used the gas cooker in the kitchen. The cottage had two rooms downstairs, a living room and a kitchen, with an outside toilet. A door from the living room hid the stairs that led to the two bedrooms. We always visited on a Sunday and it was Uncle Ben's ritual on the Sabbath, to retire to bed for a short nap in the afternoon. It made no difference who was there, he would disappear through the door to the stairs and not reappear for about an hour.

There was no electricity in the cottage, but it had gaslights that you had to light with a match or taper. It was well into the 1960's before electricity was installed. I was always fascinated by the radio they had, which was powered by a large battery they purchased from a local shop. I had never seen a battery-powered radio before.

It was a lovely walk down Tibbiwell Lane, it is very steep leading down to an old mill which used to be a pin factory. Aunty Gertie, being from Painswick, had worked there when she was a young woman, in the 1920,s. In the summer there was an abundance of wild flowers, growing out of the high banks at the sides of the lane. No cars and very few people passed through this lane. The area had been largely unchanged for over a hundred years.

Walking up Tibbiwell one day, on our way to the bus stop to take us home, we went into the shop at the top of the street, it was a small shop that sold a little of everything. I saw a red plastic water pistol in the window and asked Aunty Ethel if I could have it. She bought it for me and we took it home to her house. Everything she bought me I always kept at her house and never took it home. It had 'Empire made' moulded into the plastic. I didn't know what that meant, then. I later found out that they were cheap imported goods mainly from Hong Kong. I had great fun with that water pistol until it broke. Plastic was very brittle then and never lasted long.

Aunty Ethel also took me with her when she went to visit her sister, in Swindon, my great Aunt Alice and Uncle Charlie Harding. It was an epic journey to get to Swindon by bus, on a Sunday. We caught a bus to the centre of Gloucester at around 8.30. took another bus to Cheltenham, then another bus, which went to Swindon stopping everywhere in between. It took so long to get there that we only stayed about three hours, before we had to start the reverse journey home. We always had a nice tea with Alice and Charlie, they were really nice people. Charlie would keep asking me if I wanted more of everything. Sometimes Alice said to him 'shut up Charlie we haven't got anything left', we all laughed because it was just a game Uncle Charlie and I, used to play. He always knew what was all gone and always asked me if I wanted more of it. Uncle Charlie worked most of his life for the Great Western Railway in Swindon. They owned their own house, the only ones I knew of, in our family, that did. It had a flower garden at the front of the house and a large garden at the back where Charlie grew his vegetables. He was very proud of his garden and we strolled around it together, like old friends, while he showed me how his beans and vegetables of all sorts, were coming on. Their way of life was very different to our poor existence.

In 1957 the elections for Parliament were held, Aunty Ethel was a staunch Labour Party supporter. We went to a rally in support of Jack Diamond, who was subsequently elected as the Member of Parliament for Gloucester. I carried a placard with a poster stuck onto it, proclaiming 'vote Diamond Labour', printed in the shape of a diamond.

Not long after this my small world started to change forever. I was told that Aunty Ethel was moving to Matson, as they were going to demolish all of the houses in Clapham and Aunty Ethel was to be one of the first to go. When she was gone I didn't know what to do with myself. I knew where Matson was, because we passed it on the way to Painswick. It was only three or four miles but to me it seemed like a very long way. Paul Thorpe also went somewhere and I never saw him again.

Demolition began, the cranes with their wrecking balls hanging on wire hawsers and chains bashed away at the fragile old houses and soon they were reduced to rubble. For a while it was a new adventure playground, a lot of the houses were empty, I could climb over the piles of brick rubble and go into the houses to see what I could find. Things people had left behind were of great interest, but there was nothing of any value. I found a green glazed pot in a back yard. I thought it was a treasure, but when I took it home, Mum made me throw it away, it had a chip out of the rim and a crack in it. I had been so excited by finding it that I hadn't noticed any of that.

Soon it was our turn to go and that was the end of Clapham.

Chapter 2
Matson

When we moved to 18 Underhill Road, Matson, a whole new world of countryside and light opened up. We had a house, just built, so big and open, compared to what we had been used to. It had a lounge, a separate dining room and a kitchen downstairs, two bedrooms and a bathroom upstairs. There was an electric immersion heater to heat the water so we could wash with warm water without having to boil a kettle. We could even have a bath without having to bring the bath into the living room in front of the fire. The front door didn't lead straight into the living room, but into a hallway with doors leading into the kitchen straight ahead or into the living room on the left. On the right were the stairs with open banisters. Gordon and I soon started a game running round and round the house. We could run from the kitchen, into the dining room, into the lounge, onto the hall, then back to the kitchen. It was great fun that could get rather noisy at times, when Mum or Dad would shout at us to stop it and get upstairs, or outside, depending on the weather. When I looked out of the window at the front of the house, the other houses were to my left, looking straight ahead, about three hundred yards away, was Robinswood junior school. In between there was a long, thin strip of grass. To the right was a cornfield, big and golden. I had never seen anything like it. All of life seemed bright and golden.

Best of all, I was again close to Aunty Ethel. Her flat in Whiteway Road was just down the road. We could visit each other again as often as we liked.

For reasons that have always seemed ridiculous, I was not allowed to go to Robinswood school, although I could see it from our front room. Apparently, it was for children who lived at the top end of the estate and I lived at the top of the bottom end, so was out of the catchment area. They were to build a new school for us but until then I had to stay at Widden Street and so at the age of eight, I had to travel, on the bus to Barton Street, where I got off and walked up Sinope Street to school. On the corner of Sinope Street and Barton Street, there was a shop called The Barton Press, a stationers, they had all kinds of fountain pens, at all prices and beautiful colours of ink to go in them, my favourite was Royal blue. I bought a bottle and used it for my schoolwork. There were no ball point pens allowed. Royal blue was lighter and prettier than the usual Indian ink.

There was a small shop on the corner of Napier Street that sold sweets and tobacco. I went in there whenever I had some money to spare for a bar of chocolate. Sometimes, the old lady who owned the shop took a long time to come from the back room and I started to help myself to some things from the display. I did this a few times, then one day, showing a remarkable turn of speed, the old lady ran towards me shouting, 'I saw you take that, you thieving little sod. Come back here.' I was already in full flight, there was no chance of me going back there. Not now, not ever. The experience frightened me to death. I never went near that shop again.

Instead I went to a shop in Millbrook Street, they sold the same sweets there and they also sold penny buns, fresh sticky, currant buns. I loved them. After school I wandered around the area with Keith Burnham, who was in the same class as me. We would explore the railway and go up to the Horton Road crossing, to watch the trains go by. The Great Western Railway was a great source of interest, with such beautiful green liveried steam locomotives. The Castle class was the most common of the named locomotives. Clun castle was a regular through Gloucester. The most impressive, by far, was when one of the King class came through. They were one of the largest and most powerful steam engines ever to run in this country.

Instead of getting the bus home from Barton Street, sometimes we would walk to Chequers Bridge, where we could climb up the railway embankment to get close to the trains. We put pennies on the line and waited for a train to come along to flatten them. We put them on as many times as we could to see how big they would get before they disappeared to who knows where.

When it rained hard, the dip in the road under Chequers bridge, regularly got flooded, it was so deep the traffic couldn't get through. We could walk through, because the pavement didn't dip in the same way as the road and stayed above the floodwater. One day it was particularly bad and I had to get off the bus there and walk the rest of the way home. It was about two miles, a long way for a small boy, in the pouring rain. I was so wet that it didn't make any difference what I did, I couldn't have got any wetter, so I enjoyed the walk, splashing into the deepest puddles I could find. When I got home, Mum was beside herself with worry, because I was so late. I was in such a sorry state that she hugged me and cried with relief, that I had got home safe.

Aunty Ethel took me to a summer fete at the recently built avant-garde St Aldate's church in Reservoir Road. It was a short walk from her flat in Whiteway Road, to the Church on the corner of Reservoir Road and Finlay Road. We looked around all the stalls, with their jumble, crafts and home baked produce. There was a stall selling confectionery, I spotted a black box with Black Magic written on it. Aunty had asked me if I wanted anything and this was it.

She said, 'I don't think you'll like those, they are dark chocolates.'

They are not chocolates, it says it's magic on the box, I replied.

Aunty explained that it was just a name for a box of chocolates and not a magic set as I thought it was, but I didn't believe her. The fact that they were on sale at a confectionery stall hadn't registered either. In the end, Aunty gave in and bought them, to prove to me that she was telling the truth. Thankfully, I did like them although I was disappointed that it wasn't magic.

That summer we went on holiday to Scotland again, back to Aunty May's, Dad had a Wolsley 10 now, it had a strangely tinted rear window, making it very difficult to tell the colours of the other cars, though most of them were black, as was ours. None the less, Gordon and I played a guessing game for hours on that journey.

It was a brilliant, long, hot summer, we visited all our usual places. We went to Qeensferry at the Firth of Forth and took the ferry across the river and went to Dunfermline for the gala day. A gala in Scotland is like a carnival, with a parade of floats and carriages. I took my first photographs here with a little camera I had been given for my birthday. We visited a lot of relatives all around East Lothian. We went to Prestonpans where there had been an historic battle between the Scots and the English. Uncle Dod and Aunty Rachel lived there. They had two children, my cousins, Robert and Moira.

Uncle Den, Aunty Ina and Hugh were here, on holiday as well. We all went, including Uncle Bill, Aunty May, Victor and Jennifer and granny Wilson, into the hills, for a day out. It was a day to remember, running in amongst the ferns, playing in the burn, (stream) it was so remote we never saw another soul. Uncle Dod showed us how to guddle for trout. He got in the water and put his hands under the bank and felt for the trout taking the shade of the overhanging bank. Very soon he pulled out his hands holding a good-sized trout, which he promptly threw clear of the water, where someone killed it. We all got in and had a go, it seemed there were fish all along the burn and very soon I had one. When we had caught enough a fire was made and they were cooked and we ate them. They were absolutely delicious, but my conscience bothered me. I never caught a fish again.

The day was soon over and it was back to Aunty May's, where exhausted, we went off to bed.

I was lying in bed the next morning and could hear the radio playing. Cliff Richard was singing his first hit record, 'Move it.' That song started off what was to be a love of Rock and Roll and Rhythm and Blues music that would stay with me for the rest of my life.

That day I was in the garden playing Cowboys and Indians with Gordon, Victor and Hugh, when I noticed the replica Colt pistol that Victor had. I had a chrome plated gun that broke in the middle to put a roll of caps in. Victor's was brown and solid, much heavier than the one I had. It looked like a real gun, unlike mine, which was obviously a toy. I was envious of that Colt and never forgot it.

Back at home, during the six-week summer break from school, Dad bought me a bicycle, so that I would be able to ride to school and not have to rely on the bus. The only thing was, I had to learn to ride it. Dad gave me some instruction, then held the bike by the saddle and ran alongside me to hold me upright while I pedalled. Up and down Underhill Road, he puffed and panted, I think he was close to collapsing a couple of times. After a while he started to let go without telling me. When I realised he had let go, I promptly fell off the first few times, but eventually I got the hang of it. There was no danger because there was no traffic at all. Only my Dad and Mr Greening across the road had a car.

I soon got to enjoy riding that little red bike. It broadened my territory. From the time I learnt to ride I cycled to school, all the way from Matson to Widden Street and back, every day, at the age of 9. I could also explore Matson and Upton St Leonards, much quicker. It was my first independent means of transport. One of the best places to go was the Wheatridge, on the other side of Painswick Road. It was a really beautiful place with glowing fields of corn and little babbling brook with small bridges leading into the fields. That summer, I went up there often, when the sun was shining, to sit on one of the bridges and watch the stream flow by. I sat there alone for hours, just watching, hardly seeing another soul, it was so remote and quiet there. I enjoyed the solitude and never got bored. There was no one to argue with about when or where to go. No one to spoil the atmosphere, with the noise of unnecessary conversation.

Further on was Bowden Hall, it was a reform school for girls then, but I was much more interested in the conker trees that grew in the grounds. I was chased off once or twice, but it was worth the risk for good conkers, to take to school. Most of my schoolfriends were still city boys and good conkers were in short supply. There were a few trees in the park, but there was always a big demand. Every day, they were all picked up, while at Bowden Hall there was as many as I could carry. I was on my way home from one of these expeditions, walking up the ashpath leading from Matson Avenue to Underhill Road, when I decided to climb a tree, for no other reason than, it was there. It was a tall, thin tree with lots of short spiky branches on the lower part of the trunk, giving hand and foot holds. I got up a fair way, when I lost my grip and started to fall. I fell a little way, then one of the short, spiky branches went up the leg of my short trousers. There I was, literally hanging by a thread. All of a sudden there was a ripping noise when the material started to tear, ripping right up the leg, through the waistband, catching my shirt as I fell and ripping it from bottom to top. I hit the ground with a thud, but was unhurt. When I got up, I had a scratch that ran up my leg from the knee and continued right up my body, to the shoulder. I looked at my clothes and they were ripped to shreds, I had to hold the shorts together and run the short distance home. Mum said she despaired of me and that I would probably kill myself one day.

Closer to home was an even better source of never ending entertainment. Robinswood hill was on my doorstep. It was wild and untamed then. A short walk up Matson lane, past the church, I could get through the hedge, straight onto the lower slopes of the hill. Close to this entry point was a pond, it had railings round it, but there were a few ways in. At the right time of year, it was absolutely teeming with toads, mating and then spawning. The water went thick with the sheer volume of toad spawn. A bit farther up was a wood, with bluebells covering the floor. It was a great place for playing Cowboys and Indians, lots of places to hide, or to spring ambushes from. Once I got to the top, it was time for a rest and take in the view. On a hot summer day, if Mum knew I was going up the hill, sometimes she would make up a bottle of orange squash to take with me. I would sit on the top of the hill, by myself, take a drink and take in the beauty of it all. It was unusual to meet anyone else then, as most of the access to the hill was over private land.

A rag and bone man came round the street with his horse and cart, he shouted 'rag bone, rag bone. Mum gave me a bag of old clothes to take to him, to exchange for a goldfish. I got it and rushed in to show her what I had. I was delighted with it. We bought a round bowl and kept that goldfish for years.

One hot summer day we went to Stroud Lido, we all splashed around in the water to keep cool. Gordon and me ran around the pool and jumped into the shallow end and paddled about. All of a sudden, I slipped and went into the pool head first and banged my head on the bottom, splitting my forehead open turning the water red with blood. I had to be taken to the hospital to have it seen to. They decided not to stitch it and just bandaged it up. To this day I still have the scar from that tumble.

About this time, my cousin Hugh, Aunty Ina and Uncle Den were rehoused by the council, but instead of going to Matson, they went to Tuffley Court Estate. They got a prefab in Sixth Avenue. I soon found my way there, over the top of the hill. From the top, it was down past the old quarry, through some fields, until I got to Stroud Road. Once across the road, I could make my way through the estate to Hugh's house. The prefabs were prefabricated bungalows built cheaply after the war to fill a large upsurge in the need for decent council housing. They were detached, set in a good-sized garden, with a combined shed and coalhouse. They had built in cupboards, throughout the house and the kitchen was fully equipped with a cooker, fridge and a boiler for washing your clothes. The coal fire, in the living room, heated the water and there was a fitted immersion heater for when the coal fire wasn't lit. They were excellent houses in their time.

Back on the hill, over on the Matson side I could get into the back of the army camp, sometimes I would get through the fence and wander about, looking in the old brown wooden huts. On one of these expeditions, I saw the first comprehensively equipped gym I had ever seen. I was creeping between the huts, when I looked through a window and saw some soldiers throwing a medicine ball from one to the other. There was a vaulting box and a pommel horse and different sets of weights. I had to be very careful because if I was spotted I would have to run like hell to escape capture, but that was all part of the fun of being there.

On Matson lane, past the church on my right. Selwyn girl's school was on the left. It was an unapproachable place for a small boy like me. On the right, at the side of the road was the Red Well. There was a constant stream of water running down the road, summer and winter. All around the well was coloured bright red from the iron in the water. Farther up, on the left, was Captain Peacey's farm. He owned the land, including the fields I used, to get onto the hill. I was always worried that he would catch me walking on his land and playing in the wood, but I think the fear was greater than the reality, I don't think he minded innocent use at all.

In the winter the water that constantly ran down the lane, increased to a steady flow that could be turned into a great game. Gordon and I often went there and made series of dams out of mud. Some with small gaps in them, so that we could float sticks down the stream, the speed of the water steering them through the gaps in the dams. All this was on the side of the road. There was no traffic to interfere with what we were doing. We got covered in mud doing this and were dreadfully told off when we got home. But it never stopped us doing it again and again.

A little further up the lane was Sneedhams Green, there was a lovely little pond there, full of newts and sticklebacks, with moorhens and ducks swimming on it. It was covered over with rich green floating weed in the summer.

Further still was the old army shooting range, I used to get in there and search for empty shell cases and spent bullets. I sometimes listened to the rifles being fired and longed to be able to try one. The nearest thing I could get to a real gun, were the spud guns, Mum had bought for us. Gordon and I ran around with a large potato in one hand and our guns in the other, firing at each other and reloading as fast as we could. They were great fun though.

I had a small bow and some arrows, with suckers on the ends. I found that to get them to stick, the target had to be smooth. The best place I found, was a panel of the front door. This was fine until one day, an arrow went right through the door. Dad went mad when he saw it, he had to call out the council and ask them to repair it. He said, 'whatever you do, don't tell them, you shot an arrow through it.' We had to say we didn't know how it happened. It must have been someone from outside. The workmen duly arrived and replaced the panel and repainted the door. We were quite pleased with the end result. The door looked better than it did before.

At the bottom of our back garden, there was a stick fence. On the other side of the fence, the Robb family lived, they had two boys, about the same age as me. David and Jimmy, I became good friends with David and we played in each other's houses. One day I went into David's house and saw a television. It was the first television I had ever seen. It had a tiny 9' screen inside a large wooden, free-standing cabinet. When it was switched on, it took ages to warm up, then a small black and white picture appeared. I was mesmerised by it, even though there wasn't very much on. The potter's wheel seemed to be on, more than anything else, but when a program came on, it was a thing of wonder. We sat on the floor and watched anything.

I was climbing over the stick fence to get home from David's one day, when I caught my foot on the top and fell forward onto the ground, putting my hands out to break my fall. Unfortunately, what broke was my arm.
I went into the house and said, 'Mum! My arm hurts'!

She said, 'In the name of the Lord Harry, what have you done now'?
She took me down the Ash Path to the bus stop in Matson Avenue, to get the bus to the hospital. While we were waiting for the bus, the milkman came along in his van. Mum flagged him down and asked him if he would take us to the casualty unit at the hospital. He agreed, so we got in the van and off we went. My arm was x-rayed, pronounced broken and put in plaster for six weeks.

I told Dad it wouldn't have happened if we had a television of our own, but he said we couldn't afford it. Dad was working for the GPO now, he still drove coaches in his spare time and he also started driving a taxi, so he should have been able to afford it. We kept on and on about it and eventually he gave in. I came home from school one day there it was, a little 9' black and white television, rented from the link. The link was an early form of cable television. We didn't need an ariel, the set plugged into a little box screwed to the wall. It received BBC and ITV television and also a radio station. It was the beginning of life, as we know it. In the evening, there was a program called Gun Law on at about nine-o clock. It was a western featuring Marshall Matt Dillon and his deputy, Chester. It was on, way past our bedtime and we weren't allowed to watch it. I crept down the stairs and watched through a crack in the door. Mum and Dad caught me and told me off so many times, that they gave in, as long as I went to bed at the normal time and came back downstairs when it was time for the program to start. I had to promise not to wake Gordon or tell him what was going on, as he was younger than me and needed more sleep. I also had to promise to go back to bed as soon as Gun Law was finished.

Dad had been a cricketer, all his life. Now that he worked for the Post Office, he played for their team. They played on Sundays, throughout the summer and we were all dragged off to wherever the team was playing, sometimes going on a coach to the away matches. The only time we watched the game was when Dad was batting and then only when we noticed. I found cricket to be the most boring thing I had so far encountered, in my young life. It is something I have never changed my mind about.

Gordon and I went exploring, as soon as we could get away. We usually came back in time for tea, depending what we found to do. One Sunday we had been stuck around the pitch, we were running round and round the pavilion, shouting at each other, when we were told to stop it and sit quiet, at least for a while. I settled into a deck chair and promptly started rocking it. All of a sudden, the chair collapsed, trapping the fingers of my right hand between two of the folding wooden parts of the deck chair. I couldn't pull them out, because I was still sitting in the chair, with my weight bearing down on my fingers. I was yelling at the top of my voice and Dad came running off the pitch and lifted me off the chair, releasing my fingers. Dad put my hand into a rainwater butt at the side of the pavilion, so the cold water could soothe the pain. Nothing was broken, but it left scars across my finger that took years to fade.

All this time, the Moat junior school was being built, I knew that when it was ready, I would be one of the first pupils to go there. It was a short walk from my house and I watched its progress, while on my general wanderings around the area. It was like no school I had ever seen, completely different in design to the old red brick Victorian building at Widden Street. The Moat School was to be a modern showpiece, set in it's own grounds. with light open classrooms. It would have a football pitch, gardens and landscaped features.

During that summer, Mum was informed that the school would be ready for the new autumn term and that I would be able to attend. Mum was told that I would need a new blazer, so that I would fit in with everyone else and that approved blazers could be purchased from the Golden Anchor clothes shop in Southgate Street. Mum couldn't afford to go out and buy new clothes for us without saving up for them. The only other alternative she had, was to take out a Provident cheque, so that I could get the blazer and new shoes. A Provident cheque was a form of credit. An amount would be agreed and a cheque for that amount issued. It had a section on the back, where an approved shopkeeper could enter items and cost. The cheque could be used in any approved shops, until the transactions on the back, reached the total amount of the cheque. A collector called at the house every week, until the sum borrowed, plus interest, was repaid. Ron, the Provident collector became a sort of friend of the family, but sometimes we had to hide from him when he knocked at the door, if Mum didn't have the money to pay him, that week.

We took the bus into town and went to The Golden Anchor where I got my new blazer, complete with Moat School badge sewn on the pocket. It was my first new jacket and I felt really proud of it. The shoes here were very expensive, so Mum said 'let's go and try Yarnold's in Barton Street, they take Provident cheques', so off we went, up to The Cross, turning right, into Eastgate Street, walking past the swimming baths, all the way up to Barton Gates. The gates were closed and we had to wait for the train to come past, always a magnificent sight, when it was a passenger train, hauled by a GWR Castle class engine. Barton Gates were huge twelve bar gates, hinged at the sides, with a small wicket gate on one side so that pedestrians could walk through, up to the last minute before the train came through, when they locked automatically. There was a signal box close by, so the signalman could watch the gates to make sure everybody was clear when he closed them. They always seemed to be closed for ages before the train came along and stayed closed for ages, after the train had gone. When the gates were eventually opened, we made our way on up past the Barton Press and into Yarnold's gent's outfitters. I had my feet measured by Mr Yarnold, a pleasant man, very distinguished looking, with greying hair, swept back in a fifties style. We chose a pair of black Clarke's school shoes and Mum handed over the cheque for Mr Yarnold to fill in the details of the sale. I would really look the part, on my first day at The Moat, wearing my new shoes and blazer.

I went to the Matson Boy Scout meetings a few times but never felt comfortable with it. Although only a child I often felt that some of the activities were too childish. When we were outdoors, around the campfire, or following trails on Robinswood Hill, it was very enjoyable, but when in the scout hut, the games they played just seemed too ridiculous, to me. I'm afraid I was a little disruptive at times and wouldn't listen to the scout leader, when he told me to play the games or leave. When he eventually got annoyed and told me to leave and to come back only when I was ready to fit in. I went out of the hut, which in reality was a small red brick church hall at the side of the old Matson infant's school. I went into the playground of the school where I had seen an old corporation handcart, left there. It was very heavy and for someone my size, difficult to move, but I managed to wedge it into the porch of the church hall, so that the door couldn't be opened from the inside. I climbed up to the window at the front of the building and banged on it. The scout leader shouted at me to go away, but I made faces at him. He finally had enough of this and went to the door to come out and get me, but the door wouldn't budge. They tried for ages, getting more and more violent, but without success. I laughed and laughed, which made them even angrier, but they still couldn't get out. I went home and left them in there. I don't know how long it took them to get out, but I know Mum was told to make sure I never went there again. There wasn't much likelihood of that anyway. Mum told me off for doing it, but it had been worth it.

The time came for my first day at the Moat school, it lived up to all we had heard about it. Everything was new, it felt like a real privilege to go there. The headmaster was Mr Stephenson, who lived just up Matson Lane, at Robins farm. He was a good man, who always seemed to have time to speak to everybody. He welcomed us to the school and we were shown all around. There was a mural on a wall that had been specially commissioned. It was the first real painting I had ever seen. I was fascinated that someone could create something so impressive. I was introduced to my form teacher, Mrs Millard, who lived up on the Wheatridge in one of the large houses. She was really nice and encouraged me in every way. I would take my eleven plus exam, here at the Moat and she told me I would have no trouble passing it, if I worked hard and took it seriously. I found most of the subjects quite easy and in any of the tests that we were set, I was always near the top of the class. I made my first real model, here. In the Crafts class, I made a Lockheed Lightning fighter aircraft, out of balsa wood. It took weeks to make, shaping the twin bodies and the wings, with sandpaper. I painted it in the correct colours, that I got out of a book and cut some round discs of clear perspex, to simulate the propellers in flight. I made a stand for it, so that it looked as if it was flying. I was really proud of it and it must have been good because it was chosen to go into the first Moat School craft exhibition. During the exhibition it got slightly damaged, I never knew how. Everyone said, don't get upset, you will easily be able to repair it. But I was upset that someone could have been so careless. As soon as I got it back from the exhibition, I threw it away.

The Moat was the first school I had attended, which had a playing field. I was introduced to football and wasn't very impressed. A feeling which has never changed. The boots were big brown things with hard toecaps and were as stiff as a board. It took an age to clean the mud off them, then rub 'Dubbin' in after every game. The worst thing about it was the weight of the ball when it had been raining. This brown leather ball, soaked up water like a sponge. It became so heavy I could only kick it a few yards. One such rainy day I was encouraged to head the ball. When I made contact I heard a crunching sound in my neck. I thought it had knocked my head off. I thought, 'this is a stupid carry on, I don't think I'll make a habit of this.' I always tried to avoid playing football from that day.

I started having school dinners, but I have always been a fussy eater and often didn't like what we were given, I can't eat any meat with fat on it, or worse still, get a piece of gristle in my mouth. The head of the table told me I had to eat some of the things I didn't like, but there was no chance of that. My first stand against authority was about to happen. One day I tipped a packet of orange crystals, into my glass of water. The head of the table told me, I was never to bring anything like that into the dining room again. I replied that I would never come into the dining room again and I never did. I kept my dinner money and spent it at the off licence at the Musket, buying crisps and sweets, every day.

In the playground, we played marbles, most of the marbles were plain glass, or had a coloured twist in them, some were old pop alleys, that had come out of old pop bottles. I also liked racing cars and my favourite one of all was a 'Vanwall' painted in the historic British Racing Green. Tony Brookes and Stirling Moss, who was every boy's hero, drove them in many World Championship races. I had a Dinky Toys 'Vanwall' which was my prized possession, it was far more stylish than any other car of the period and had an engine that had been made from four 500cc Norton motorcycle engines. We sat in the playground with these cars and imagined we were famous racing drivers.

I had never seen a race, but at the Saturday Minors at the Odeon picture house in Eastgate Street, the Pathe Newsreel had shown clips of Stirling Moss speeding over the finish line and wearing the laurel wreath of victory.

The Saturday Minors at the cinema was an exciting outing. We queued up in a long line that stretched from the front entrance in Eastgate Street, up the street and round the corner, along the alley at the side of the cinema. I often went with my cousin Hugh and sometimes with Andy Collingwood, it cost us 6d each to get in and was good value, for a morning's entertainment. There was a film and lots of cartoons and serials. Flash Gordon was always a favourite. There was always a cowboy serial as well and usually a comedy, like Abbot and Costello or Laurel and Hardy. It could get a bit noisy sometimes and boys threw things at each other in the dark, the worst thing was when someone dropped ice cream on you from the balcony above. When it got too bad, the lights came on and the manager walked out onto the stage and told everybody to settle down. The show wouldn't restart until order was restored. There was always a lot of booing and hissing, while this was happening, but the show always came back on in the end.

About this time, 1960/61, fashion started to rear it's ugly head. I had managed to persuade Mum that I could no longer be seen in short trousers and I started trying to style my hair into what was the Teddy boy style. I had difficulty with this because my hair is naturally fine and whatever I did to it, it didn't want to stand up, into anything like the result I was trying to achieve. I wanted to look like Elvis, but it was just wishful thinking. I plastered Brylcreem on it in vast quantities, or a cheaper equivalent that came in huge jars, from Woolworth's. With the help of this greasy white goo, I got something like the style I wanted, but it was never very good. I got some stuff from Pete Baldwin's barbershop in Barton Street, which was a thick, off white liquid, with a strange smell to it. I put that on and achieved another minor styling success. The drawback with this one though, was that it went rock hard when it dried and if it rained, it softened up again and ran off the hair and down your face. I found out that it was a type of sugar and water mixture so had a go at making my own. It worked as well as the shop bought stuff, but suffered from the same drawback. The only thing it had going for it, was that it was cheap, but I couldn't put up with it for long and soon it was back to the Brylcreem. The down side of Brylcreem, especially when used in vast quantities, was that everything my head came into contact with, became covered in the stuff. No chair back was safe and my pillows were a nightmare for my Mum. It was like trying to wash an oil slick out of everything.

Andy Collingwood had great hair, he could get it into a real style and I was always envious of it. We were walking along one day, when he said to me, 'you'll have to do something about that hairstyle if you want to hang around with us.' It came as a shock to me, because I didn't think there was anything wrong with it. I just said 'okay', but I knew there was nothing I could do. I brooded over it for a while, but then just decided not to worry about it and went my own way. It was my first 'what will be, will be', decision. 'Que sera sera.'

One Friday afternoon, my cousin Hugh turned up at our house. He had come over Robinswood hill, to visit us.
He said, 'why don't you come to my house for the weekend.'
I asked Mum and she said it was okay as long as Aunty Ina knew about it. Hugh assured her that she did. We set off to go back over the hill to Tuffley, when we got near the top, the weather started to change and black clouds were looming up. We heard thunder rumbling in the distance and decided we had better get a move on. We didn't want to get caught in a thunderstorm on the top of the hill, so we started running. We ran all the way down the hill, to Aunty Ina's and made it before the storm started. When the storm broke, it was very fierce, thunder and lightning and heavy rain that went on for hours. The next day, it was bright and sunny again, with no sign of the previous day's storm, we went to the minors, in the morning, then in the afternoon we decided to go back up the hill. We went along to the quarry and found there had been a landslide, some huge chunks of the top of the quarry had broken away and fallen down to the next level. It made me think about the times I went close to the edge to look down, because there were always cracks in the surface, as far as two or three feet from the edge.

Back at home, on Monday it was time for school. This was the best time I ever had at school, most things at the Moat were made fun, but as with everything, there are always some things you don't like. Despite my protests, I was given a leading part

24

in the school play. The very thought of it filled me with dread. I was adamant that I didn't want to do it, but they insisted. Eventually it was agreed that I could take a more minor role, that of a 'troll', with very little to say, but even that was too much for me to bear, so I kept getting it wrong. On the day of the performance I refused to go to school, saying I was sick. They weren't very happy about it, but they should have listened to my protests.

On a lighter note, the school had a charity fund-raising drive, asking us to think of ways to raise money on an individual basis. I asked Mum if she would bake some biscuits and cakes, so that I could sell them at school. We had a week to raise as much money as we could, so on Monday I took a tin full of goodies Mum had made, to school and sold them during the break. They were so popular that they sold out almost immediately. When I got home I asked Mum if she would make some more and she agreed. I gave her the money for the new ingredients and kept the profit. At the end of the week, my Mum's baking was a legend and I had made much more money than anyone else had. I won a poetry book as a prize for my efforts, a possession that I still look at with pride. It reminds me of my Mum and what a lovely a person she was, nothing was too much trouble for her to help someone in any way she could, let alone do anything for her two sons.

Mum got a part time job, at Walkers Stores on the shopping parade at the top end of Matson Avenue, she met lots of people, through this job and was very popular. She held regular parties for her women friends, they came to our house one evening, most weeks and Mum supplied cakes, meringues, sandwiches and biscuits, all home baked. They sat around talking or played cards. Gordon and I were in bed while all this was going on but sometimes we came down for a look and they would let us stay for a while.

Mum was working one day and Gordon and I were playing in the house alone. Dad was working and we were left to our own devices. I had started to do something, which was potentially very dangerous. Over the front door, there was a concrete weather canopy. I could get out of the bedroom window and drop onto the canopy and from there, I could swing by my fingertips and drop to the pavement at the front of the house. I had done it many times, until on this particular day I caught my foot on the window ledge as I was getting out and I fell, head first out of the window. I hit the canopy, then rolled off, landing flat on my back on the concrete below. I don't know how long I was lying there, or who was there, but I remember seeing Mum running down the road towards me. I was starting to recover by then and soon got up. She took me into the house, where I assured her I was all right.

She didn't know whether to tell me off, or hug me to death. My back was extensively bruised, but I was okay, although my back still gives me trouble sometimes. She made me promise, never to do anything so stupid again.

On my way to school one morning, a rodent ran across in front of me. So I went after it and managed to catch it. I thought 'wow! This is the biggest mouse I have ever seen.' I held it tight, even though it struggled and tried to bite me. I thought that if I could get it home, I could keep it as a pet.
I shouted, 'Mum, Mum! I've caught a mouse.'
She came into the kitchen and screeched, Oh my God, it's a rat, throw it out. I said, 'what's a rat, it looks like a mouse to me.'
She just kept shouting, 'throw it out, throw it out', but I wouldn't. In the end she got a cardboard box and told me to throw it into the box and get my hands away quickly, so that it couldn't bite me, which it was trying to do all the time. I managed to do that and she said she would keep it for me until I got home, so I hurried off to school. When I got home the rat was gone, Mum told me it had died and she had buried it. I never knew what really happened to it, but I was very upset about it.

I had my first real fight, on the grass outside our house. It was with the boy next door, Jeff Davis, I can't remember what it was about, nothing of any consequence, I expect. Jeff was a big lad, we were the same age but he was much bigger than I was. We were rolling around on the ground, punching each other, when Mrs Davis came out, I was surprised when, instead of stopping it, she started encouraging Jeff, shouting 'go on Jeff give it to him.' Just then I caught him a good blow to the nose and started it bleeding. He seemed to lose heart for the task at that point and I knew I could beat him. I carried on punching him and Mrs Davis became hysterical, screaming 'stop it, stop it' and started shaking uncontrollably. She was screaming that I was a bully and for me to leave Jeff alone. She seemed to have forgotten, that a few minutes earlier she had been encouraging her son to bash my head in. I think she had a lot to put up with, living next to me. Her children, Jeff and Pauline were much better behaved than I was.

Christmas came and things were much better now, there seemed to be more money, we had better clothes, a television and toys to play with. I was soon to have my eleventh birthday in January 1961 and I didn't want just toys this year. I had been given a Meccano set last year and had made a chair lift, which I set up on the stairs, one of us at the top, the other at the bottom. We made the chair go up and down by turning a handle. This year I wanted a steam engine so that I could power the chair lift. I woke up early on Christmas morning and there it was, on my bedside table. Mum had made the mistake though, of supplying the methylated spirits, needed to run it. I tried to fill it up and get it started, all without getting out of bed, because it was so cold, that morning. I lit a match to light the burner and set fire to my hand and the tablecloth, that covered my bedside table. I managed to put it out without too much damage and my hand wasn't badly burnt, it stung a bit and went red, but was okay. I couldn't hide the burn in the tablecloth. Mum went mad at me and called me a lunatic.

I was also given a pair of blue denim jeans and a pair of Danny Kaye boots. Clothes were just starting to matter to me. I was starting to want to look cool.

It was 1961 and this year I had to take my eleven plus exam. Everyone said I would have no trouble passing it. They had more faith than I did. My teacher told the class to make sure we all have a good nights sleep and a good breakfast on the day of the exam.
I thought, what's different? I do that every day.
I didn't realise that other people didn't live the same way we did. Mum always made sure we went to bed at the proper times and that we always ate well, starting the day with corn flakes or porridge. I sat the exam and came away from it with some confidence of a pass. There had been nothing in it that had worried me. Now all I had to do was wait for the result.

Dad came home with a dog for us. It was a little black and white shaggy haired terrier, that we unimaginatively named, Terry. We played with him, running round and round the house, but he kept biting us all the time. When Mum fed him, he wouldn't let anyone into the kitchen, so he had to be fed outside. He got so vicious, that we had to start shutting him in the shed. We didn't realise, but Terry was a mad dog, getting worse as he grew older. One day I came home and Terry was gone. Dad had taken him to the vet's and had him put to sleep. I cried for ages over it, even though I hadn't been able to get near to him for some time.

My last term at the Moat school finished and the summer holiday started, soon the exam results would be here. One morning, the envelope arrived; I couldn't wait to open it. I had passed, with a good grade and would be going to my first choice school, which was the Crypt grammar school in Podsmead. We had to go to the school to discuss the requirements for the first term. They gave Mum a list of the new clothes I would need, it worried her to death.
She said, 'how am I going to afford all this?'

I needed a new blazer and badge, a cap, new shoes, new trousers, sports kit, including two rugby shirts, one in school colours, one in white. We had never come across, such regulations before. Fortunately they had a school fete where other parents, sold the kit their sons had grown out of. We managed to get some of it there, keeping the cost down. For the rest, it was back to Ron for another Provident cheque, followed by another trip to the Golden Anchor.

Dad had also promised to buy me a new bike if I passed the 11 plus and true to his word, he took me to Halfords, in town and I chose an American style bike, it was red, with a bent crossbar and a three speed hub. It was a modern design, very different to the traditional style. It was my first new bike and I was very proud of it.

Chapter 3
Dark Times

On the first day of the new school term, full of pride and hope for the future, I rode my little red bike to my new secondary school, down Cole Avenue into Podsmead Road, to the front entrance of the Crypt school. I would be one of the smallest boys at this school in amongst a mixture of older boys, some good, some bad, some bullies. I was to encounter bullying here, the like of which I had never experienced before. I arrived and put my bike in the bike sheds and walked up the drive towards the playground. I didn't know anybody, I felt very alone and very vulnerable, I had that 'butterflies' in the stomach feeling. I hadn't got very far when some older boys started to take the mickey out of me, I wasn't very amused and told them to bugger off. They thought this was very funny, coming from a first year. John Haines, a second year student, who was later to become a good friend, swiped the cap from my head and wouldn't give it back, they were all laughing and giving me the run around. I had a job getting close to John, but when I did, I punched him as hard as I could. A fight started and we fought until a master dragged us apart. It was not an auspicious start at my new school.

I found the masters very forbidding, not at all friendly or supportive, like they had been at my other schools. Not at all like Mr Stephenson, the headmaster and Mrs Millard my form teacher at the Moat. I had been a popular pupil at school and had a good relationship with the teachers, who had always told me that they expected me to do well academically. The teachers at the Crypt all seemed to treat us like we were rubbish. Shouting for any reason, no matter how small and taking every opportunity to belittle us or to try to instil fear into us. I very quickly thought, 'I don't like this place very much. Bullies in the playground and bullies on the staff.'

I had always been very strong willed and could never stand for any kind of bullying. The more the staff tried to bully me, the worse I got. I don't think I had ever been in trouble at school before I came to the Crypt, now I was in trouble all the time. I was determined that no one would bully me.

I can't remember any of the teachers names except for Bert Beddis, the religious instruction master. He was the only one I remember who treated me in a decent manner. The rest were a bad lot and I have erased their names from my memory. There was a particularly nasty science master. All I remember about him, apart from his attitude, was that he was a tall man, with a big nose and a habit of rubbing both sides of his nose at the same time. The first two fingers of his right hand making the form of a V sign, while he paced around the classroom daring us to incur his displeasure. The rest I have just blotted out.

It was too far for me to get home at lunchtime, so again I was supposed to have school dinners. I refused point blank, so I started taking a lunch box. Mum packed it with sandwiches, a biscuit, an apple and maybe one of her cakes. The rules at this school were that all food was to be consumed in the dining hall, whether it was brought in or was a school dinner. There was no chance of them making me sit in the dining hall, to eat my sandwiches. I ate them sitting on the sports field, or under cover, in the bike sheds if it was raining. The teachers caught me doing it many times, but couldn't make me stop. They gave up in the end. I was starting to get to them because unlike most of the boys, I couldn't be intimidated. Once I decided on a course of defiance, I never gave in.

I was starting to think more about girls in a sexual way. There were very few sex magazines about then and what there were, I didn't have the nerve to try to buy. I went into a shop in High Street, Tredworth, on the corner of Moor Street, across from the Golden Heart. They sold second hand comics at the far end of the shop. Next to the comics were second hand nudist magazines, such as Health and Efficiency and Spick & Span. The owner tried to keep youth's away from that pile, but he couldn't always watch close enough. Every now and then I managed to slip one up my jumper. I would pay for the comic and walk away. I couldn't wait to get somewhere quiet, so I could have a look at my prize. In these magazines, the women's private parts were always retouched out of the photographs. It was years before I realised that women had pubic hair. One day I got greedy and stuck two or three of these mag's up my jumper and started to walk out. The problem was, they were made of shiny, slippy paper and trying to keep them trapped up my jumper, without looking too conspicuous, proved impossible. I exerted great pressure with the side of my arm, but they kept slipping down. Just as I got level with the counter, they fell to the floor. Quick as a flash, I bent down, picked them up and ran out of the shop, jumped on my bike and was gone. I don't think the shopkeeper even realised what had happened, but I didn't risk going there again.

We were sitting in our living room on weekend, not long after I had started at the Crypt, when we heard a terrible banging and bumping in the hall. We ran out to see what had happened and found Mum slumped at the bottom of the stairs. She was conscious, but her speech was slurred and she was obviously not well. She came out of it and insisted that she was all right. But she wasn't all right, it was the first sign I had seen of an illness which was to affect all of our lives. The dizzy spells and blackouts became more and more frequent and she was becoming ill for longer periods. Her parties stopped and most of her friends faded away. Granny Wilson, Mums mother, arrived from Scotland and moved in with us to help Mum with her illness and help look after us. I didn't appreciate what she was doing at the time, I later found her to be a lovely woman, but as a young boy, she brought with her, a new regime, much more strict than I had been used to and I didn't like it. It wasn't long before we were arguing almost continuously. At it's worst, we had a fight, with brooms, both of us striking and parrying most ferocious blows. I caught her a blow to the leg and she threw her broom down and said she'd had enough and was going home. We compromised a little, after that encounter and we started to learn to live with each other. She was a great help to my Mum, in the early days of Mum's illness. I didn't appreciate gran until years later.

It soon became dangerous for Mum to go up the stairs at all and Dad asked the council if we could get a move to a bungalow. They offered us a prefab, close to where Aunty Ina lived, so we did a swap with the family that lived in the prefab, at 98 Fourth Avenue, Tuffley.

The house next door to No 98 had been burnt down before we moved there. It had originally only been in a block of two, so it was left on it's own, quite a long way from it's nearest neighbour. Gran went back to Scotland, as there was nowhere for her to stay now. The prefab wasn't big enough. We settled in, Gordon and me in one bedroom and Mum and Dad in the other. We hadn't been there long when Mum took a turn for the worse and was taken to Frenchay hospital, in Bristol. It turned out she had a brain tumour, that was inoperable and would have to be controlled by drugs. She was there for what seemed a very long time. Gordon and I were left mostly to our own devices. Dad was always at work, somewhere or other, so we had to fend for ourselves.

I had little or no parental control or guidance from this point. I would make my own decisions from now on.

Soon after we moved here, we got a little brown, mongrel puppy. We named her Tina. She was a wonderful dog, so full of love. She would become my best friend for many years to come. I took her with me, everywhere I could. We went up the hill together and wandered all around the estate, we became inseparable. She was an independent dog though. I never kept her on a lead, so wherever we went she just walked along with me, doing her own thing. Sometimes she would decide to go home and just head off on her own. I never worried when she did this. She was always there when I got back.

A few months later, it was coming up towards Bonfire night. My cousin Hugh knew everybody around so we soon got in with the local boys. The bonfire was to be the joint effort of all of us in the gang. We collected anything that would burn. The bonfire was built on the waste ground next to our house so I had to watch it as much as I could, in case a rival gang set it on fire before the big day on November 5th. Hugh knew where to get the best wood from, so we went far and wide bringing large amounts of wood, stacking it higher and higher. It was huge by the time we finished. When it was lit, there was a large crowd there, of all ages, from all around the area. It was a real social occasion. We had food brought by some of the Mums and potatoes to bake in the fire. It was the best bonfire night I ever had.

Hugh was into making kites, he made some so big that when they flew, we had to be careful not to be carried into the air. They were mostly traditional shaped kites made from two canes in the shape of a cross, covered in brown paper. We carried them to the top of Robinswood hill when the wind was strong. They were difficult to launch, but once they were up, they flew to tremendous height. It could be very exciting, if not a bit frightening. The power of the wind was awesome as we held on to each other in an effort to control the big kites. I hung on to Hugh so that he wouldn't be carried into the air, we were both dragged along struggling for control. We soon realised that when the wind was that strong, we would have to stake them to the ground or risk being dragged along. It was really good fun. That hill was a great playground. We made dens in the ground. We had secret places that we had excavated. They were well concealed and were rarely found by anyone else, although there weren't the amount of people using the hill then. It was still difficult to gain access to it without crossing private land. We got inside these dens, lit candles and made ourselves at home. We sat around in our little hole in the ground and told jokes or stories of our bravado and finally emerged blinking into the sunlight, filthy.

It was nearer to school from Tuffley than it had been from Matson, but things were no better, I was starting to struggle with the work and was becoming increasingly belligerent towards the teachers. For reasons only known to himself, a boy Dave, who was a year older than me, was repeatedly bullying me. He tried to make my life a misery, but I was becoming increasingly independent and tougher every day and he never succeeded in wearing me down. He continued until I became a dangerous prospect, then he gave up. I never paid Dave back for the way he treated me, but that was only because our paths never crossed until my rage had subsided a little and in later years, I thought of him as being insignificant.

John Ewers was a good friend to me, although he too was a year older. He was an inoffensive type, so was unable to help with the bullying problem, but he was supportive, because I think he had had some of the same treatment. I didn't make many friends at this school and have forgotten most of the other boys there.

As the days went slowly by, I became increasingly isolated at school, I didn't like it there and I didn't want to bother with it. It became more and more of a problem for me to fall in with the rules. They sent letters to my home, but Mum wasn't there and Dad didn't care very much. He had his own problems to worry about.

After numerous incidents, I set off a small bomb, made from household chemicals. For some time I had been experimenting with a particular chemical mixture and had pretty well perfected it. I put it up against the door leading from the playground into the gymnasium. When it exploded, it blew a hole through the bottom corner of the door. Some teachers came running out, to see what had happened, but I made no attempt to escape. I just stood there and said, 'how did you like that then.' I was taken to see the headmaster, who decided, it was time I was referred to a psychiatrist. After the consultations with the psychiatrist, his report stated that I was not unbalanced, but in my own interest, it would be best if I was removed from the Crypt school.

Because of the problems at home, with Mum being in hospital and Dad working, it was recommended that I go away to a boarding school. Dad wouldn't be able to afford it, but I was offered an assisted place at a school in Sussex.

I was undecided about this, but on balance I thought it might be a good opportunity, so I agreed to go.

I can't say anything good about my experience at The Crypt except for going to see the school play. It was the most professionally presented play I had yet seen. Up to then I had only seen children's productions, but Shakespeare's Merchant of Venice acted out on the school hall stage was absolutely superb. I can still see the bright green light sparkling off Shylock's emerald ring. That school undoubtedly had a lot going for it and maybe it suited some of the boys but it didn't suit me. They tried to teach through domination and intimidation, when what I needed was encouragement. It was like trying to mix oil and water.

Chapter 4
Leaving Gloucester

So it was decided, I would go away to school somewhere in Sussex.
I had to have a few new things to take with me, things that I had never had before. Dad took me into town and bought me a pair of slippers and a dressing gown, which were requirements of the school. It was the only time I ever remember going shopping, with Dad. He took me into the old Eastgate Market, for a drink at Mr Fitch's refreshment stall, near the back entrance which led to Bell lane. I had a ham sandwich, with very thin slices of ham and thin sliced bread, cut across to make triangles. Dad had a cup of tea and I had a glass of orange squash, from one of those coolers that had a glass top with a paddle in it to keep the squash moving. I said to Dad, how nice the squash was, he replied that it was only cheap stuff and weak at that. He said rather sharply, that what we got at home, was far superior. I suppose it was the fact that it was chilled that made the difference. We had never had a fridge at home. There was one fitted into the kitchen in the prefab but it was a gas one and we never got it to work.

Carrying a small, brown suitcase, packed with my clothes, including my new slippers and dressing gown, I was escorted to my new school by a social worker. We took the train from Gloucester to Paddington, then the underground to Victoria, where we boarded another train destined for Brighton. About half way between London and Brighton, we got off at Haywards Heath, then took a taxi to my new home, in the village of Lindfield. The home was called 'Beckworth', a huge old house set in acres of it's own grounds. It had football pitches, tennis courts and large gardens full of trees from all over the world. We went in through the front entrance, something I would rarely do for the rest of my stay here. We were shown in and I was introduced to Mr and Mrs Harrison, the House Master and Matron. Mr Harrison was a very large man, who had in his younger days, been a bodybuilder, but had now gone to fat. Mrs Harrison was a small, slim woman, who was always dressed in a blue uniform.

It was 1962, I was 12 years old and my independence was growing stronger every day.

We went through the large front entrance, into an entrance lobby. Mr Harrison's office led off one side from this lobby. Straight on through large double doors, was the main hallway of the house. It had a number of doors off it, leading to the main social room, the dining room, the study, the kitchen area, a toilet and some stairs leading to the cellar, which was used as a changing room, for when we came in from outside. This was the way I would use, to come into the house on a day to day basis. Everyone had a locker here where shoes or slippers would be kept, to change into, when going in or out. Upstairs was split into many dormitories, toilets and wash rooms. I was put into a dormitory with five boys of around my own age.

When they had shown me around, Mr Harrison suggested that I go outside and meet a large group of boys who were playing a friendly game of football. I went outside and walked up to the touchline and watched for a while and quite soon they invited me to play. I had never liked football but I thought I had better show willing. As we ran around, they soon passed the ball to me. As soon as I got it I was kicked and knocked over by one of them, they thought it was hilarious. This happened a few times, so I walked off the field. I shouted, 'very funny, you bunch of bastards.' I went into the cellar, the way I had come out and up the stairs. I went into the toilet to relieve myself and wash off some of the mud. I soon heard someone behind me. I turned a saw a boy I would later know as Tiny. It seemed he was the tough guy in my age group and he had been sent in to test me. He said, 'who do think you are to call me a bastard, I'm going to teach you a lesson.' I hit him straight between the eyes, grabbed him by the hair and bashed his head against the basins. There was blood everywhere, I threw him to the floor and walked away. The fight had only lasted a few seconds. When I opened the door, there was a gang of lads waiting to congratulate Tiny. I didn't have a mark on me and wasn't even breathing heavily. There was a stunned silence as I walked past them. I had made my first mark. I had also learned that if violence is inevitable, strike first and strike hard. All is fair in love and war. In future I would win at all costs, whatever it took. Even if I lost the first battle. From now on, anyone who took advantage of me, would never be safe. I would never be the hardest guy around, but I was likely to be the most dangerous.

Beckworth housed about forty boys and was at the southern end of the picturesque Sussex village of Lindfield. The school we all attended was about a mile and a half away in Haywards Heath. We walked to and from school every day. It was a large school with approximately 800 students, male and female. The buildings were light and modern, surrounded by playgrounds and sports fields. It was nice to be back in a mixed school. The teachers were more like I had been used to, at my junior schools. They were more approachable, not stern and hard, as they had been at the Crypt.

There was a dramatic turn around in my schoolwork, everything started to go well, again. I came near the top of the class in most of my subjects, I was regularly used as an example of how a new boy could come in and do well. I never felt menaced by the staff, or by the students, during my time there I had the sort of troubles, many boys must have, but their was little malice intended and I dealt with them in my own way. Once they had got over the initial mickey taking, about my accent, it was a much nicer place to be. In general, I felt much better about things. I quickly got a reputation as someone not to try to take advantage of. I was to come across some boys who felt they had to prove themselves, but it wasn't anything to worry about. It was just the sorting out of the pecking order that young males of all species indulge in.

Completely different to bullying, was the initiation ceremony I knew was to come. Compared to things that had already happened to me in the past, it was nothing and I knew that when it came I would take it in good heart. The older boys subjected all the newcomers to it. There was a horse trough on the edge of the common, at the end of our drive. They waited for winter until the first ice formed on the trough, then stood around on the fateful morning to catch a newcomer. They grabbed me as I came through the gate and carried me to the trough, where the ice was broken with my head as it went through into the water. There was nothing malicious about it, they even supplied a towel to dry off with afterwards.

We were not allowed to leave the grounds very often, except for Saturday and Sunday afternoons. We walked into the village, but there wasn't much to do there. One sunny afternoon I went for a walk into the countryside, beyond the village. I was with Malcolm, whose full name was an impressive Malcolm Donald William Hamilton Burgess. We reached a bridge across the River Ouse. We climbed a gate into a field and walked alongside the river. Soon we came to a place where there was a small island, only about ten feet from the bank. We thought it would be great fun to get onto that island, to explore it. There was an old tree fallen across the gap, so I decided to scramble across. I was halfway across, when with a resounding crack, the tree gave way and I fell into the water. I grabbed one of the smaller branches and managed to haul myself onto the bank. I was soaked to the skin and very bedraggled, my clothes were a sorry state. It was a glorious day, so I decided to take my clothes off and lay them on the ground to dry in the sun. we were lying there, soaking up the sun when I heard a grunting noise.
I said 'what's that noise Malc?'
He replied, 'I don't know, but I don't like the sound of it.'

We got up and looked over the grassy earth bank we had been lying on and there, only a few feet away, were three huge sows. We jumped up, I grabbed my clothes and we ran like hell, leaping over the gate into the field without breaking stride. Once in the safety of the other field, we turned and looked to see if the sows were close behind us, but it seemed they hadn't been interested at all. They were still where we had last seen them, snuffling away at the ground. We laughed great belly laughs, with tears rolling down our cheeks. I was standing there with no clothes on laughing my head off. My clothes had dried out by now so I put them on and we walked back to Beckworth.

I was still making the same bombs I had used to such good effect at the Crypt. I made one using a large size Brylcreem jar and took it to the local common. A few of my friends came with me, fascinated as to what it would be like. They had never known anyone who could make a bomb. We all retired to what I thought would be a safe distance, it went off with a huge 'BOOM.' Everyone burst out laughing with the excitement and perhaps a bit of nervous energy. I don't think they had expected anything so powerful. I started to walk forward towards the hole in the ground when I noticed a large spike of glass embedded in the thick lapel of my school blazer. I treated explosives with a bit more respect after that. But the fascination with things that go bang has always stayed with me.

We stayed in the grounds most of the time, playing tennis, or snooker, with varying degrees of success. I hated football and never joined in after that first day. I played chess regularly in the common room and became quite a good player. We had some modern games too, my favourite was Buccaneer, a game of pirates sailing the seven seas in search of treasure. There were always things to do, but I started to want more, than just games.

In my class, there was a little girl called Nina, she was a really sweet and gentle person and was to become my girlfriend. I asked Mr Harrison if I could go to Nina's house for tea on Sunday. He said it would be all right, as long as I was collected and brought back. On the big day, Nina's father arrived, in a large car to collect me. He drove out into the country and stopped outside a most beautiful half timbered cottage. We went in and Nina's mum made me very welcome. They were lovely people. They owned a beautiful country cottage, I had never met anybody who owned anything like this. I thought they must be so rich, I couldn't comprehend it. Everyone I knew, lived in a house, rented from the council. I was overwhelmed by the thought of it. We had tea with sandwiches and cakes then retired to Nina's bedroom where she had a record player. We played her records all afternoon, until it was time for me to return to Beckworth.

Nina and I were sweethearts for what seemed like ages but probably wasn't. Because of the rules of the house I couldn't get to see her very often, so I think she just got fed up and dumped me. Neil Sedaka was in the hit parade singing, 'Breaking up is hard to do.' It was particularly poignant, at the time. We remained friends while I was there though and I think of her very fondly, even now, not having seen her since 1964.

Shortly after our breakup, my class were waiting in line, outside a classroom, for the teacher to arrive. Some of the boys were messing around, pushing and shoving. A lad next to me leaned over and punched the big ginger haired boy who was standing on the other side of me. Ginger turned and punched me a heavy blow on the nose causing blood to spurt everywhere. We started to fight, but when the teacher came up the stairs, shouting for us to stop fighting, Ginger stopped and looked towards the teacher. In that split second I hit him with a mighty blow that knocked him to the floor. The teacher went mad at me. I just said that Ginger had deserved it.

We were both taken to the headmaster, Mr Bulled, a rather apt name for the large overbearing man that he was. Mr Bulled caned us both, on the hand. I knew that this was the first and only time I would allow anyone to inflict corporal punishment on me, without fear of retribution. I looked at Mr Bulled with murder in my heart and said, 'you'll never do that to me again.' As he started to speak, I turned and walked out of his office. Normally he would have called me back but I think he thought better of it.

I think that this was the time that the honeymoon with Beckworth came to an end, I soon started to resent the rules that were imposed on me.

I came home, for the summer school holidays, Mum was home, it was lovely to see her, but she was not well. She could only walk with the aid of a stick. Sometimes she had to use a wheelchair and be pushed around because she had no strength to propel it herself. But the day I got off the train at Gloucester, she was standing there to greet me, with a huge smile on her face. It was one of the most memorable things of my life. I can see her standing there, longing to hug her son. It was a very emotional reunion.

All the time I was at Beckworth, I wrote letters to Mum, wherever she was and to Aunty Ethel, to reassure them that I was all right and to let them know how I was getting on. Aunty Ethel sent me regular postal orders, so that I would never be short of money. They both loved me and I couldn't wait to get to Matson to see how Aunty Ethel was. She was 76 now, but was still very much alive. I never realised, how old she was, until I thought about it, years later.

It was just as well that Aunty Ethel sent me small amounts of money regularly, because every weekend, we were supposed to be given half a crown for pocket money. Everyone was to be given the same. Parents had to lodge a sum of money with the Housemaster every term and he would give it out at the correct rate, every week. Mr Harrison called me in on many occasions to inform me that Dad had failed to lodge any money in my name and that he was unable to give me any. I felt hurt when this happened, but was never surprised. Thankfully, Aunty's money kept me from appearing too poor to the rest of the boys.

Still, I was home now, with six weeks, with nothing to do but enjoy myself. This summer I got to know a lot of the local kids of my own age. Although I was only around for short periods of time, I made some good friends. Down in Westbury Road, I met Phil Newman and his sister Linda. There were three girls who all lived in Westbury Road, Christine, Glenda and Susan. They were all good friends, I was always trying to snog with Christine, round the back of the garages, just down the road from her house. A bit further up, in Arlingham Road, lived John Jones, he became a good friend. We did lots of things together later.

We had a large area of waste ground, next to our prefab. We called it 'the dumps', because it was made up of piles of earth, dumped from building works, years earlier, now grown over with grass and weeds. Gordon and I rode our bikes over the dumps, it was a natural scramble track for us to ride and jump, round and round. Further along, the field flattened out and we shot out bows and arrows on it. I had a six-foot English longbow, with arrows that I bought from Fletchers sports shop in the Oxbode. I shot at targets, put up at different distances and was pretty good with it. The most stupid thing we did was to shoot up in the air, so that the arrows went out of sight. Then wait until they hit the ground and measure who had got the closest to the group of archers. We stood in a group, looking up, trying to see the arrows. We never thought that if we got too close, the arrow would go right through the top of our heads. We must have done this hundreds of times, without injury, more from luck than judgement. I had got hold of my first air rifle. It was a low powered, battered old .177 BSA. I shot at tin cans in the back garden. I balanced them on the fenceposts, as they were the only part of the garden still visible. Dad hadn't cut the grass, or done anything in the garden, since we moved here. I don't think he ever did anything to the garden, the whole time we lived there. It was a constant source of annoyance to Mr Hooper who lived across the road. Mr Hooper was a keen gardener and had taken over the garden of the burnt down prefab next to us, to grow his vegetables in. He was fighting a constant battle against the encroachment of weeds from our garden, but he was a nice man and rarely said anything. The grass in our garden in summer was about three feet high. Sometimes Dad managed to catch the council grass cutters when they were doing the dumps next to our garden, with their machines. Dad would give them a couple of quid to come in and do our jungle. He even pulled the fence down so that they could drive the machine straight in.

This was my rifle range, we had an apple tree just outside the back door, but they were cooking apples, no good at all to me. I used the apples as targets. Trying to shoot them off the tree. The rifle was quite accurate, but was so feeble that if anybody wore a coat, a direct hit, was hardly noticeable. One day Gordon was running around on the dumps, I took aim and got him, in the leg while he was in full flight. He fell to the ground, like a wounded soldier and made a terrible fuss about it. I took a look at it and there was only a small red mark. I told him to shut up and take it like a man. A typical big brothers' unsympathetic attitude, but there was no doubt, that I would never have done any harm to him, or allowed anyone else to harm him, if it was in my power to help him in any way.

Further down the fields, there was a brook. We had a swing tied to the branch of a big old tree, so that we could swing across the brook, landing in Grange Road. Opposite this swing was a field leading to an orchard. I don't know who's it was but it was one of our scrogging targets. Turning left to the end of Grange Road, across Stroud Road there was an old derelict house, we all knew as 'the old house.' We went there often and played in the ruins, you could take a girl there and get some privacy, in the early evening. I rode my first motorcycle in the grounds of the old house. I can't remember who's bike it was, but it was a small hand gearchange BSA. I tore up and down the field and I was hooked, I would be a biker for the rest of my life.

My cousin Hugh was building a pigeon loft in his back garden and needed some bricks for the foundations. We went to this old house over a period of three or four evening to get some. We took Hugh's old wooden cart so we could wheel the bricks home. It was hard going though, because we carried them through a large concrete pipe which ran under the Stroud Road and emerged in Grange Road, fearing detection if we went above ground. We loaded them onto the cart and pulled it across the fields to Hugh's house.

One day I was in the field where we had a swing across the brook, when a woman came striding across the field. When she got to us she grabbed her son and said, come with me, I've told you you're not to play down here with him, pointing towards Gordon. Taken by surprise, Gordon asked her what was wrong, but instead of answering, she slapped him. I was standing next to her when she did it and gave her a hefty slap that really shook her. She started shouting that she knew where we lived and she would return with her husband, to sort me out.

I went home and went into the bedroom to wake Dad up. I told him what had happened and that there might be trouble. Soon there was a pounding on the front door. I looked out of the window and could see that they were out for blood.

Dad got out of bed, wearing his regular night attire. A collarless shirt and a pair a baggy Y fronts. He went to the door, with Gordon and me standing behind him. It was quite a sight from behind with his spindly, pure white legs sticking out from the bottom of that old shirt. God knows what they thought when they saw it from the front. They started shouting that I had hit the woman, but Dad wasn't having any of it.
He said, 'bugger off before I belt the pair of you.'
They knew they weren't going to get anywhere with us so they beat a retreat shouting that they would get the police.
Dad just repeated, louder this time, 'go on bugger off.'
They never came back.

Along Grange Road there was a railway bridge. On the right, just before the bridge was King's farm. On the far side of the bridge, there was Lovell's orchard. The apples there were absolutely gorgeous. We went scrogging there too, but didn't risk going under the bridge and having to climb through the formidable hedge. Instead we went into a tunnel which had been cut into the railway embankment to allow the brook to flow through. The tunnel seemed very long then, it had a bend in it so you couldn't see light from the other end until you got halfway through. But it was worth it. The tunnel came out directly in the corner of the orchard. We filled our shirts until they were bulging like a man with a beer belly. Then we made our way back through the tunnel to enjoy our feast.

I was into rock and roll, Elvis Presley was my idol. Mum took me into town and bought me a pair of winkle picker shoes, a black shirt and my first leather biker style jacket.

To finish off the rocker ensemble, Aunty Ethel bought me a hand made studded belt. It was made especially for me at Cantillions leather shop, in King Street.

Soon it was time to go back to school, I set off on the train to London. I was becoming a seasoned traveller now. I got the bus from Haywards Heath, to Lindfield and walked in through the school gates. Matron was the first member of staff to see me in my new outfit of black shirt, leather jacket and winkle pickers. She was horrified and I was told that I was not to wear that sort of clothes as long as I was at Beckworth. The jacket was to be put away and returned to me when I was going home, next time. It took me a long time to find where they had put it, but find it I did and wear it I did. I already knew the house inside out. I crept around in the dead of night, down the back stairs, into the kitchen to raid the biscuits in the larder. From the kitchen I could get anywhere without being discovered, as long as I was quiet. I started sneaking in and out of the home, they caught me occasionally but no matter what they did I couldn't be stopped.

One morning I decided that I'd had enough. Instead of going to school, I walked on, past the school gates, to the London to Brighton Road. I started to thumb a lift, I was a bit shy about it at first, this being my first attempt at hitch hiking. I soon got a lift in an old van. The driver was going to Mitcham, it was a good first lift. When he dropped me off, I started walking up the A23 towards Central London. The plan was to wait until nighttime and make my way to Covent Garden, where I thought there would be lorries, loading for Gloucester or nearby. Covent Garden was a fruit and vegetable market then. At night, lorries were loaded with fresh produce for delivery the next morning.

I didn't get another lift into London so I kept walking for hours and eventually found myself in the West End.

It was too early to make my way to Covent Garden, so I thought I would have a good look around Soho. I was only thirteen and hadn't seen anything like it before. The lights in Piccadilly Circus were particularly fascinating. I wandered around for hours, just taking it all in. At around 9-o clock I was looking in a shop window, in Shaftesbury Avenue, when a man tapped me on the shoulder.

I turned towards him and he said, 'can you tell me the way to Trafalgar Square.'
I replied, 'No! Sorry mate, I'm a stranger here, just passing through.'
He produced a warrant card from his pocket and grabbed me by the shoulder.
He said 'read this card.'
I said, 'it's okay, I know who you are.'
He said, 'read it son; don't take anyone at face value in this town.'
The warrant card proved that he was an officer with the Metropolitan Police. He said, 'are you satisfied that I am a police officer',
to which I replied, 'yes.'
He said, 'okay get in the car.'
I hadn't even noticed the other officer in the car, which had quietly drawn up close to where we were standing.
I got in the car and off we went through the streets of London, to Bow Street police station. They took me in through the front entrance, into a large office, full of policemen and women, milling around. I was taken to a desk and told to sit down. They brought a WPC who sat on the other side of the desk. They asked me my name, where I was from and what I was doing in the West End at night.
I refused to answer any of the questions.
They were very nice, not at all oppressive, but I was determined to say nothing.

At about 1 o clock in the morning they gave up and took me to a cell. We went through a locked door into a tiled corridor. The cell doors were all on the right hand side of the corridor. On the left were small washbasins, screwed to the wall. I was taken past most of these doors, almost to the end, when I was told to go into one. Inside was a bed with a mattress, a blanket and a toilet. I was left there, with the lights on. The cell was decorated with the same tiles as in the corridor, green and white. The window was so high up no one would ever have been able to see out of it. It was cold, I wrapped the blanket around me, but I still sat there all night, shivering. I tried to get some sleep, but it was impossible. My mind was racing, thinking of what might happen next, wondering if I would get a chance to escape. It was a very long boring night, I sat there looking at the blank, tiled walls, thinking, if I stay in here too long, I will go mad.

Eventually I heard the key rattle, in the door at the end of the corridor. Footsteps tap tapped along the stone floor, until they stopped outside my cell door. The key rattled again and the door opened. A policeman stood there, holding a tray with a mug of tea, two boiled eggs and two slices of bread and butter, on it.
He said, 'have your breakfast, I will be back later and we will have another talk.'
I was starving and I ate with vigour. The tea went down a treat and warmed me up.

I didn't have a watch, so had no way of knowing what the time was, but it seemed like an age that I was waiting for the policeman to return. I sat there, looking round the cell, my brain screaming with boredom.

When he did return, he took me back into the office I had been in the night before. I saw a clock and realised that it was nearly mid day.

They asked me the same questions they had asked me the night before, but again I wouldn't answer.

After a while the WPC suddenly said, 'do you know this gentleman.'

I looked round and standing behind me was the social worker, who had taken me to Beckworth, a year earlier.

I said, 'yes I know him.'

I knew the game was up. I was secretly very relieved that I was going to get out of this place.

He took me out into the street and asked me if I was hungry. I said that I was, so we went into a café. I had a plate of fish and chips, followed by strawberries and cream. Then it was off to the station and I was escorted back to Beckworth.

They asked me why I had absconded. It was the first time I had heard the word absconded. It sounded much more grand than just running away. I told them I had had enough and wanted to go home. They told me that I would have to stay at Beckworth and make the best of it and not to do it again or I would be in big trouble.

Winter came and the beautiful village of Lindfield, was transformed from a picture postcard scene to a winter scene equally as pretty. It was the most beautiful place to live I could ever imagine. I envied all the local people I met and thought how lucky they were. This winter the village pond froze solid. It was a large pond in the centre of the village; it had a island in the middle where ducks nested. But this year the ice was so thick, the villagers were skating on it. I was lucky enough to borrow some skates from a friend and I learned to skate on ice, a skill that I never lost.

The Christmas holiday came and we went to Haywards Heath Railway Station to catch our respective train's home. Quite a few of my friends were catching the same train as I was, a fast train, through to London, from where we would go our separate ways. I had kept a handful of bangers from November, which we threw out of the windows as the train sped through the small stations, packed with commuters. We could see people shaking their fists and shouting as we disappeared into the distance. We thought it was a great wheeze and laughed uncontrollably.

Home again, this time for Christmas. Mum wasn't there; she was back in hospital, this time in Edinburgh, near her family. I was told she was doing really well there. I remember it as a cold, lonely time of wandering the avenues of Tuffley on dark nights. Anything to keep me out of the house. Aunty Ethel gave me a small transistor radio for Christmas. It was a modern miracle then. They were very expensive and no one else I knew had one. It had an earpiece so I could use it privately when necessary. I wandered around the estate in the evenings, no matter how cold it was, wearing the earpiece, trying to tune the radio to Luxembourg, the reception was terrible, with lots of squealing and fading in and out. But it was the only station playing the sort of music I wanted to hear. Radio Luxembourg was a commercial radio station, complete with advertisements, the most memorable was the one by Horace Batchelor, of Keynsham It had a slogan that was repeated over and over again, every night. It was for a football pools system. Whether it was any good I have no idea, but if the advertising was anything to go by, Horace should have made a fortune

I took this radio back to Beckworth with me and used it a lot. I had to keep it quiet, because I knew I wouldn't be allowed to have it in the dormitory in the evenings, which was the time when the best music programmes were on, so it was important to keep the radio a secret. I got into bed and put the earpiece in, to listen to the latest records in private.

It was 1963 and a new sound had just hit the music scene that was to change everything. I heard The Beatles for the first time. This was to be the biggest ever year of change to hit youth culture. The Beatles made Love Me Do, followed quickly by Please Please Me and From Me To You. The Rolling Stones released Come on, which I thought was the greatest record ever, at that time. It was the start of a revolution, which would carry me with it for years to come. We were listening to British groups, instead of Americans. The British music scene was to go on to dominate the world.

An even bigger thing that would make me stand out from the crowd for a long time and make me a well known figure, was my decision from the first sight of The Beatles and later Brian Jones of the Rolling Stones, to grow my hair long. This was something the older generation could not accept. I washed the grease out of my hair and let it hang down. When I had washed the grease out, it was already longer than was acceptable to the school and I was immediately told to get it cut. I was to have this problem for the next few years, but I never gave in to their threats.My euphoria with the new music was to be short lived, I hid the radio, in my bedside locker during the day, thinking it would be safe. I went to locker one evening and it was gone. I couldn't believe it. The loss of this musical lifeline was devastating. I asked all the boys, but nobody had seen it. I had to go to Mr Harrison to report that my radio had been stolen. He wasn't very happy about the fact that I'd kept it without his permission, but after he finished telling me that it was my own fault for keeping a valuable item in the house, he agreed to investigate the disappearance.

I was very depressed about it. It wasn't the fact that I no longer had the use and enjoyment of the radio. What was getting to me was that I would have to tell Aunty Ethel, that the radio she had given me had been stolen. I felt as if I had let her down by not looking after it properly and I couldn't bring myself to tell her. I knew she would be sympathetic, but that didn't help, I still felt that I had let her down. I was feeling pretty low at this time, it was to be the first time I considered suicide. I walked to school in the mornings along the main road and stood at the edge waiting for a large vehicle to come along, but I never had the courage to take that step.

Two weeks went by, then Mr Harrison called me into his office. There was a policeman with him and I could see my radio on his desk. I felt so relieved to see it, I had a big grin on my face. That joy was soon to turn anger, when the policeman picked up the radio and told me that they had caught the boy responsible, but that he had damaged the radio beyond repair. The policeman handed me the radio and I knew immediately that what he had said was true. It was as light as a feather, the insides were completely missing. I asked, why had the boy done such a thing? They said they couldn't explain it. They wouldn't tell me who the boy was, or why I couldn't be compensated, which made me even angrier. I had lost my radio, they knew who had stolen it and he wasn't going to be made to pay for it. My first lesson in justice, or lack of it, which would influence my decisions for the rest of my life. Never rely on other people's rules. I would forever live by my own strong sense of what is right and what is wrong, whatever the law said. The law, truly is an ass.

Only a few days later I heard a rumour, that the police had been seen, talking to a boy who was a year older than me. It didn't take a genius to work out why. I went to him and even though he was bigger than I was, I asked him straight out, why he had taken my radio, then smashed it to pieces. He said, 'piss off you little prat or I'll smash you as well.' I said okay and walked away.
The boys in my dormitory knew it would not end there. They all wanted to know what I would do, but I just said I would deal with it. Later, I went to the boy and said, in front of his peers, I'm going to take you now, or outside, wherever you like.

He had to make a choice, or look a coward in front of his friends, I was smaller than him, which made it even harder for him to back down.

He said, 'we will meet in the old field at 6 o clock.'

I agreed.

A buzz went round the whole house. My friends said, I must be mad going up against him. He certainly didn't seem to be worried about the prospect.

The appointed time came and it seemed as if the whole house was there. I had already decided, there was to be no more talking. As soon as we faced each other I launched a ferocious attack, punching, kicking and butting him, as hard and as quickly as I could. In no time at all, it was over. He was lying on the ground, in the worst state I had ever seen anyone. He was covered in blood and had to be carried back to the house. The story that everybody, quickly decided on, was that he had fallen, head first, from a tree.

I saw him the next day and he was black and blue, so bad I almost felt sorry for him, but it was a fleeting emotion and I soon steeled myself against it.

My reputation was growing, but now I encountered people who wanted to get a reputation themselves, by beating me. It was a nuisance at times, but made me even stronger.

There were a lot of things happening in the world at this time, or maybe I was just starting to notice them, The Great Train Robbery, happened not too far away from Lindfield, so we took a particular interest in that.

The Profumo scandal broke and was of special interest to us as we were reaching the age of sexual awareness. It made Christine Keeler and Mandy Rice Davis into household names, which I will never forget.

Another name which became a part of the English Language, to mean bad landlord, was Rachman. The story of Rachman, a slum landlord taking advantage of the poor was big news in 1963.

Martin Luther King made his famous, 'I have a dream' speech.

Henry Cooper knocked over Cassius Clay and we all knew Henry had been robbed.

Later this year John F Kennedy was shot and killed in Dallas, Texas.

One morning we got out of bed and went into the nearest washroom, to find Mr Harrison waiting there. One of the sink plugs had gone missing and we all had to turn out our wash bags, in search of it. I turned mine out and to my horror, the plug was there. Someone had put it there, to get me into trouble, Mr Harrison asked me what it was doing in my bag. I replied that it was not the missing plug. I said my Mum had given me the plug, because when she had been in the RAF, she had been to many places where the plugs were missing and it made it easier to have your own, just in case. It wasn't true, but it was the sort of thing Mum would have thought of.

Mr Harrison accepted this explanation, even though I don't think he believed it. Shortly afterwards, he called me into his office and told me that he was moving me from the dormitory, into a small single room, with it's own facilities, so that I wouldn't have to mix with the other boys. I was absolutely delighted, with this prospect. Mr Harrison thought it was to be an imposition, but it was entirely the reverse. Later, he tried to put me back into a dormitory, but I refused. I loved that little room, it was the first bedroom I had ever had that was my own.

I came down to breakfast one morning to find there was a relief House Master on duty. Something was obviously wrong. We all went into the dining room and waited to find out what had happened. Finally matron came in with tears in her eyes. She announced, very bravely, that Mr Harrison had died during the night and that she would be leaving. We were soon to have a new House Master and Matron, until then we would have a relief.

 A few weeks later Mr and Mrs Irwin arrived to take over, they were from South Wales and were strong supporters of rugby union. Coming from Gloucester, I soon found we had a lot in common and we got on well from the start. We talked more on equal terms than I had been used to. Mrs Irwin had a collection of Penguin Books, which although she had some reservations that they would be too adult for me, she let me borrow. That was the start of a lifelong addiction to historical novels.

Soon after Mr Irwin's arrival, they decided to introduce rugby to the school sports curriculum. Until now they had only played cricket and football. Both sports I detested and thought of as an utter waste of time. I suddenly found that I could outplay anyone in my year. It showed me the value of knowledge and training. I had played rugby and enjoyed it immensely, at my other schools. Even after they got the hang of the game, I could run rings round them. My experience was too great for them to overcome in a short time. It was so easy to score sometimes I used to laugh like a drain.

Summer holidays came round again, I got the train again to London and I had a bit of time to spare, before my connection to Gloucester, so I got the underground to Trafalgar Square. There was an escape artist doing his act, all trussed up in chains, his accomplice putting him in a white sack and fastening it up with chains and padlocks. As I stood there fascinated by this act, a girl walked by wearing a minidress. I had never seen anything like it, all the girls I had seen up to now all wore full skirts to below the knee. This was the latest fashion and was the sexiest thing I had ever seen. The dress was made of a predominantly blue and red multi coloured, silky material, it was tight and followed every contour of her body, so shapely and sexy that I had to follow her for a few minutes just to take it in. All thoughts of the escapologist completely forgotten.

Soon I was back in Gloucester, meeting all my friends, it was particularly good this time as there had been such a dramatic change in my appearance. My hair was not greasy any more and already longer than any of the other boys. The girls loved it and I started to play the field. Chatting up the girls was easier than it had ever been. They all wanted to hear about what was happening in London, the most swinging place in the world at that time. I was the only one they knew who went there regularly. I started going to the youth club on Friday evenings, at the Tuffley Rovers building, in Lower Tuffley Lane. In the corner of the hall, there was a small record player set up on a table,. We took our own records to play on it and dance the latest dances. I knew most of the people here, it was a good way to spend an evening. I met Bobby Grant, who would become a lifelong friend. There were the sisters Shirley and Rose Cunnigham and Bridget Maloney, who was so nice, it frightened me off, Ted Whittle, Alan Boughton Andy Powell, Chris Rogers and many others, all equally as important.

All this was a different and much more exciting world, than I had at Beckworth. When I went back to school, I was to become even more resentful of the restrictions placed upon me. The regime meant, much more isolation from the things I felt were important, like girls, music and dancing. We were encouraged more to academic study and sport. I couldn't think of anything I wanted to do less, than study or play games, when the girls were getting more attractive every day.

At school things were going much the same as they had since I came here, my grades were good and I only had a couple of problems with boys who needed to prove themselves as tough guys. One lad who had been pushing me for a few days, without any response, decided that he would trample my little plot, in the school garden. We all had a plot to grow vegetables in. He came across and walked all over the seeds I had just planted, scuffing the earth up as he went. He must have been pretty stupid when I think about it. Fancy antagonising someone when they have a garden fork in their hands. I stuck him in the leg with the fork and he started screaming that he had been stabbed. The teacher came running over to see what had happened. I said I had been breaking up some earth with the fork, when the boy had stupidly come alongside me and I had accidentally stabbed him. There was an inquiry over it but the boy never said anything different. He had more respect for me, after that.

The All Blacks were on tour, playing South Eastern counties at Hove. Mr Irwin called me aside and told me he had a ticket for the game but was unable to use it. He said I could go instead if I would like to. He gave me the money for the train and off I went on my own to Hove. It was a great day out and an act of kindness I never forgot. But it couldn't make up for my perceived lack of freedom. It was time for me to make a break for home again.

I told my friend Stuart Bennett that I was going and he asked if he could come with me, he was from Gloucester as well. I told him I didn't think it was a good idea, as he was a good student, pretty contented with his lot at Beckworth. He wasn't constantly at odds with authority like I was. Stuart kept on, so I gave in to his pleas. I told him I would be going the next morning.

The morning seemed to me to be the best time to go, as it gave us all day, up until teatime at 5-o clock before we would be missed. I decided to give London a miss this time, after my previous experience. I worked out a route across country, through Horsham, Guildford, Basingstoke, Newbury and Swindon, to good old Gloucester. It was slow going, the lifts were few and far between at times and we didn't make very good time. When we got to Basingstoke we decided to take a short train ride to Newbury. We were in a compartment with a city gent type and he started asking question about our journey. We told such outrageous lies he must have thought we were mad. We got off the train and resumed our hitch hiking, walking along the A4 towards Swindon. Progress was still slow, so we decided to get into a field and spend the night tucked up under a hedge. Although the weather was warm, it went off very cold in the night and we didn't sleep much, with nothing to cover ourselves with, but at least it was a rest.

The next day we were up bright and early and on the move. We got a couple of good lifts and we were in Gloucester by lunchtime. Stuart asked me if I would go with him to his house. I didn't think it was a very good idea, but he pleaded with me, I think he thought there might be safety in numbers. He was wrong though because his mother started telling him off almost as soon as we went through the door. I made a hasty exit and made my way home. Much to my surprise, Dad was home. He had been contacted by the police and told that I was probably on my way.

He said. 'Took your time, didn't you'?

I didn't reply.

He said, 'you know you'll have to go back, don't you.'

I said, 'I'll never settle there Dad. It's time I came home.'

He said, 'I'll see what I can do.'

I stayed at home for a few days, going round seeing my friends and having a laugh about my adventure, then I took the train back to school. I spent more and more time in London every time I went through. I was starting to know the city quite well. I went to Carnaby Street to see the fashion shops, they were really something. Carnaby Street was a small cobbled lane then, with little shops, full of the latest styles. Lord Johns tailors was just a single fronted shop, but was famous already. I walked up and down the street in awe of it all.

I got back to Beckworth and things carried on as normal for a while, then one day, I was called into Mr Irwin's office. There was a social worker there, who wanted to talk to me. He said, that taking everything into consideration, I would be able to go back home, as long as I agreed to go to Linden Road secondary school. Although it was well below the academic standard I was used to, with my record, it was the only school that would take me. It was to be my choice, to go or to stay at Beckworth.

I made what was probably the worst choice I would ever make.

I chose to go home.

I didn't appreciate the benefits I could have had if I had stayed, but life was out there and I needed to live it.

Chapter 5
Back Home

I was pleased to get back to Gloucester and wasn't worried about going to Linden Road school, as I already knew some of the boys and girls there. My dog Tina was pleased to see me as usual, her tail wagging incessantly. She didn't leave my side for days after I got home. I had always worried that she would take offence at me going away and leaving her, or forget me, but my fears were unfounded, she was always delighted to see me whenever I came home and I had no intention of leaving again.

This was my third senior school but I wouldn't need a new uniform this time. I was past that. My uniform at Linden Road was my Leather jacket or a Donkey Jacket and a pair of hob nailed army boots that I got from the Army and Navy stores at the bottom of Westgate Street. The boots were cheap, lasted forever and delivered a terrible blow when applied to an adversary during a fight. The Donkey jacket was big, again lasted well, was warm and was cheap to buy.

Mum wasn't home at the moment, she was still in Scotland, but was doing well. Things were a bit rough and ready at home. I hardly saw Dad, so I came and went as I pleased. Dad hardly knew if I was there or not. He was still working nightshift at the post office in George Street, by day he was driving school buses for Cathedral coaches and driving a taxi for Thomas taxis. It didn't leave a lot of time for him to take much interest in what I was doing. He gave me some money to live on and left me to it.

I was becoming more independent every day. I started to feel that I didn't need anybody.

Bobby Grant lived in Tennyson Avenue, Podsmead, on the route I would take to school. I often called in on her in the mornings. Mrs Grant would give me a cup of tea, while we chatted. They were a lovely family, it was like a breath of fresh air to me to sit and talk with them. Bobby and I set off for school on our bikes, riding to the Lannet together, where we had to split up, Bobby carrying on to Derby Road to the Central Girls School and me turning down Balfour Road to our school entrance.

Linden Road school was an old red brick building, with a tall chimney that could be seen from a great distance. It was surrounded by black iron railings, with the gate to the boys entrance, off Balfour Road. The girls entrance was in Linden Road. Everything was small and dark, it was like going back in time, with the high windows, you couldn't see out of. Old fashioned sloping desks with inkwells in the corners. A boy would be assigned to filling these inkwells at the start of a lesson. No ball point pens were allowed. If you didn't have a fountain pen, a pen would be issued to you, then handed back when you left for the next class. These pens were a stick with a nib fixed to one end, which had to be dipped into the inkwell, every few words. There was usually a horrendous mess on the page after one of these was used. These pens were much more use as darts. They could be very accurate with practice, the nibs were sharp and stuck into wood or anything soft. Many battles would be waged across the classrooms with these so-called pens. This school had an anarchy that I was unused to but would embrace and exploit to the limit.

Girls also attended Linden Road, but unlike my last school, the girls here were completely segregated, the two halves of the school were separated by railings in the playground, with an exclusion zone, either side of the railings to keep us apart. The exclusion zone never worked though, we were always hanging over the railings at break times. I chatted to Jackie Worral across these railings. Jackie didn't seem to be worried about these silly rules either and I fancied her like crazy. Inside the school, the girls used all of the building on one side of the main hall, which doubled as the gym and the boys used everything on the other side. Some of the classrooms had their doors off the main hall, so when we came in or out we could see the girls doing the same on the other side. It was a bit like East and West Berlin. A completely ridiculous situation.

Once again, on my first day, the school tough guys, Paul Wellington and Dave Simmonds approached me. Although they were a year older and reaching the end of their school lives at the age of fifteen, I stood my ground and showed no fear. After this stand off I had no further trouble with them. I was now fourteen and had about a year and a half, of schooling left. I couldn't wait to get out of this place. It had just turned 1964 and these boys would be leaving school at Easter. It would soon be my turn.

By now my hair was something to behold, the school just wasn't ready for it. From the day I arrived, they started telling me I had to get it cut. I told them they had, 'no chance.' They tried the 'try to be a credit to the school' approach. They tried the 'we'll cut it for you approach', but nothing was ever going to work. My hair made me an individual. Parents wouldn't allow their boys to grow their hair long and schools certainly wouldn't allow it. Even working men couldn't get away with it. Employers wouldn't allow it. Anyone who wanted their hair long would have to be strong of character to resist the pressures and the taunts from people who couldn't come to terms with it. This was a revolution as far as they were concerned and it threw them into confusion. It's hard to imagine such a fuss now, over something we would regard as trivial, but these were different times. This was long before the Hippie period when everyone wore their hair long. At this time, there were only two other people in Gloucester with hair in the same league as mine. They were Elwin Edwards, who played in a rock band and had to have special permission from his employers, the GPO, to have his hair long and Paul Cantillion, who was a boxer and didn't have to worry about what other people thought. That's how rare it was. Hair as long as mine wasn't just a fashion statement, it was a show of rebellion against traditional values. The people of Gloucester had never seen anything like it except for rock bands on the television.

My hair and my individual sense of style was to bring me into a lot of conflict with what we later called, the straights. They were people who couldn't come to terms with the 60's youth revolution.

At school it was seen as constant problem that wouldn't go away, they saw it as a challenge to their authority as guardians of the morality of the young people in their charge. How could having long hair be considered a danger to the morality of the nation? I don't know, but that how it was. In 1964, the Rolling Stones went to the USA and were ridiculed by the establishment because of their appearance to such an extent, that they were unable to get their talent across to the kids.

The teachers at Linden school were a very mixed bunch, from the stern Mr Sterry, the maths teacher to the over familiar, rather bohemian art teacher, Donald Mann, who was always saying, give us a fag Balli, refusing to believe that I didn't smoke.

Herbie Wayne, the English teacher, seemed to me, the best teacher they had, he didn't care what I looked like. He appreciated my skills and capacity to learn and never treated me badly. His storytelling had great expression, he could hold the attention of a class without threats because he was such an interesting man. He made it interesting to learn. He was my idea of what teachers should be like, but such men were rare. Unfortunately he left the school later in the same year I started there.

Mr Rickets was my first form teacher. He was more like the archetypal teacher, stern and hard, shouting the odds. It got him no respect at all. We just thought he was an asshole. To make things worse it came to my knowledge that he was spreading lies about me to the other teachers, trying to get me into trouble. Most notably that he had seen me smoking in the bike sheds. I was guilty of a lot of things, but smoking wasn't one of them. It seemed a waste of time and money to me. Why did a man in his position do such things? Respect rating zero.

Colin Charter, the science master was okay, although he had his moments. We did used to play him up terribly at times.

Mr Kelly, the metalwork teacher was a lovely old man, who retired soon after I arrived at the school. He was replaced by Derek Hendry, who wasn't an awful lot older than we were. He had worked at Walkers stores in Matson as a delivery boy until he went to college. My Mum worked there at the time and wanted me to take over the delivery round when Derek left, but I was just too young. He was all right, was Derek. He had young ideas and knew where I was coming from. I never had a problem with him. In fact I took evening classes in metalwork at Linden, after I left school.

Norman Talbot, the games master was okay too, some didn't like him because he had a habit of grabbing boys by the sideburns and tweaking the hair when he was trying to make a point. He picked me for the school rugby team a few times. The first match I played was against my old school, the Crypt. In the first half, I got a hard knock on the nose, which started it bleeding heavily, so I had to leave the field. I came back on when the bleeding stopped and we went on to win. That win was immensely satisfying. I think picking me for the team may have been in part, a ploy to persuade me to get my hair cut, because before long, Norman took me aside and said, I couldn't continue to represent the school, while my hair was long. So it was bye bye rugby.

I politely told him where he could stick his team. He got a bit angry about it, but who cared. When I think about it, he had a lot to put up with. I think Norman had come up with the plan, of picking me for the team, hoping he would be able to bring me into line. Like every other plan they devised, it didn't work.

After this incident I hardly played games again, only when I couldn't escape on the journey from school to the sports fields at the Black Bridge where we always had games on a Wednesday afternoon. We assembled in the playground for the register to be taken to make sure we were all there. We formed a crocodile to walk about three-quarters of a mile, to the playing fields. A teacher led the way and another brought up the rear, but there were places where the teacher at the rear couldn't see us. We took our chance to leap over a wall, or dive behind a hedge, to hide until the crocodile had passed out of sight. The boys left in the crocodile laughed uncontrollably at the sight of us diving left and right into the bushes. The teacher would shout at them to be quiet, but never seemed to realise what was happening. Quite a few boys disappeared on that journey every week. We often walked up to that spot during the lunch break to hide our bikes in the bushes so that as soon as we were free, we could ride off to do what we wanted.

On one of these occasions, Chris Rogers and I went down to the stream at the bottom of Masefield Avenue. It was countryside down there then, the stream was clear and fast running, full of wildlife. Beautifully coloured small fish, sticklebacks and others I can't remember the names of. There were also different species of newts there. It was a tranquil spot and we spent the afternoon, watching the wildlife, going about its day to day existence. A memorable afternoon, much more memorable than another games period.

Chris was at my house one day, we were going out somewhere and I needed some money. Dad was in bed asleep as he often was during the day. We both crept into his bedroom, so that I could steal some change from the pocket of his trousers. As we crept past him,
Chris said, 'oh no! He's awake.'
It scared me for a second, until I looked round and saw that Dad was sound asleep.
I put my finger to my lips and said 'SSSSSH.'
I went on, into the room, picked up Dads GPO issue trousers and took half a crown out of the pocket. When we got out of the bedroom,
Chris said, 'but he was watching us.'
I replied, 'no he wasn't he always sleeps with his eyes open.'
I was used to it and hadn't thought to mention it to Chris. It did look a bit spooky if you weren't used to it.

My old red bike was by now much too small for me now and I had no chance of buying another. I asked around everyone I knew and managed to scrounge enough parts to put together a bike, big enough for me to ride to school. It had a huge old frame, odd sized wheels and an old fashioned, very large saddle, which I covered in fur. It looked like a bears head. The handlebars came off a motorcycle scrambler. They were bent and no use for racing any more, but I straightened them enough to use on my bike. The tyres had holes in them, which I plugged with bits of other worn out tyres, cut into strips. The ride was a bit rough where the tyres were so lumpy, but it got me around. When I was riding up Wilton Road one afternoon, on my way home from school, I came across a rag and bone cart. I saw a wheel and tyre on the back, that looked better than the one I had, so I dragged it off the pile and rode off. The ragman had seen me though and came running out of the house shouting at me to come back with his wheel. Some hope! I was riding like the wind. The wheel turned out to be an aluminium racing wheel, with a 12 tooth fixed gear. It took some starting off, but once moving it made the bike really fast. It was fun to ride too, but it had its disadvantages, you couldn't stop pedalling to take a rest. It was good fun to get up some speed, then stand on one pedal with my leg straight, making my body go up and down, up and down, it looked really comical. I was doing it in Kings square one day, when the chain snapped and I hit the crossbar with a resounding thump that brought tears to my eyes. Worse still, I had no money to repair it, or to get home. So I went to the cycle park, on the corner of King Street and using a small knife, managed to prise a split link from another cycle and repair my own chain.

I rode that bike everywhere, I would sometimes wait for a bus to leave Kings Square and try to race it to Tuffley. I could beat it most of the time, sometimes getting in the slipstream, then overtaking as it slowed to pick up passengers. I was doing this one day when a policeman on a big black cycle with a 3 speed hub gave chase. I saw him coming and wondered what he wanted. I kept going, pulling away from him until we got to Stroud Road hill where by using his gears he had the edge. I still had my old fixed wheel, which was hopeless going up hills. When he caught me, he was all red in the face and sweating. He asked what I thought I was doing trying to get away from him.
I said, 'sorry I didn't think you were trying to catch me. I thought you must have been in a hurry to get somewhere.'
He said, you haven't got a rear brake on that bike.
I said, 'I know, you don't have to have one with a fixed wheel.'
He said, 'oh bugger', turned around and set off back down the hill.

I was riding along Parkend Road one afternoon when I got it wrong crossing the railway lines. The lines crossed the road at an angle of about thirty degrees, while the safe angle for a bicycle to cross them was ninety degrees, so cyclists had to go out into the road slightly and cut back to cross the lines at a better angle. I had done it many times, but this time my front wheel went down into the railway line,

58

resulting in me being thrown off at speed. I tore my jacket and trousers and skinned my knees and elbows. It was a well-known hazard.

I was going home on the bus one Saturday morning with my cousin Hugh, when the bus suddenly braked hard. We were half way down Seventh Avenue, almost home. We sat and waited to find out what was wrong and could hear people saying that a child had been run over. After a while the conductor came up the stairs and told us there had been an accident and we would have to get off. As we went through the door, which was at the front, we couldn't help but see that the child was lying behind the front wheel, his leg having been run over. It was only the briefest of glimpses but it was enough. We walked the rest of the way to Hugh's house. When we went in, Aunty Ina said, 'what's the matter with you two, you are as white as ghosts.' I was in a cold sweat. It was the worst thing I had ever seen.

I was going to the youth club regularly now, it was the Friday night highlight at the start of the weekend. Ready Steady Go was a new pop program on the television. It featured all the new artists, like the Beatles, the Rolling Stones, The Kinks, The Animals, Manfred Mann and some of the Americans like Ike and Tina Turner, P J Proby, Gene Pitney and one of my particular favourites, John Lee Hooker. They also had a weekly new dance lesson. I watched that first and then it was out to the club, to try out the latest dances. There were lots of pretty girls there to dance and talk with and I always enjoyed the company of pretty girls. Shirley Cunningham who had blond hair and her sister Rose who had strikingly beautiful jet black hair were still regulars at the club and so was Bridget Maloney, who was so nice I don't have the words to describe her.

I was talking with my friends when Bobby Grant arrived with her cousin Mary. None of us had ever seen Mary before, she was so beautiful we were all struck dumb for a moment, then all we could talk about was Mary.
I said, 'I'm off to talk to them.'
My pals said, 'you've got no chance there.'
I was in with a head start though because Bobby, who was also beautiful and therefore unapproachable to many of the boys was already a good friend, so it was natural for me to go to talk to her. She introduced me to Mary and we hit it off right away. I walked her home that night, full of pride.

I saw her many times and gave her lifts home on the crossbar of my old bike, Eventually we both moved on, but she is still a wonderful memory, it was all so innocent compared to today.

At the club one night a youth started picking on my friend John Ewers, I had never forgotten that he had been supportive when I was having problems at the Crypt, so I kept an eye on what was happening. Things were different now and I would take on anybody. I had never heard of John ever having been in a fight and he was obviously worried. I didn't want to make him think any less of himself by my stepping in too early, but I said to him. If it happens John I'll be there. It did happen and I went outside. This youth took up a karate stance and was egging John to make a move. Just then John laid into him and gave him such a battering, we all stood back in amazement. I needn't have worried at all.

Back at school, most days merged into one long round of boredom. A highlight of the day was during the morning break there was always a rugby scrum around the small window that served as the school tuck shop. We would go up to the back of the scrum and grab one of the small boys. We'd tell him what we wanted, give him the money and throw him over the heads of the other boys, to the front of the queue. Nobody objected because they knew who had done it. The small boy didn't object either because he got what he wanted too.

I hadn't been there long, when the election for the captaincy of the four school houses were held. I must have made an impression with my peers because I was asked if I would like to stand as the captain of Drake House. I was very pleased to accept the nomination and was duly elected. I must have been more popular with the boys than I was with the teachers.

The teachers were horrified by the decision and tried to block it, but it was a democratic election and it would have been very wrong to have changed the decision, so after initial rumblings, they accepted it.

On one of the few times I made it to the afternoon games period, Mr Rickets was in charge instead of Mr Talbot. He split us into rugby teams and was to be the referee. Our side was soon winning by a mile so he decided he would help out the opposing team. That was a bad mistake because he soon started taking a battering. I took the ball and was making for the goal line when he committed the sin of tackling me around the waist, I had seen him coming and already half handed him off, but he hung on until I punched him in the face, when he let go and I went on to score. He went mad at me but I insisted that it was a fair hand off and seeing as there was no referee, who could say any different. Revenge was sweet.

I was having a pen fight with some of my classmates one day when we ran into the hall. My target was running up the hall, away from me, I took aim and threw a long shot. Just as I let it go. Digger Wolfe, a large, rather eccentric man with a booming voice, came out of a door to see what all the noise was about. He looked away from me and shouted at the boy running away, to walk. My missile hit him in the back and stuck in, but the tweed jacket he was wearing was so thick he didn't even feel it. He walked off down the hall with the pen stuck in his back, with us all trying to get out of sight in case he turned round.

I stole a few of these pens and took them home to use as darts, I put pictures on the wall of our bedroom and threw the pens into the pictures. Gordon was doing something that annoyed me one day and I threw a pen at him and got him in the arm. He ran off shouting that I had stabbed him, but there was no one listening.

In Mr Charters science lab, I always sat at the back. One day some of us were flicking rolled up bits of paper at him with elastic bands. After a lot of shouting and threatening, he picked on me and told me to get out of the class, threatening that he would deal with me later. I went outside, but as it was almost the beginning of a double period, I thought I'm not hanging around here until break. So I went to the Seymour café for a cup of tea. All would have been well, if I hadn't got back too late for the class to be dismissed. When I got there, the class was empty except for Colin Charter.
I walked into the class and said, 'where's my milk Mr Charter'?
We had a third of a pint of milk at breaktime every day.
He answered, 'where have you been'?
I said, 'no Mr Charter, that's not the answer. I asked where my bottle of milk is. I seem to have missed it.'
He repeated, 'where have you been'?
I said, 'we're not getting anywhere here are we. I wasn't standing outside all that time so I went to the café, but I'm still entitled to my milk so where is it'?
He exploded with rage and shouted at me to get to the headmaster's study. I just laughed and walked away. I got my bike out of the bike sheds and went home. This was something I would do more and more often whenever they tried to discipline me.

I often went to the Seymour café at lunch times, for egg and chips and a cup of tea. Either there or the Seymour fish and chip shop. This was strictly against the rules, but hey! What are rules for?

61

The one time I did end up in the headmaster's study, I felt rather sorry for the incident which led to it. I must have been feeling particularly belligerent on this day, because the teacher I had the argument with was quite a nice old gent known as Slicky Wyatt, who I rather liked. During the lesson he asked me a question which I answered, yes.

He said, yes what.

I said, yes, that's right.

He said, you must answer, yes sir.

I said, not any more. I'll never again call anyone sir.

After a slightly more heated exchange, where he got no further forward, he ordered me out of the class. He followed me out and started to rant and rave. I had never seen him like this before and was rather surprised. When I responded with a bit more cheek, he lost his cool completely and slapped me round the side of the head. In an instant, I slapped him round the side of the head, with such force it knocked him over. I went to the Headmaster's study, where he gave me a lecture, which came to the point where he stated that this was a caning offence. I stopped him there and told him it would never happen. I told him he could try, but I would not let it happen. I also pointed out that Mr Wyatt had struck me first. I had been here long enough to gain a big reputation, so he decided to back-pedal saying that this time he would let me off with a caution.

After that, whenever I was sent to see the headmaster, I never bothered. I just left the school and came back the next day. I did it so often the didn't say anything about it.

One such occasion was when Mr Sterry blew the whistle to signal the end of break. I happened to be walking past him when he blew it. The rule was that all activity stopped on hearing the first blast, then on the second blast everyone made their way to their respective classes. I had never taken any notice of this rule and always continued with what I was doing. This time I was too close to Taffy Stevens, the woodwork and technical drawing teacher, who happened to be in the playground. He saw his chance to pull me up and He grabbed me by the shirt collar and shouted stand still, catching me off balance and pulling me backwards. I straightened up and turned to face him. We were almost nose to nose,

I said to him, 'if you ever lay a hand on me again I'll drop you without another word.'

He started to argue so I said, if you want it, take off your glasses and we'll set to, right now.'

He shouted for help, to Mr Sterry who was standing close by.

I said, 'he won't save you, I'll take you both.'
Mr Charter came over next and I knew the odds were now too great,
I said 'yes I know. Go to the Headmaster's study.'
So off I went. They must have known I wouldn't bother. I went through the door nearest the heads study, on through the changing rooms, out of the door the other side of the building and away. I came back the next day, nobody ever mentioned the incident.

One afternoon we were waiting in line to go into the changing rooms for a PT lesson with Mr Talbot. Some boys were messing around, pushing and shoving and slapping each other with their daps, when it got a bit more serious, between Roger Merrett and me, though I'm sure it would have come to nothing. We were going at it when Mr Talbot appeared. He said, if you want to fight, we'll do it in the gym. We got changed and put on the boxing gloves. I wasn't very keen on the idea, Roger was a police cadet and had some boxing training. I was a street fighter and had no experience of fighting to any rules. I knew I could be in trouble, without the use of the head and the boot. The fight started and we were soon knocking each other all around the ring. After the first round I sat in the corner sucking air into my lungs. I could hear a buzz going round the crowd.
I heard Rob Jessop say, 'I think Cliff's finished, he'll never last.'
But I knew different, I wasn't at all worried about my fitness. We resumed the fight, I got in a few good hits and started to think I might be in with a chance, but I got over confident and Roger caught me with an uppercut to the chin, which knocked me over. I was more surprised than anything and there was no damage done. I jumped up and said I was ready to continue. Mr Talbot made me take a mandatory count, then stopped the fight and declared Merrett, the winner. I protested and said look at the state of him; he only hit me once, which was a bit of an understatement. But Mr Talbot had got his own back on me and we all knew it. That decision irritated me for years, although it was probably fair.

During my last year at Linden School, I committed the only act of bullying that I can ever remember doing. Mick Fisher had for some reason brought a guitar to school. I was so jealous of him with this guitar that I belittled his achievements and menaced him, in the playground. Nothing more came of it, but I always felt bad about it and would like to take this opportunity to apologise to him.

I never wanted to bully anybody, although unknowingly I may have intimidated some people and to them I would also like to apologise.

The world was changing, the Vietnam War had started, the Mods and Rockers were fighting each other on the beaches and seafronts all along the south coast. This was a particularly confusing time for me, because I wanted to be in the forefront of the Mod trend, but I was obsessed with motorbikes and had worn a leather biker jacket for years. I wasn't old enough to have a motorbike or scooter yet so it didn't really make much difference. I loved the whole Mod scene and embraced it fully. Martha and the Vandellas, made a record called Dancing in the street. Cheltenham had a dancing in the street party on The Promenade, with a disco playing all the latest music. It drew a huge crowd and was one of the best events I ever attended. I hitch hiked over to Cheltenham, something I would do many times, until I got my own transport.

I met Penny Taggart, a pretty girl who lived in Longlevens. We started going steady. We arranged to meet in Gloucester, under the Bon Marché clock. Lots of courting couples met here, sometimes you could see a boy or a girl who had been waiting too long and paced around wondering if they had been stood up. Penny turned up and we wandered around looking in the shop windows, ending up at the Roma coffee bar in Westgate Street. The Roma was open until 10 o clock so we sat in there with one bottle of coke each for as long as we could. We sat and talked and met other friends. It was a great place. The owner, Tony Pelopida was one of the nicest men I have ever met. I only knew him through the coffee bar, but for thirty years I occasionally went into the Roma for a coffee and a roll and Tony always remembered me with a smile and a friendly hello. I was a regular in 1965, Tony didn't mind us not buying very much, as long as he wasn't too busy and we weren't too noisy. The Roma was the first coffee bar in Gloucester with an espresso coffee machine. It was so big, covered in shiny chrome, it dominated the counter area. The cappuccino with froth on the top, sprinkled with chocolate was wonderful. The food was also of a very high standard and has remained so to this day. It was my favourite place of that time. We came out of the Roma and wandered around the town before heading for the bus stop to catch our respective busses home. Penny was a lovely girl who went off to London to make her way in the world. We lost touch but I often wonder what happened to her.

It was all so innocent, window shopping, walking around town, going to the park and sitting in the little wooden hut in the corner, so we could talk and kiss and cuddle, with a little privacy. Perhaps calling in to the youth centre at the Rickenel, for a chat with our friends.

I went out with lots of wonderful girls during my teenage years. I feel very privileged to have known many of them. Some of them I still meet occasionally, perhaps at a dance or while shopping. Some of them seem to have vanished for ever, moved away like Penny did, maybe.

My cousin Hugh had started working for John Harker, as a deck hand on one of the fleet of oil tankers which came up the canal, then into the river up to Worcester. While on school holiday I went for a trip with Hugh, on the Rosedale from Gloucester to Swansea and back. All of the Harker tankers were named after the Dales, some I remember were the Arkendale, the Ribblesdale, the Rosedale and the Wyedale.

On the day before we were due to leave, Hugh and I, went to Llanthony stores to collect the grocery order for the ship. We walked along Llanthony Road with the box of groceries to where the Rosedale was moored at Monkmeadow. We boarded the ship and stowed the food in a locker, ready for the trip. Hugh showed me around, taking me into the engine room. It was only a small tanker, but none the less impressive. I was feeling very excited at the prospect of the forthcoming journey.

We left Gloucester early the next morning, sailing down the canal to Sharpness. We had to wait until following morning for the tide to be right to let us out into the Bristol Channel, we spent the evening drinking in a pub at Sharpness docks. Then it was through the lock, into the Bristol Channel and on around the coast to the refinery at Swansea to load with oil for the return journey. I felt terrible on the outward journey. Once into open water, the round bottomed vessel, rolled from side to side, even in the calmest of seas. I went a pale shade of green, had a cold sweat and felt as sick as a dog. I tried going below, but that didn't work. Eventually I went forward and sat on the bow with the fresh sea breeze blowing in my face. After a while the seasickness went away and didn't return for the rest of the trip. We anchored in Swansea bay until we were called in to load. While waiting in the bay, Hugh put a fishing line over the side and caught a huge skate, which he cleaned and cooked for dinner that night. On the way there and back, we went under the Severn Bridge which was still under construction. It was an enjoyable experience, my first of mixing with men in a working environment. They treated me as an equal, not a child.

Hugh bought a Triumph Tiger 100 combination. It was an ex AA patrol bike and the sidecar was a big toolbox, shaped like a coffin. It had been painted black, over the AA yellow. Hugh rode it around, lifting the sidecar wheel high up, off the ground when he went around corners. We went out for a ride one day, Hugh on the front, me on the pillion and Ady Hayward in the box, which had no comforts, such as a seat. It also had a lid which had to be held up, when you sat in it. When in the box you had to hang on for grim death to stop yourself being flung around and the lid crashing shut, plunging you into darkness. Once wedged into that position it was very difficult to get the lid open again from the inside. We were going through Painswick when a policeman stepped out and stopped us.

He said, 'what's he doing in that box, it's not made to carry people.'

We protested but the policeman made Ady get out of the box and we had to leave him behind. Ady turned and started to walk home. We went a little way down the road, turned around and went back for Ady who hadn't got very far. He jumped back in the box and off we went, giggling like schoolgirls.

I went to see John Jones, one afternoon. When I got there I saw a striking blue Triumph 21 motorbike parked outside. I went in and asked John who's bike it was. He said it belonged to his Sister Barbara's boyfriend Roy 'Tich' Cambridge. I had heard of Tich Cambridge but had never met him. He was a very well known character, a bit like me. But he was about five years older and was a man. We talked about the bike for a few minutes, then he roared off. He made an impression on me, I liked him and the bike. Roy would later become one of my best friends and we are both still riding motorcycles more than thirty years on.

I started moving away from the youth club in Tuffley, for the bigger scene. I started going into town more often, to the Swan and Falcon, in Longsmith Street. I had just turned 15 and thought I knew it all. I had all the confidence in the world. The Swan and Falcon was a pub that held regular dances, on Thursday and Saturday evenings. You were supposed to be 18 to get in, but I had no trouble getting in as long as I could pay, which wasn't very often. Most times I had to try to get in without paying. One way was to wait in the side bar of the pub until someone I knew came out of the dance to get a drink. I could have a look at the hand stamp which they continually changed. Sometimes it was easily forged with an indelible pencil, sometimes we could wet the stamp and press our hands together to transfer the mark, albeit in reverse. The entrance to the dance was dark so if I waited for a crowd to go in, the doorman didn't take much notice, as long as the mark was there. When all else failed I would just wait for a crowd and crash my way in. One way or the other usually worked.

I was on my way to the Swan & Falcon one dark night when I took the short cut along Mercers Entry, an alley that runs from Westgate Street to Cross Keys lane. I never had much money at this time, not more than four or five shillings, so when I pulled my handkerchief out of my pocket and all my money fell out, clattering to the ground, it was a disaster. It was so dark in that alley, I couldn't see a thing. I was scrabbling around the ground trying to feel anything when I saw a light coming up the alley, I could see it was a policeman. I thought, 'yes, here comes my saviour. When he got closer, I could see he was a huge constable with a big fat belly and a very large handlebar moustache, which was going grey.

I asked him, 'would you shine your torch on the ground for me please? I've dropped all my money.'

He never even slowed from his stride and as he pushed me roughly aside,

he said, 'Fuck your money' and slowly disappeared out of the alley into Westgate Street. Another less than successful encounter with the forces of law and order. Respect for the police was getting less and less every day.

I started to meet a whole new set of people at the Swan & Falcon, all kinds from all over the city. Hard men, who were much older than me. I stood out from the crowd, with my long hair and I was already well known to many, so introductions were made easily. Big Ernie Hannaford, Terry Freeman, Jasper Davis, Aggsy Hayes, they were all there and many others besides. Soon everybody knew who I was. They had live bands on there, all playing the same sort of music. Rock and Roll and Rhythm and Blues. This music has stayed my favourite all of my life. The Trespassers would hammer out High Heeled Sneakers, Reelin & Rockin and Dimples, at great volume. I was in heaven.

I met Roy Hemmings at one of these dances, we were to become good friends and for a while, went everywhere together. Roy was a good-looking boy, very popular with the girls, I was famous, with my long hair and also popular with the girls, so we made a good team. Everywhere we went, we caused a stir, dancing and generally making ourselves high profile. We almost always went home with a girl each.

Roy and I were out on New Years eve, we had been somewhere that had closed early and we had slipped up by being miles away from the parties with no way to get to them. We were walking along Coney Hill Road when I looked at my watch and said to Roy, 'well that's about it Roy, the New Year's about to start.'

Just then, the front door of a house flew open and dozens of people spilled into the street. They all linked hands and started singing Auld Lang Syne. We were grabbed and urged to join in. We had an instant uplift to our previously sagging spirits. We danced around and sang with them until they started to filter back into the house, then we started to walk off.

Mr Greaves ran up to us and said, 'come on in boys, you are very welcome, help yourselves to anything you want.' I was overwhelmed by his family's generosity. We stayed for hours, eating and drinking and had a really good time. I had never met Mr Greaves before but I recognised him. I think he was a bus conductor who had a distinctive way of calling out, 'move along the bus please', when the bus was full. He was quite a personality. I never met him again but will always remember that incident vividly. Thank you, the Greaves family, for a memorable New Year's eve.

The club at the Barnwood church hall was another favourite for a while. It was in the cellar, down some narrow stone steps. The cellar had lots of small booths where you could sit and talk with small groups of friends or in the more secluded ones, could kiss and cuddle with a girlfriend. I was there one night with Ann Bell, who was a striking young girl, very desirable. I think one of the locals took exception to my being there with her. As I went up the steps to get to the toilets, he barged into me.

I said, 'look out mate, be a bit more careful.'

He punched me on the nose starting it bleeding. I grabbed him and we fought our way down the steps, finishing up in on of the small brick booths. This was my kind of fight, in an enclosed space. I managed to get him by the hair and bash his head around the walls. I finished him off and went upstairs to clean up. I had blood all over me. The person in charge took me aside and told me, the lad I had just fought was a well-known local hard case and he was sure to come after me. I was unconcerned but decided to take her advice and leave. I was walking home when I saw him coming up behind me, I just kept walking hoping he would go away, but waiting for him to make a move. He followed me for a while gradually catching up. Soon he was too close and I had to stop and turn to face him.

He said, 'I'll have you now you little bastard.'

I pulled out a flick knife and said, 'oh yeah. I'll fucking kill you first you bag of shit. Go on take a chance.'

He was a strange type, quiet and slow of movement, but with a menacing air about him. He didn't say anything, he just turned and walked away. We saw each other many times over the following years, there was always an atmosphere you could cut with a knife until finally we stood next to each other in the toilets at a dance. We looked at each other, both smiled and said, 'all right?'

But that night I had proved to myself the value of being armed, for defensive purposes. Something I would almost always be, one way or another, from now on.

Chapter 6
A Gloucester Boy

I was fifteen now, so one day I went to school and told them I was going to leave. They said I couldn't leave until the end of term, but I had found out that if I had a job to go to, I could leave early. I had already lined up my first job as a warehouseman, for The Western Trading Company, working at the Pillar warehouse, in the docks. The school, to my surprise, advised me to stay until I had taken my exams, as it was likely I would get good results, but as usual I wouldn't listen. Dad didn't care, in fact I'm not sure he even knew for a while. So I started work on a weekly wage of £4.

It was many years later before I realised how foolish I had been, wasting the chances I had of a good education. Like most youngsters, I thought I knew it all when in reality I knew next to nothing.

Mum came home again and seemed a lot better. Her stay in Scotland seemed to have done her good. She was well but there was something else on her mind. Before long she asked me if I would leave Gloucester and go to live with her in Scotland. She was going to leave Dad and take Gordon and me to live with Gran in Tranent. My answer was, that I loved her but I would not leave Gloucester again. I was a Gloucester boy and I would stay here with Dad. She decided to stay with us, she was the most unselfish of people, but when I look back, she should have left us and gone back to her homeland where she was happy. She gradually started to go down hill. I don't know why she slipped back into her illness, but slip she did. It was heartbreaking for me to watch. Since Mum had become ill there hadn't been any joy in our home lives and as the illness got worse I don't think Dad could handle it and neither could I. Mum was liable to collapse or stumble around in what looked like a drunken state, complete with slurred speech. Sometimes she would wander off and eventually be brought home by the police. Sometimes it took a long time for her to be found, because people thought she was drunk. I found this aspect of her illness particularly distressing. One day she was found wandering in London and had no knowledge of why of how she had got there. I became increasingly hardened to these bouts of illness until I got to the stage where I ignored them, or left the house as soon as I saw it starting.

Life was pretty bleak, there was very little happiness at home. One evening, my brother Gordon and I were having an argument, when suddenly, Dad leapt from his chair and went for me. His arms were outstretched, with his hands open, his intention was obviously to go for my throat. As he came forward I hit him on the bridge of the nose, right between the eyes. The blow knocked him backwards and brought him instantly to his senses. He was still pretty mad though and started yelling at me to get out of his house. Mum said no, don't go. I told him, if you want me to leave, throw me out. He wasn't in a position to do that so he just let it go.

Mum was getting boxes of tablets, in lots of 500 at a time from the Doctor, there didn't seem to be much in the way of care, just keep her doped up as much as possible to keep her quiet. I never agreed with all these tablets but it wasn't my decision. I think Mum got a better standard of care in Scotland, which is why she improved whenever she went there.

I had never had much affection or bodily contact with my family and Mum's illness made the thought of any contact even less attractive. I developed a coldness, bordering on a phobia about bodily contact, which I have never completely shaken off. I still can't tolerate illness and have to get away from it. I still don't like people to physically get too close to me, or to touch me, unless I know them well. If someone does get too close, I have to move away as quickly as I can.

I came home one day to find my Uncle Charlie there. I hadn't seen much of him, over the years I had been growing up. He was what we called, a gentleman of the road. A gentle man he was too. Although he often lived rough or in hostels, he didn't drink and was no trouble to anyone. He was a soft spoken man, with fine features and deep blue eyes. Apparently he had been having a rough time of it, so he was going to stay with us for a while. Dad had set him up with a job, which he didn't really want. Uncle Charlie hadn't worked for years and didn't really want to. He went out every morning, supposedly to his new job, returning late in the afternoon. A couple of weeks went by, then he just disappeared. He had never shown up to the job. He must have just been wandering the streets, passing the time until he could come home. That's just the way he was, he didn't want any responsibility. But he achieved happiness in his own way.

He got a regular bed at the Church Army Hostel in Great Western Road. They were very good to him and looked after him for years. Whenever I bumped into him, I always gave him something.

He used to say, 'don't let anyone see you give me anything, they'll think I'm begging.'
He had been arrested before for begging and was always worried about it.

How times have changed, with beggars on every street.

My new job gave me even more independence, the wages were small, but it was money that I had never been used to. I could now go out every night, as long as I was careful. I started to go to the Locomotive public house, (now The Famous Pint Pot), but then just a small pub. In the back bar I got to know Stuart Crowther and Bill Rand, we went around together for a while and had some good times. They were to become lifelong friends, even though we only bump into each other occasionally.

I saw people in that back bar, tattooing themselves with a needle and a bottle of Indian ink. I made another really stupid decision here, I decided to have a go myself. I got the ink and the needle and tattooed a swallow on my left hand. It's not even very good, I don't know why I thought it would be, as my ability in art was always pretty poor. But I did it and I still have it today.

Stuart, Bill and I walked down Sandhurst lane to the Globe some nights. The Globe was a cider house then. We went into the small front bar, there always seemed to be the same round faced man sitting on a stool. His face was deep red and his nose redder still. It fascinated me every time he lifted his glass to take a drink. His hands shook so much it was a major achievement to get the glass to his lips. If his glass was anywhere near full it was impossible for him to take a drink without considerable spillage. The old joke that goes, 'Do you drink a lot? No I spill most of it' could have been written about him. The cider was cheap and very strong. I was only fifteen and a couple of pints of rough cider had me rolling. We used to stagger back to town, singing and laughing, all the way to the bus stop, where we caught the bus home.

Sometimes I would be the worse for drink and I would make my way to the docks, where I worked. We used to pack the china sanitary ware in straw, when we loaded it on the lorries. The straw was kept in the cellar below the warehouse. I had a key to this cellar and used it to get some sleep, if I had missed the last bus home.

I hadn't been working there very long when on my way home, the chain came off my bike. As I bent over the bike to try to fix it, my wage packet fell out of the top pocket of my shirt. I put my foot on it, as I was using both of my hands to get the chain back on. I got it done, jumped on the bike and rode off. When I got home I went to my pocket and realised what I had done. I got back on to my bike and went back to where I had lost the money, but it was gone. Out of the four pounds I earned, I only got just over two pounds and ten shillings and it was all gone. It doesn't sound much now, but it was a big loss to me.

When I worked in the docks, it was a very different place to what it is now. It was alive with all kinds of commerce. The Western Trading Company that I worked for had three sites. Pillar warehouse, another larger warehouse in the main dock area and the showroom which had it's back entrance in the docks and it's front entrance on Southgate Street. Alongside this showroom was the showroom of rival builders merchants Haine and Corry. Gopsill Brown, the sack makers occupied another of the large warehouses, employing many women. Also employing many girls and women, was the Carpet works, in High Orchard Street, just up the road from where I was working, in Merchants Road. The girls were all around, during lunchtime and packed into the Spa café, or sometimes in the Goat public house in Llanthony Road. Although I was only fifteen, the landlord Frank Mathews would always serve up a pint of cider, seemingly without a second thought. I used my lunchtime trying to chat up the girls, I would have done anything for a job at the carpet works, but never managed it, unlike my friend Roy Cambridge, who has many stories of his own, to tell about his time there.

Ships were constantly coming up and down the canal. For some, Gloucester was as far as they could go. Their cargo, offloaded here, to be moved on by road. West Midland Farmers had a Grain store, not far from Pillar warehouse and I often watched the grain being loaded onto the ships, from a chute on the side of the building directly into the hold. Two fleets of oil tankers ran from Gloucester docks. One by John Harker, the other by the oil company 'Shell.'

My job at Western Trading, was to load the lorries with all kinds of plumbing supplies, They held stocks of bathroom suites, copper cylinders, belfast sinks and flatpack kitchen units, which were on the top floor. I wasn't used to the long hours and physical exertion required for this job, so I got tired in the afternoons. I started climbing up onto the top of the large stacks of flatpack units and getting some sleep. Sometimes I would hear Barry Day, the assistant manager calling me. He had realised I was missing and was searching for me. He always came up in the lift, a floor at a time, opening the door, shouting for me, having a quick look round before closing the lift door and moving on to the next floor. As soon as I heard him, I nipped down the narrow back stairs and ended up below him. I would get on with something, on one of the lower floors or in the cellars, until he found me. It was a very easy going job, perhaps that was why the wages were so low. But I enjoyed it, it wasn't a bad first job.

A policeman called at the house one evening and told me I had been reported for shooting an air rifle at a man in Seventh Avenue, this man was the father of a boy I knew and he knew who I was. I was very distinctive in appearance and would have been very easy to identify. I was mystified as to this accusation, I didn't know what the policeman was talking about. He asked me where I had been at the time of the offence. I thought for a while and remembered that I had been at a metalwork class at night school. They checked and found that I couldn't have done the shooting. I was off the hook, but on any other night I wouldn't have been able to prove where I was. Luck had been on my side. I never found out why that man had identified me, I couldn't be mistaken for anyone else. It was very odd.

Shortly after this incident I went to a dance at St Barnabas Church hall, in Stroud Road. There was nothing memorable about it except that when I was walking home, I met Gerry Blackford and a friend of his whose name I can't remember. As we walked up Tuffley Lane towards the Railway Bridge, Gerry's friend ran across the road and went into the telephone box. We kept walking and he came back across the road carrying the handset from the telephone. We both told him what an idiot he was, but he didn't care and threw the handset away. We carried on under the bridge, turned right, through the alley into Fourth Avenue. Gerry lived a short distance from the alley so I said goodbye to them both when they went into the prefab and continued on my way home, which was probably another half a mile away.

The next morning a policeman came to the door. He said I had been reported for vandalising a telephone box. I said I knew nothing about it, but they had already been to Gerry's and had his name and the name of his friend and they had said that I had done it. I thought, this has nothing to do with me, why are they saying I did it. In my inexperience, the policeman had tricked me, he knew who they were but they hadn't said it was me at all, they had said nothing. I thought, I don't even know this person so why should I worry about it. It was his own fault anyway, so I gave them a statement as to what happened. Gerry hadn't done anything either.

We all had to appear in juvenile court charged with vandalism of GPO property. I still had faith in British justice, so I thought, the truth will come out and Gerry and

I would be found not guilty. But I hadn't reckoned on our local Special Constable. It transpired that just before I met the other two, they had passed his house in Slimbridge Road and they had been a bit noisy. This man said, on oath, that he had followed us and that we had all been involved in the vandalism. He had continued to follow us until we all went into Gerry's prefab, which I had never done. Most of his story was a complete fabrication. I had met him before at the youth club and didn't think much of his overbearing manner then. I thought even less of him after this.

We were all found guilty and I was put on probation. I found this particularly galling because I have always had a respect for property and would never have indulged in vandalism of any kind. I treat all property as I would expect my own property to be treated.

That copper was marked down for future retribution, I knew that one day I would pay him back for his lies.

Gerry and his friend thought that I had betrayed them and unwittingly, perhaps I had. Shortly afterwards I went into the back yard of the Pilot Inn in Southgate Street, to get to the 41 Club which was upstairs at the back of the pub. Gerry and a gang of his friends were in the bar and they saw me walk up the passage. They came out and set upon me, knocked me to the ground and gave me a kicking. I had to go to the hospital to have some stitches in a cut to my lip. A policeman came and asked me who had done it. I told him to 'fuck off.' My experience with the police and the law, hadn't been very positive, to date.

Some of the men who had given me the kicking, later realised they had been a bit harsh in their judgement and apologised to me. I had more respect for them, than I did for the law.

The 41 Club was always a pretty rough venue, probably the roughest place I went to on a regular basis. There seemed to be fight after fight every time I went there . I was never involved in one myself but I saw some spectacular wild west style fights, with chairs and anything they could get hold of, being used as weapons. I was going in one night when I got to the bottom of the stairs, looked up and could see that a fight was already in progress. I could see it was a big one by all the stuff flying about. I stood at the bottom of the stairs thinking perhaps I'll give it a miss tonight, when I saw a girl hit another girl on the head with a tubular chair. She came rolling down the stairs, ending in a heap on the floor. When the fight started to spill down the stairs, I decided it was time to leave. I'd had enough entertainment for one night.

On another occasion, I saw Ernie Hannaford fighting with somebody outside the Pilot. They were going at it hammer and tongs. As they came towards me, I cracked the bloke on the head with my pint mug. That was the end of the fight.
Ernie turned to me and said, 'Thanks mate.'
I said, 'that's all right Ernie, anytime.'

I left my job at Western Trading and went to work as an office junior at Weddel and Co, in Longsmith Street. Keith Bowers worked there, he was a year older than me and had a Vespa scooter. Although I admired it as the epitome of the mod culture, I still longed for a motorbike. Soon I would be old enough.

The meat trade was very different then. There were three meat company's along Longsmith Street. Swift's, Armours and Weddels. The lorries and vans were all loaded, directly off the street. There was no problem with traffic congestion. Meat would also be taken from these wholesalers, in small high sided trolleys called 'dillies', pushed by a meat porter, across Southgate Street, up the cobbles of Bell Lane, into the back of the old Eastgate market, to Butcher's such as W T Johns & Sons and Langley's.

When I finished work on Friday afternoon, the weekend was for fun. That summer I had some great times with my friends. I had money in my pocket and plenty of things to do.

In the simmer of 1965, Terry Gardner was going out with Jean Precious from New Addington, near Croydon. Terry, John Jones, Andy Powell and I regularly went there for a weekend. One glorious sunny day we drove up the M4, on our way to a party. We were singing the song by The Loving Spoonful,

What a day for a daydream
What a day for a daydreaming boy
What a day for a daydream
Dreaming about my bundle of joy

It was one of those unforgettable times when everyone was as happy as you could imagine. It was a fabulous party with lots of food and drink and great hospitality. When the party ended we all went back to the Precious household and continued for the rest of the night. In the morning, Mrs Precious came down and made us a breakfast of eggs on toast. We spent the rest of the morning recovering, then set off for home. I needed a weeks rest to get over it. Terry married Jean and moved to New Addington, we never saw each other again for many years. But I have some good memories of our friendship.

On Saturday nights I started going to the Guildhall dances, with Roy Hemmings. The ballroom was really big then, with a sprung wooden floor. It was five shillings to get in and in return for that princely sum, there was a different pop group every week plus the regular Peter Tilley Showband. No such thing as a disco yet. We danced all the time the pop group was on stage, then when the Showband came on it was time to go off to get a Coke. The Guildhall had a strict no alcohol policy, soft drinks only. They were great dances and we soon knew all the regulars. Roy and I were both high profile characters. We moved in on the girls in pairs, danced with them and chatted them up. We did all the latest dances, very proud of our skills. As well as these new dances where you didn't touch your partner, jiving was always popular, we could really show off. I can still see Les (Ernie) Hannaford jiving with two girls at once. He was really great at that. It was very impressive. Dave Orrit was always there looking like he owned the place. Dave was everywhere, everybody knew him, just as they knew me. We were both slightly eccentric, although in different ways.

I had my distinctive long hair, which was still very popular with the girls but caused a lot of adverse comments from some quarters. Sometimes I had to fight over it, when others took the mickey taking too far. It was always strangers who had never seen anyone with long hair before. One night in the Guildhall, there was a rugby team from somewhere in Wales. They were getting more and more boisterous as the evening wore on, even though there was no drink for sale. At one stage they surrounded me and were taunting me with things like, 'give us a kiss sweetie.'
I was getting annoyed and told them it was time to pack it in.
They said, 'who's going to make us, boyo.'
I pointed to behind them and said, 'they are.'
The Welshmen looked round and they had been surrounded by a very large number of hard men. Instead of backing off, they decided to push their luck a bit further, but it was a bad move and a brawl started, that they couldn't win. The weight of numbers against them, gave them no chance. They tried to make their escape down the stairs and into the street, but it wasn't going to be that easy. They had upset too many people in there and we were out for blood. The fights continued up and down

Eastgate Street. The police arrived with dogs, which spread the fighting further afield, as far as King Street and continued until the last of them had been beaten up or escaped.

Roy and I came out of the Guildhall at midnight when the dance ended and made our way up Barton Street to the Imperial café, also known as Otto's. It was one of the few places open at that time of night. We went in for our egg and chips to finish the night off. There was often trouble in there as it was full of drunks and hard men.

The same man came in week after week, covered in blood. I often wondered what had happened to him, but I never found out.

One night a drunk came in and went round everybody's plate, stabbing chips or sausages off them, with a large sheath knife. Nobody argued with him and he thanked everybody he took anything from.

Another night, we were sat eating when Knocker Dalby came in and walked up to Dave Knight and said Hello Mr Knight. Knocker picked up a bottle of sauce and emptied it all over Dave's meal. Dave immediately threw it in Knockers face and a fight broke out. John Williamson who was a regular card player there, came rushing out of the back room and all hell let loose. It was a wild west scene, with crockery flying and chairs being broken over peoples heads. We all started piling out of door, when the police car could be seen coming up Barton Street. We all ran off and scattered to the winds.

From Otto's we made our way up Barton Street, forking left at the India House, up India Road, through an alley, then across Eastern Avenue into Coney Hill Road, where Roy lived with his mum and dad. I often slept in the spare room at Roy's house. It was a different world to my own home. Mrs Hemmings came into the room in the morning with a boiled egg and a cup of tea, for my breakfast in bed. She sang at the top of her voice, which was so bright and happy. It was a very happy house. She was a lovely woman, I'm sure Roy appreciated her.

I started going to London again, to the clubs that were a world apart from the provincial scene. All the latest fashions were there and all the clubs that were so exciting. I frequented The Marquee Club and The Flamingo, both on Wardour Street, where a lot of the big time bands had started their rise to fame. Georgie Fame always put on a great performance, as did The Good Goods, one of the best bands to come out of Gloucester. I saw many great acts, the names I have mostly forgotten, but the atmosphere and the energy of the performances will stay with me forever. The Rolling Stones had been regular performers at the Marquee, but before my time. During the next couple of years, bands such as Ten Years After, John Mayall, Jimi Hendrix, Alan Bown and Geno Washington all appeared at the Marquee, it was one of the greatest venues of all time. The Marquee and The Flamingo were open all night, something unheard of at home. I would hitch hike to London, change my clothes in a station toilet, leave them in a left luggage locker and be ready for a wild weekend. I went back to Carnaby Street, which was getting more famous every day, it was already changing from when I first came here two years ago. The shops were almost all clothes shops now. Full of stuff we would never get in Gloucester.

The fashions came to Gloucester much later than they did in London then. It was a real big deal to go all the way to London for clothes. It was so far away to most people. Most girls and boys of my age had to wait until the fashions came to Leslie Hull's shop in Eastgate Street, next to the Odeon cinema. They were the ones who made the most effort to keep up with what the young people wanted. Without them, Gloucester would have been an even sleepier backwater than it was. We went to see Tony Armstrong or Phil Mathews, who was our own age. They always tried their best to get the latest stuff in, but it had nothing compared to the trendy shops in London.

It seemed very important to me at the time, to be right at the cutting edge of fashion. I loved having the latest clothes and strutted around thinking I was the top man.

More and more Mods were coming out now. Froggy Taylor and Graham Midgeley were also at the forefront with their full-length leather coats in bright colours never before seen on a man. Froggy looking supreme on his scooter festooned with mirrors and foglamps, complete with foxes tail fluttering from a whip aerial. Gloucester was slowly coming alive.

One weekend, my cousin Hugh and I went to London, we had a bad time hitching, sometimes the lifts just didn't come. But we got there in the end. We went to an all nighter at the Flamingo in Wardour Street. We took our good clothes with us, changed when we got there and put our stuff in a left luggage locker in a tube station. When we staggered out in the morning we made our way to the station for a wash and brush up and changed back into our travelling clothes for the journey back. The Club was packed to the seams. As the night wore on, some even managed to grab some sleep in a chair at the edge of the dance floor, despite the deafening noise that never let up. A black soul band was hammering out some great numbers. I wish I could remember who they were, because they had great stage presence and made a great night. Unfortunately a lot of things around this time are a bit vague in my memory. There was a compliment of huge bouncers, dressed in dark suits and wearing tight black leather gloves. Every now and again, the lights would come up and the bouncers would rush through the crowd, grab the troublemakers, drag them to the door and unceremoniously throw them out into the street. But it was a hell of a place.

One night at one of the Guildhall dances, Roy Hemmings and I started dancing with two girls, then chatted them up. We got on well, but Roy had got the one that I wanted. We walked them home, had a snog at the gate and made our way home. I was really disappointed that I hadn't got the girl of my choice, because I really fancied her. The following Saturday, fate took a hand. I was riding my bike along Eastgate Street when she walked across in front of me. We saw each other and stopped for a chat. She was dressed in the uniform of a W H Smith shop assistant. She was a Saturday girl, being still at Central girls school. Before long we made a date for that night.

Jill was different to the other girls I had been going out with. She was something really special to me and we started going steady. I was really proud to be seen with her where ever we went.

I went out with her for what seemed like ages, but in reality was only a few months, but I was obsessed with her. Unfortunately I didn't want to go anywhere. I just wanted us to be alone together all the time. Jill's mum let us use the spare room, or sometimes we would go to my house when there was no one home. Jill soon got fed up with this, but I didn't see the signs until they hit me in the face. Our friends had got used to seeing us together, so one evening when I was out alone, I bumped into a gang of friends at the fair in the park.
One of them said, 'I'm sorry to see you have finished with Jill.'
I said, 'what makes you think that?'
He told me that she had been seen out with Dennis.
I was absolutely furious because I was friendly with Dennis and hadn't expected such treachery. I felt betrayed by both of them.
I walked to where Dennis lived. He was a bit older than me and was old enough to have a scooter. It wasn't there, so I knew he wasn't at home. I walked a little further up the road and sat on the pavement, up against a hedge. It was dark and I

was hidden in that darkness. My mood as black as the night. About an hour passed, when I saw Dennis arrive home. It was about 11-o clock. I got up and walked towards the house and went round the back. Dennis had just gone into the kitchen so I knocked gently on the door. He had a look of surprise on his face as he opened it. I stepped past him, giving him the hardest punch in the stomach I can ever remember throwing. Just the one punch sent him to the floor, retching and gasping for breath.

His mother shouted from upstairs, 'what's going on Dennis', but Dennis was in no condition to answer. I said nothing throughout this episode. I just turned and walked away. We both knew why.

My love affair with Jill was near the end. My affection for her has never diminished though. She married a good man and had a lovely family. They are both still my friends. I don't see them very often, but it is always a delight for me when we meet.

One of the best places around was the Blue Moon in Cheltenham. I loved going there, I met Mickey Clarke there who was later to become the drummer in a band along with Wanger Wainright and some other friends. They were a tremendous band, but that's in the future. The Blue Moon was the, 'in place' everyone who mattered was there. I took my first purple hearts here one night. I had the most incredible high. I loved it, I thought I could do anything. My senses were heightened to a degree that I can't describe. I danced closely with a girl and thought she was the most sensual thing I had ever felt. I can't remember her face, just the incredible softness of the dress she was wearing. I regularly took pills of all sort and qualities for a while. Mostly purple hearts and french blues. I had no knowledge of the harm that drugs can do, I think we were much more innocent about it all. I had never heard of such a thing as a drug addict. The pills just made things seem so much better than the reality. I saw some great acts there too, Acts that were great whatever my state of mind. Julie Driscoll, Brian Auger, Long John Baldry and Rod Stewart made up 'Steampacket.' I loved Julie Driscoll and hardly even noticed Rod Stewart. Lee Dorsey also came to The Moon, hammering out, 'Ride your Pony', now that was a great record! Lee used a real 45-calibre revolver, firing blanks during that record. He sang SHOOT, (BANG) SHOOT, (BANG) SHOOT, (BANG). We had a special dance for that song, which involved a lot of arm movement and could be a bit dangerous if you were too close to the next dancer. I also saw the Good Goods, TheGroundhogs, The Drifters and the mighty Spencer Davis Group with Stevie Winwood. Regrettably, I missed John Mayall at the 1965 Christmas Eve party, they say it was a great show. I resolved to see John Mayall at the next opportunity.

Further along the High Street in Cheltenham, was the Aztec coffee bar. It too was above a shop and was reached by going through a narrow doorway, up a long flight of stairs. It could be a bit rough in there sometimes but it was often the only place open late at night. I was always conscious of the fact that only a couple of years earlier, one of my all time rock hero's 'Brian Jones' had been a regular visitor to the Aztec.

I used to hitch hike to Cheltenham to get to the Blue Moon, I was still only fifteen and had no transport. I was with Hugh one night when a middle-aged man gave us a lift to Gloucester. He said he could take us as far as his home in Escourt Road. When we got to his house he invited us in for a drink, we saw no harm so we thanked him and went inside. He got us a drink and went out of the room. When he came back in, his intentions dawned on us pretty rapidly. He was homosexual and was propositioning us. We declined his offer to stay the night and made a hasty exit. It was my first encounter with anything of that nature, apart from seeing Chummy around the town.

Chummy, whose name was Derek Barrow, was a well-known transvestite. I first saw him walking along Severn Road. I was on the back of Hugh's motorbike. As we went past him, Hugh shouted to me, that's Chummy there. I almost broke my neck, swivelling round to get a better look. I couldn't believe my eyes. He was wearing a tight sweater and a short tight skirt and was tottering along on high heels, at an astonishing rate.

He often went into the Westgate Café, another of the few places that stayed open very late at night. This place was basically a transport café but was as rough as any place I have ever been in my life. It attracted all kinds of humanity. The food was terrible, there really was nothing to recommend the place, except that it was the only place open. I never went there through choice, only if I was with a gang of lads after a night out.

I met Dave Keveren, who rode a gold coloured 1964 Triumph Bonneville, we became friends and Dave carried me on the pillion, all over the place. We decided to go to Bournemouth one Sunday. On the day, the weather didn't look too good, it was cold and foggy, but the forecast was good so we went anyway. The fog got thicker and thicker, we got slower and slower. It took hours to get there, which was

particularly annoying when we were on such a fast bike. A couple of miles from Bournemouth, the sun came out and suddenly it was a warm summer's day. But it had taken so long to get here that we only had a couple of hours before we had to start back. We travelled that couple of miles outside of Bournemouth, when the fog closed in again and it took us even longer to get home than it had to get there. But I had some great times with Dave, on that bike.
I wanted one.

I lost my job at Weddel's for being cheeky to Mr Brooman the area manager. Fred, the branch manager didn't want to see me go but he had his orders. I had answered the phone to Mr Brooman, in my usual polite way. He was an offensive man who was used to his rudeness being tolerated,
He shouted, 'FRED.'
I replied, 'yes sir I'll see if I can find him for you, who shall I say is calling', although I knew who it was, by his rudeness.
Mr Brooman shouted, 'just go and get him NOW.'
I put the phone down.
A few minutes later, it rang again, I answered the same way as before. This time Mr Brooman bellowed for Fred, I told him I wouldn't be spoken to in that manner and put the phone down again. A few days later, Fred told me I had to leave, but to go to the British Beef Company at the cattle market in St Oswalds Road and to tell them he had sent me. There was a job there doing the same thing, but the money was slightly better. So I finished at Weddel's on Friday and started at British Beef on Monday. I had another office junior's job. It turned out to be a good place to work, I made lots of friends there. I was re acquainted with John Haines, my old adversary from the Crypt school. John was a trainee manager and things were very different between us, we became good friends.

The man who interviewed me and ultimately gave me the job was John Miller. He was a quiet man who often didn't say very much, but when he did it was some of the most stimulating conversation I have ever had. As I got to know him over a period of time, I looked upon him as a great role model. He was very educated and had made the most of his life. He had travelled to Australia and lived there for a while doing all sorts of work and once I got him going, the stories he told will live with me for ever. He taught me to spin a coin with great accuracy, something I still do all the time. He left British Beef to go to teacher training college. During the last week of our time together, I persuaded him to bring his clarinet and saxophone to work, to give us a tune. He had always resisted my pleas, until the last minute. When he started playing, I was overawed with it. It was so good I couldn't understand how anyone could hide such talent, but to John it was nothing. I last saw him during the sixties in Bristol where he had gone to teach at a school. I lost touch after that. He had a profound effect on me and I will never forget him.

A few weeks after I started at British Beef, I saw Mr Brooman picking some meat from a rail of sides of beef. I wandered past him, smiling.
I just said, 'Hello'!
I never spoke to him again.

As soon as I turned sixteen, Dave Keveren found my first motorbike for me. He took me to see it. An old maroon coloured, C12 side valve BSA. I bought it for five pounds and started to learn to ride. It only lasted a couple of weeks, when on the way to Swindon, it packed up and I had to leave it at Cirencester and get a ride home on the back of the Bonneville.

At work the next day I asked the boss 'Roy Evans', if he would let me take a van and driver to Cirencester to collect the bike. Roy Evans was a really nice man and was especially compliant to a request of this nature, in the afternoon, after he had returned from the Bell & Gavel. Roy said it was okay, so I asked Dennis Birch if he would take me. He agreed, so of we went in the meat van. We put the bike in the back, tied it up and took it home to Tuffley. On our way back to work we were going up Southgate Street when Dennis spotted a girl wearing a particularly short skirt. He opened the sliding door of the van so he could hang out for a better look. All of a sudden there was a bang. The traffic in front of us had stopped. So had we, but only when we hit the car in front. It couldn't have happened at a worse time, we had to explain to Roy what had happened, but he was all right about it and didn't moan too much.

I knew nothing about the workings of motorbike engines, then. After due deliberation I decided to cut my losses and I sold it for two pounds. It turned out that a valve had broken and it was soon repaired. But I was not sorry to see it go. It was so feeble compared to Dave's Bonneville. He had to wait for me all the time.

That winter, it was very cold. Things were not very good at home, it was always freezing. Everywhere in the prefab was bitterly cold except for the living room when the coal fire or the paraffin stove was on. If you moved more than a few feet away from the heat source, it was still freezing. The windows would often have ice on them, on the inside. The bedrooms were absolutely bitter cold all of time. At bedtime we got our clothes off as fast as we could and dived into a bed which had as many covers on it as we could pile on. Everything went on the bed, including the old GPO greatcoats that Dad had been issued with during his years at the post office. When we woke up we could see our breath, we put our heads under the blanket to warm our noses up, then jumped out of bed and dressed as quickly as we could. Mum wasn't doing very well, things were getting on top of her and I was getting more and more distant when she had a bad day. I couldn't stand to see it, I had to try to ignore it or get out of the house. I loved her but her illness was taking it's toll on all of us.

One morning in April, Gordon had arranged to go out with Hugh. He got out of bed and went into the living room, where he found Mum slumped on the settee. He looked at her, unsure as to whether she was asleep or not. Gordon left the house and went to meet Hugh and told him that there was something wrong with Mum, that it looked like she had collapsed. Hugh told his mum and dad, then came to our house with Gordon. Uncle Den went to the phone box and called for an ambulance. Hugh asked Gordon for a mirror, which he held to Mum's mouth, but there was no sign of life. A few minutes later, Gordon came into my bedroom and woke me up.
He said, 'get up Cliff, I think Mum's dead.'
I said, 'don't be so daft.'
But I got up and went to see what had happened.
I went into the living room and saw Mum lying half on the settee, with a leg hanging off the side, falling to the floor. She was an awful blue colour and was obviously dead and had been for some time.
When the ambulance men came in, they took a look at Mum and put her on a stretcher to take her to the ambulance. As they went through the front door,
I said to one of the ambulance men. 'Will she be all right'?
He replied, 'we'll do what we can.'
We all already knew she was dead.

I got on my bike and went to the Post Office in George Street, where dad was working. I went in and asked to see him. Someone brought him to where I was waiting. He immediately asked what was wrong.
I said. 'Dad, Mum's been taken to hospital and this time it's bad.'
He said. 'How bad is it, son.'
I said. 'I think she's dead, Dad.'
He almost collapsed, he grabbed my arm to steady himself. It was one of the few times I can ever remember him touching me.

A few days later Mum was cremated at the crematorium in Coney Hill.

85

Even though she had been ill for so long it was no easier to accept. Hugh was very distressed and couldn't join us in the car for the return journey after the funeral service.

I felt even more alone now. We had only been together on and off for the last few years, but her loss weighed very heavily on me. I withdrew into myself, while the rage that burned inside me gradually subsided.

There was an inquest, because she had died suddenly. The inquest showed that Mum had died of barbiturate poisoning. The tablets they had been giving her had built up in her stomach and ultimately, killed her. This happened because the level of care had been so poor. She was ill and had been left to her own devices to ration the pills to the correct dose. She had been unable to do this as often she didn't know whether she had taken them or not. The verdict of the inquest was accidental death. I was burning with anger and publicly accused her doctor of negligence.

I had never fully understood the nature of Mum's illness and only now was it dawning on me that there had been no tumour. Mums illness had been a mental illness, brought on by her inability to cope with dad's constant affairs with many other women. I had been too young to realise what had been going on. I thought he was always out at work. There was never anything said about it, in front of Gordon and me, so we had no perception of what their personal problems were.

It was only later that I realised why Mum always got better when she went to Scotland, it was because they looked after her so much better and she didn't have the problem of dad's unfaithfulness to deal with. Why didn't she leave us and go there. She knew what the truth was.

I suppose I will never fully understand her reasons. I suppose she just couldn't bear the thought of leaving her sons behind. She paid for that loyalty with her life.

Life went on. I was even more independent now. I came and went as I pleased, stayed out at nights, got drunk, got into fights. Life would never be the same again. It was 1966, I was sixteen and I had my own life to live.

Chapter 7
Girls and Bikes

I got on the bus going home from town to Tuffley. As I reached the top of the stairs, I saw a beautiful girl, sitting close to the front of the bus. She had long dark hair and was wearing a lime green coat and a black wide brimmed straw hat. The seat behind her was vacant, so I took it. I started talking to her, she already knew who I was. We talked until it was time for her to get off the bus at St Barnabas Church. It wasn't too far from home, so I decided to get off the bus and walk with her. She lived in Cherrywood Gardens, off Firwood Drive, so it was on my way. Before long I had managed to make a date with her. Her name was Angela and we arranged to meet at the end of her road at a prearranged time. I took her out, to the downstairs bar in the Duke of Wellington. We sat and talked and it came out that her surname was Talbot. I was stunned for a moment, because as soon as she said the name, I knew, that she was Norman Talbot, my old games teacher's daughter. After the initial shock, I found it quite amusing. We started going steady, but it was very difficult at first, because she wouldn't let me come to the house, in case her dad saw me. Eventually, I insisted that it couldn't go on, her dad would have to find out some time. So she agreed that I could call for her. Right from the start Norman wasn't amused and wouldn't let me past the front door. We went out with each other seriously for a long time, but Norman never once made me welcome.

I had bought another BSA during this time and took my driving test. The test was a nerve-wracking experience, though when I look back on it, I have to laugh. The examiner and I came out of the test centre in Denmark Road and walked towards the bike. He looked at it, then pointed at a car about 25 yards away and asked me to read the numberplate.
I said, 'don't you think that's a bit far away.'
He said, 'all right, go a bit closer then.'
I edged forward until I was close enough to read the numbers and the examiner seemed satisfied. He told me to ride down Cheltenham Road, turn right at the roundabout, right again into Kenilworth Avenue and back up to London Road. I was to go around and around this same route until he indicated for me to stop. As I rode along, I could see the examiner hiding behind the trees in Kenilworth Avenue, taking notes. Next time around he was hiding in a different place. Eventually, by stepping into the road and waving his arms, he signalled for me to stop. The next test was to ride alongside him at walking pace. Then he told to continue riding the

same route until required to perform an emergency stop. Again I could see him hiding behind a tree. After a couple of circuits, he jumped out in front of me, giving me plenty of time to stop without risk of running him over. It was obvious that he didn't want to become an accident statistic. The final test was to answer questions on the Highway Code. He described a couple of road signs, which I had to identify and that was that. I had passed.

Angela hadn't been very happy about the bike, as all of our friends were getting scooters. Now that I had passed the driving test, I could take a passenger but Angie wouldn't go on it after the first few times. She just didn't like it.

I loved it, this was a real bike, even though it only had a 250cc engine. It was a BSA C15 SS80 sports star. I bought it from my cousin Hugh, who had moved on from motorcycles and had got a car. This blue and chrome machine was a leap forward in my biking life. It went like the wind compared to the old side valve C12.

There was always some conflict between the two rival groups of teenagers at this time. The Mods and the Rockers were separate entities that were never supposed to meet except in battle. I thought it was a ridiculous situation, one that I could never reconcile. I loved the clothes and the whole Mod scene, but I also loved the leather jacket and the speed and thrills a motorbike could give me. I didn't see why I had to abandon the Rocker culture in order to embrace the newer Mod culture. I wanted the best of both worlds and I think I managed to achieve it. I made many friends in both camps and never got into any of the mindless violence that occasionally broke out between them. They were all my friends.

I was riding my C15 to work one day when I was passed at terrific speed by Paul Hayes, riding a 650cc Triumph Thunderbird. It was done up in racing style with Clip On handlebars and Rear Set gearchange and brake levers, so it was ass up, head down and ride like the devil. I was blown away by the speed at which he came past me. When I got to work, he was standing by his bike, so I said, 'give us a go Paul.'
To my surprise he said, 'go on then.'
I got astride it, immediately feeling the sheer size of it compared to my BSA. I straightened up the T'bird and blipped the throttle, Paul told me to give it plenty of revs and drop the clutch, so I did just that. I took off with such unexpected force that my feet flew backwards, off the footrests and I slid back on the seat, just managing to keep a hold on the handlebars. I was flying up the road hanging on to the handlebars for dear life. I was accelerating so fast that as I was being forced off

the back of the bike, I was rolling the throttle open even more as I was trying to drag myself back towards the front of the bike to get to the brakes. I eventually got it back under control, turned it round and had a more controlled run back. It was a white knuckle ride that I wouldn't have missed for the world.

I rode my C15 into town one evening and parked in the Bike Park on the corner of King Street. When I returned to the bike to go home, I turned the petrol tap on and saw petrol pouring out from the carburettor. I had a special end cap, on my Amal Carb. It had a Perspex window in it so that the float could be seen working. Someone had taken a fancy to it and had unscrewed the three screws and stolen it. I was stuck. I decided to walk to the Northend Vaults, where my friend Paul Hayes' father was landlord. Luckily, Paul was at home. I told him what had happened and he took me to his shed, where he riffled through his spares and found a standard end cover that would fit my bike. We walked up to Kings Square and fitted the new cover. I was back on the road again. Thank God for friends.

I was even more determined to get a big bike after my experience on Paul's Thunderbird. I went to Lundegaards motorcycles, on the corner of Southgate Street and Parliament Street. As soon as I saw it, I knew this was the bike for me. A 1965 Gold BSA Lightning Clubman 650cc, one of the fastest bikes on the road. It was big and bold and it was love at first sight.
The salesman said, 'it's a very hairy machine.'
He took me out for a ride on the back of it, he wouldn't let me ride it myself. It didn't matter, I had to have it. I had to raise the money some how. It cost just over £300, it was a year old with 3000 miles on the clock. I could trade in my C15 as a deposit, but I had to get finance on the rest. I was classed as a minor so I had to get my Dad to stand as guarantor, for the hire purchase agreement. He refused at first, but I nagged him until he gave in, grumbling that I would probably kill myself and leave him with the debt. I went to the shop to collect the bike. I was more excited than I had ever been in my life. They wheeled it out of the workshop, into Parliament Street, I got on it and kicked it into life. The sound sent a thrill right through me. I put it into gear and moved gently off, towards Brunswick Road. The greatest impression I have of that first ride, is of looking at the twin clocks, (speedo and rev counter) above the chrome headlamp, thinking how big it all was.

I rode up Brunswick Road towards Eastgate Street, then headed for the open road so I could give some welly. Once out of town, I had to see what it would do. I screwed every ounce out of it and did the 125 miles per hour on the clock. WOW! What a bike. When I got home later that day, Dad came out to have a look at it.

To my surprise, he said, 'let's have a go on it then.'

He got on it and kicked it over and asked where the gears were. I told him they were, one down, three up. He snicked it into gear and roared off up the road like a demon. He was only wearing an old white collarless shirt and the ubiquitous GPO trousers and shoes. He came back a few minutes later, his shirt tail flapping in the wind and his hair swept back all over the place. He screeched to a halt outside the gate and had the biggest grin on his face that I can ever remember him having.

He said, 'yep, that's a beauty', then walked back into the house. That was the last time he ever rode a motorbike. Dad had learnt to ride, when he was in the army. Before the war, some of the 9th Lancers had been motorcycle despatch riders, which is what Dad did before he trained to drive a tank and subsequently went to North Africa to fight against the German army commanded by Rommel.

This bike was a real thug. It accelerated at an incredible rate. It did 50mph in first gear, although at revs that high, the vibration shook my eyeballs around. Everywhere I went I rode like a madman. Out on the open road, I couldn't stand to see anyone in front of me. If I saw a vehicle ahead I saw it as a challenge, to catch then pass whatever it was.

Angie didn't like this at all, but I couldn't help it. I was a biker and she wasn't. I loved to ride at speed, Angie hated it. Never the less we had something strong between us and we got engaged. Angie's parents were not too keen on the idea and given the hostility we had between us, the prospects were never good. It was a shame really because in a way I quite liked them. I certainly had a good deal of respect for them, although true to my form, I'm sure I never showed it.

I rode my new bike to work and everyone came out to admire it. John Haines said I should come to his house to meet his brother Roger, who was a BSA fanatic. On the weekend I went round to their house in Highworth Road and met Roger, we talked about bikes and biker things and struck up the beginnings of what would turn out to be a lifelong friendship. We rode together, fixed the bikes together, drank together and chased girls together, for years.

The previous year when I had been going to London regularly, one of my friends from work, Miles MacPherson had introduced me to his brother Hughie. Hughie was a lorry driver for FMC Meat Company, he went to London regularly and agreed to give me a lift. He lived with his wife Diana and two small children Gillian and Carol, in a small flat in Ladybellegate Street. I was riding my bike along Fourth Avenue when I saw Hughie fixing a fence at the front of number 90.

I stopped and said, 'hello Hughie, what are you doing here?'
'We've just moved in', he replied.
His new house was only about a hundred yards from mine. From that time, we became the best of friends, a friendship with the whole family that would last for the rest of our lives. I took all my girlfriends to their house, we would sit and talk, drink coffee, or just watch TV. We were always willing babysitters whenever Hughie and Diana wanted to go out. Even if I was unable to bring a girlfriend, I enjoyed babysitting Gill and Carol anytime. We had some great times together. They were such happy little girls.

One night, Diana, Hughie, Angie and I, went out for a drink at a country pub. We met Mick Johns there and it turned into a bit of a session. Hughie worked part time for Mick's father, Bill Johns, at his butcher stall in Eastgate market and had borrowed the old butchers van. It was foggy when we came out of the pub, Mick got into his car and sped off. We piled into the van, Angie and me sitting on the floor, in the back. Hughie and Diana in the front. Hughie raced up the lane after Mick. All of a sudden we came to a T-junction, Hughie saw it too late because of the fog, he slammed on the brakes, but we started skidding across the road. I saw it coming and managed to grab the back doors of the van. There was a tremendous bang as we hit the very high kerb on the opposite side of the road. The van came to an instant stop, buckling in the middle, ending up shaped like a tent. The seats had tipped forward, Hughie hit his nose on the interior mirror, starting a nosebleed. As Diana was thrown forward in her seat, Angie slipped into the space left by the seat, which then fell back on top of her, with Diana still sitting in it. I got out of the back of the van and went to the passenger door. Diana was unable to open it from the inside, but it opened all right from the outside. Diana and Angie got out okay and Hughie scrambled out on his side. No one was seriously injured, just a bit battered and bruised, I didn't have a scratch. Mick Johns came back to see where we had got to, saw the van and said, 'oh my god, dad's van.' They arranged to get a breakdown lorry from Westgate Motorhouse, to take the van away. Mick gave us all a lift home. The van was a total write off. The insurance assessor said he had seen less blood in cars where people had been killed.

Hughie worked on Saturdays for W T Johns the butchers in Eastgate Market. That Market was a wonderful old building which should never have been demolished. We could take a break at Mr Fitch's coffee bar where Gaggia coffee machine spluttered away and the sandwiches were just as thin as I remembered them from when my dad brought me here a few years before. Peacocks had the biggest stalls in the market, Rigby's fish stall always put on a fine display of their wares all set out on an iced slab of white marble. You could buy humbugs from Emblings sweet stall, fruit and vegetables from Ford's, or flowers from Alfred Hurran's. It seemed like you could get anything in that market. For a short time, I too worked on Saturdays for W T Johns, preparing chickens, in a small 'cold room' in the corner next to Hurran's flower stall. There was a pretty girl working for Hurran's and we sometimes managed to snatch a bit of privacy round the back of the stall. It was worth going to work on a Saturday just to see her.

That summer I met Patti Hughes, a pretty American girl with long blond hair and the sweetest nature of anyone I have ever known. I started seeing her every minute I could. I think we were very good for each other and she loved riding on the back of the bike. Patti was here on an extended holiday, staying with Wendy Pyart and her family at Churchdown. The Hughes family lived in Rochester, New York and were friends of Wendy's family. My brother Gordon was going out with Wendy and I met Patti through them. Patti and I walked around hand in hand totally besotted with each other. We spent a wonderful few months together, before she went home. We wrote to each other for a long time but eventually stopped. Patti would have liked me to visit her in America, but I didn't have that kind of money in those days. I also secretly feared that she was from a different class and I might be a disappointment to her if we tried to continue what we had.

Things had gone downhill between Angie and me. I had been spending more time with Patti than I had with Angie. We were still supposed to be engaged but things were not so good. Angie had heard that I had been seen with another girl and it caused some rows, but I had been unable to stop myself seeing Patti. Now she was gone and Angie was giving me more and more grief. Angie went off for a two week holiday with a girl friend, leaving me and Roger Haines to run around. Roger has always been a ladies man and we had a lot of fun together. Angie was gone for the two weeks and didn't even send me a postcard. I knew we were close to the end. Roger had a lovely British racing green, Mark 2 Jaguar. We went to the railway station to pick up Angie and her friend, to give them a lift home. I didn't intend us to have a row, but that's what happened. I went completely overboard about the fact that she hadn't thought about me while we were apart. I suppose Patti had been so sweet and so attentive, I had been spoiled by it and expected Angie to be the same. Anyway, that was that, our affair was over.

The summer of 67, the so-called 'summer of love' was a constant round of parties and musical events. It was a wonderful time to be young, free and single. I heard of a party to be held at Valerie's house in Tetbury Road. It turned out to be one of the memorable ones. Val's parents had gone away for the weekend, so the party had been quickly organised. It was soon packed to the seams with people, the music was loud and the atmosphere was electric. There was plenty to drink and things soon got very lively. Clothes started to come off and people were running around the house in various states of undress. All of a sudden there was a woman banging at the door and shouting that her son, Philippe was in there and she wanted him out. They were a French family who were here on holiday. Philippe's mother had found out that he had come to this party and she didn't like the sound of it. We wouldn't let her in, but I said I would try to find him. I went upstairs into a bedroom where I had last seen him, he was on the bed with a naked girl.

I said 'Philippe, your mum is outside creating a fuss.'

He jumped off the bed, grabbed his clothes and ran out of the room. I stood at the foot of the bed and looked at the girl, lying naked on her back with her arms outstretched in the shape of a cross and her legs open wide.

I said to her, 'Philippe won't be back. What are the chances'?

She said, 'come on then, let's do it.'

I stripped off and dived on the bed, we had a great time for a while and then it was back to the party. She had only just met Philippe anyway and only fancied him because he was someone new and different. That's often how it was then. The phrase 'free love' had some meaning. There was a lot of sex happening at that time and I wanted as much as I could get. If I missed a chance I looked on it as an experience lost. The party carried on into the night, some went home and the numbers went down to a more manageable level. Somebody said we had run out of cigarettes, so I said I would go to the machine at the shops in Seventh Avenue. I borrowed Val's Vespa scooter, I was wearing only a pair of trousers, no shirt, shoes or socks, when I got on the scooter and started it up. As I was about to pull away, a girl ran out of the house and jumped on the back.

She shouted, 'take me for a ride Cliff.'

She was wearing a tiny baby doll night-dress that you could see right through, she sat on the back seat and put her arms around me, holding me tight. Off we went into the night, we rode around the estate, ending up at the cigarette machine. Once we had the cigarettes, we headed off down Seventh Avenue, to the end where it turned into Evenlode Road. There were some old garages at the end of the road, as I went past them I saw a police Panda car, parked not quite out of sight with two policemen sitting it. I could see the startled look on their faces as we swept past, the girls 'baby doll' blowing in the wind. I turned into Tetbury Road and rode the scooter straight up the side entrance to Val's house. We looked out and saw the Panda car come past looking for the scooter, but they missed us. As the night wore on we also ran out of beer so I said I would go home to get a crate that I had there.

My cousin Hugh was working for Talbot's Beer Bottlers and got me some cheap beer. I wasn't spending much time at home at this time, when I got there I was surprised to find dad there with a girlfriend. They had been out for the evening and come home late, somewhat the worse for drink. Then they had started drinking mine. I told him it was hard luck but he wasn't having any more. I took what was left and returned to the party, which carried on into the early hours of the morning. More and more people left, leaving a few of us to sit and smoke grass and get mellow. We talked, smoked and drank coffee until we decided to go to bed. There wasn't enough beds for everyone, so I ended up in a double bed with three girls. It was a bit of a squeeze with four of us in it and they played me up a bit, but it was a lovely experience. But we were wrecked after a good night and soon fell asleep. In the morning the pleasure was extended by my being able to lie in bed and watch the girls get up and do all the things girls do. I think this is one of the great pleasures in life and this morning I had it in triplicate.

Things weren't all fun, sometimes I felt depressed and had to keep myself to myself. Sometimes I stayed in bed for days and nothing could make me get up and get out. Christmas came and I was feeling particularly low. Gordon and dad were each going somewhere for Christmas day and I told them that I was going somewhere too. I left the house on Christmas morning and went into town. It was totally deserted, I sat around in the freezing cold for hours and saw no one. There were places I could have gone and people who would have been pleased to see me, but I couldn't face anyone. I sat on the wall in Kings Square with tears rolling down my cheeks. I was truly alone. Why I was crying I don't know, I had chosen to be alone and it was nothing new for me.

A few days later I went to a party in Bristol Road, where I had my first and last hallucinogenic experience, with acid (LSD). I can't remember whose party it was or very much else except that I felt like I was flying and that someone else must have been having a bad trip because she cried for what seemed like hours. But who could tell. I didn't like the loss of control so I knew that acid wasn't for me.

The 60's were rolling on. Sex and drugs and rock and roll.

Chapter 8
Flower Power

The hippie era was emerging. We began to be aware of what was happening in San Francisco, Flower Power was the in thing. Love and peace was the slogan that was all around and I was all for that. Scott McKenzie was singing about San Francisco and so were The Flowerpot Men with 'Let's go to San Francisco', even one of my favourite groups, The Animals, released 'San Franciscan Nights.' San Francisco suddenly seemed to be the centre of the universe. Jimi Hendrix burst onto the scene with 'Hey Joe' and 'Purple Haze.' Procul Harum released that great hippie single "A Whiter Shade Of Pale.' Even the Rolling Stones changed their musical direction, abandoning for a while, their R&B roots and releasing 'Their Satanic Majesties Request', an essay in Psychedelia, which included the love and peace singles, 'We love you' and 'Dandelion.'

A new club opened at the Cross Hands in Brockworth called The Dandelion. For a while it was the place to go. They had the new psychedelic lights flashing away and everyone was there. It's strange how a small club, hastily constructed in a skittle alley can suddenly become one of the premier meeting places of the in crowd. Another improbable place to suddenly become popular was The Chateau Impney, a bit farther away, in Droitwich. It had a club with soul music hammering away and large grounds, which could be used for romance on warm summer nights. Not many of us had cars so we had to crowd into any car we could, to make the journey to the Chateau on Saturday nights. There was never a shortage of cars going there as long as you knew the right people. For a time there were so many people from Gloucester there, it was as if it were in the middle of town.

The Bristol Hotel was another great venue in the 60s, when Danny Knight was the landlord. It was closer to home and was always a good night, they had some great acts featured there. Mostly local bands but sometimes a bigger name, like Jimmy Cliff, the Jamaican singer who later had a hit with 'Wonderful world beautiful people.' He had a great stage presence and was a big favourite here.

The club took the whole of the 1st floor of the Bristol Hotel. When it got too hot or if I wanted to see who was coming into the club, I used to stand at the top of the stairs leaning against the wall. There are always nasty people who come to these places and try to bully everyone. Tonight I was to come up against a well known thug from Stroud. He had been coming to Gloucester a lot and had made a reputation as a hard man. I was standing at the top of the stairs when he came striding up. He saw me and came right up close. Sticking out of the top pocket of my jacket was a Cadbury's Crunchie bar, which he grabbed and started to unwrap it. I said, 'don't do it mate.' I knew the Hippie ideal of peace and love was about to go out of the window.

He was supremely confident and continued to unwrap it laughing as he did so.

I said nothing, just watched and waited.

He put the Crunchie in his mouth to take a bite.

At that instant, I punched him on the end of the Crunchie sending it to the back of his throat. He flew backwards down the stairs, landing on his back. A second later I launched myself off the top of the stairs and landed on his chest, feet first. He was choking and spluttering and had gone an awful purple colour. John Williamson, who was the bouncer on the door came running to see what was happening. When he saw this guy gasping for breath, he turned and looked at me.

I said 'I think it's time he went home John.'

He agreed, picked the bully off the floor, took him to the door and threw him into the street.

The Bristol Hotel was mostly a good place to go, with occasional spectacular outbursts of fighting. I managed to steer clear of most of it, but sometimes it wasn't possible. I was standing next to my cousin Hugh, trying to ignore the drunken antics of Bronco Jelf and Gordon (Agsie) Hayes. They were both hard men and it was best to keep out of their way when they had this much drink on board. I had known Agsie for years and wasn't on my guard as I would have been had a stranger been acting the way he was. They were dancing, after a fashion, reeling around, bumping into people who couldn't get out of the way. I was far enough away not to be affected by this, so I was looking around, largely unconcerned. Out of the blue I was suddenly attacked by Agsie, who took me by surprise and was trying to stick the nut on me while pushing me backwards. I ducked my head into his chest and kept close, so that he couldn't hurt me and started to fight back. I was still going backwards and soon came to the stage, which was only about a foot high. As I hit it, I fell backwards with Agsie on top of me. One of the guitar players in the group had seen what was happening and kicked Agsie in the head, making him roll off me. I jumped up just in time to see John Williamson coming to sort it out. We were both grabbed, with a view to being thrown out.

I said, 'hold on John, Agsie is drunk, he had a go at me out of the blue.'

John knew it was the truth and said 'okay.'

He left me alone and escorted Agsie and Bronco, from the premises.

A few nights later I was in there again and a buzz was going round that Agsie was in the bar, looking for me. I thought, I'm not waiting for him to find me, I'll go to him.

I walked up to him and said 'what's the problem Agsie?'

He replied 'Hello Cliff, what's up'?

I told him I had heard he was looking for me because of the fight the other night.

He said, 'Oh no, that wasn't you was it? I'm sorry mate, I was so pissed I didn't know what I was doing.'

I said, I realised that and it wasn't a problem.

He was so drunk, I don't think he ever really knew what happened that night.

Hughie MacPherson asked me if I would look after the girls while he and Diana went to his Works Christmas dinner and dance. Of course I agreed, Hughie had become my best friend and I was very fond of Diana, Gill and Carol. I enjoyed being with them all. Hughie and Diana went off to the dance in a coach, which had been supplied by the company so that everyone could have a drink. I don't think they meant for anybody to get in the state that Hughie did though. I heard the coach arrive outside and opened the front door to let them in. what I saw was one of the funniest sights I have ever seen. Diana walked straight down the path and into the house, looking a little disgusted with her husband. Hughie was staggering all around the garden, unable to make out where the door was. I went to him and helped him into the house. As we went through the front door, he tried to get to the bathroom, which was straight ahead. He never made it, he was sick all over the lino. If you've ever tried to walk on wet lino, you know what's coming next. Hughie was already unsteady on his feet and had no chance at all on vomit covered lino. He skidded a few times then went down with a crash, then crawled, or rather slithered along until he got to the bathroom, leaving a trail of slimy diced carrots behind him. I went back through the living room, into the kitchen and saw Diana putting the kettle on, totally unconcerned. She asked me if I wanted a cup of coffee. I said 'Yes please, but shouldn't we keep an eye on Hughie.'

She said, 'No! Leave the silly sod to suffer.'

We sat and drank our coffee, then I helped Diana take the grips out of her hair, all the while listening to the sounds of suffering coming from the bathroom. Eventually, it went quiet so I decided to go into the bathroom to check on him. He was on his knees with his head hanging over the rim of the toilet bowl, snoring gently. He had gone to sleep.

I woke him up and helped him into the bedroom, where he flopped onto the bed and went out like a light. Diana slept in the kid's room that night. The next morning

I came to see how he was, he was up and about as if nothing had happened. It was a remarkable recovery. But Hughie MacPherson is a remarkable man in many ways.

It was with Hughie, on a trip to Taunton, that I first realised that I might need spectacles. We were travelling in an old Thames Trader meat lorry, rattling along the A38 from Bristol, towards Cheddar, when Hughie pointed to something up on a hill. I said, 'I can't see anything.' Hughie said, 'are you joking.' I assured him I wasn't. He said he thought I should go to an optician. I took his advice and found that I was quite severely short-sighted. I had always thought my sight was as good as any one else's. When I had my first glasses, it was a revelation but I only wore them when I felt I needed to. I didn't like being seen wearing them. It didn't fit my image, but I kept breaking them and soon realised that the safest place for glasses was where they were supposed to be. Sitting on top of my nose. I have never liked wearing glasses and don't think I ever will.

Hughie drove a Seddon lorry at times and I took many trips with him in it. There were very few rules for lorry drivers then. No tacograph or log books to worry about. He would take the lorry home and leave it outside the house overnight. On a freezing cold morning, Hughie tried to start the lorry, without success. He said I'll get it going and disappeared into the house. He came back with a crumpled newspaper. He told me to sit in the driver's seat and turn the engine over and give it plenty of revs when it fired. I turned the key and the starter motor got the engine turning. Hughie lit the newspaper and waited a few seconds until it was well alight, then he stuffed it down the air filter which was sucking vigorously. Suddenly there was a mighty bang and the engine was running. As I revved it there was a cloud of black smoke and debris coming from the exhaust, but it soon cleared and we were off.

The Macpherson family booked for a Sunday coach trip to Weston Super Mare. They had only booked four places, for themselves and the two girls. When Hughie's mum said she would have liked to have been able to go, Hughie and I decided we would go together on my bike and meet them there. We set off much later than they did and had a good fast run. The weather wasn't that good, we set up windbreaks on the beach and put on our costumes, but it was a bit cool and showery. Never the less, we had a good day out. On the way back, I was howling up the fast lane of the M5 motorway at around 110 miles per hour when I felt Hughie hitting me on my back. I turned to see what he wanted and he pointed to the nearside lane. I saw it immediately, how I had missed it I don't know. The traffic in the two slower lanes had been quite heavy and tucked in between the traffic was a motorway patrol car. As I looked back, I saw the blue light come on and thought, 'Oh Bollocks.' I opened the bike up as fast as it would go. We were approaching the sliproad for the A38 at Patchway so I swooped off the motorway as fast as I could and kept going. I looked behind and saw the blue light following, but it was a long way back. I kept going, slowing for nothing, the blue light was ever receding, until after five or six miles, we couldn't see it any more. We came to Falfield and saw a pub on the left. I braked as hard as I could and screeched into the car park. There was a huge Mark 9 Jaguar parked there, so I pulled alongside it, putting it between me and the road. We jumped off the bike and waited. A few seconds later the police car came flying past, blue lights still flashing. We had escaped. We laughed aloud and went into the pub for a drink and to spend a bit of time, so the police could forget about us.

In 1968 I met a young man who would become a lifelong friend. Suresh Karadia had come to Gloucester when his family had left Africa. He was a photography student, who was extremely talented and indeed dedicated to the craft he wanted to make his livelihood. We started to hang around together. I was still riding like a lunatic, but Suresh didn't seem to mind. One day we were going down Stroud Road towards town, from where Suresh lived, in St Barnabas close, when I took the bend, just past Ribston hall school, a bit too fast. We came around the bend to find a bus stopped and a car coming the other way, so I couldn't go past. I heaved on the brakes, got into a skid and down we went. When we came to rest, the bike had gone past the bus, but somehow we had ended up underneath the side of it. We crawled out from underneath the bus and checked ourselves over. We were amazed to find no injuries to either of us. We picked up the bike and that too was okay apart from the odd scratch. I kicked it over, it burst into life and we were off again.

I was giving Suresh a lift home one afternoon, travelling along Eastern Avenue at high speed. He saw me and started to turn. The chase was on. I gave the bike all I could and left the police car for dead. At St Barnabas roundabout we turned right, down Stroud Road, then left into St Barnabas Close. I turned onto the drive of Suresh's house, we jumped off and ran into the house. The police must have just caught sight of us as we turned into the Close, because they came hurtling up the road, screeching to a halt at the end of the drive. Two coppers jumped out of the car looking very angry. As they came to the door, we came out.
I said, 'hello, what do you want?'
One of the policemen said, 'you were speeding along Eastern Avenue and Finlay Road.'

I replied, 'no, not us mate, we've been here for ages, we're just going out.' The bike was creaking and gently smouldering from the heat of the chase, but I looked him straight in the eye and denied it.

He said, 'you were going so fast, I was flat out and you were pulling away from me. I know it was you but I didn't get close enough to be sure. I'm going to be watching you.'

With that, they got back into the car and left. Another victory for the motorcycle.

Two weeks later, on a warm Sunday afternoon, I was riding gently along Stroud Road at around the speed limit. I was thinking that all was well with the world, when I saw a police car parked at the side of the shops, just before St Paul's traffic lights. I looked and thought no more of it. The lights were on red so I stopped behind a small queue of traffic. Suddenly I heard a police siren, I looked behind and saw the same police car that had been parked by the shops.

He shouted, 'pull over around the corner.'

When we stopped, he got out of the car and what a surprise? It was the copper from two weeks ago.

He went into police robot speak and recited, 'I have followed you for three tenths of a mile in which you exceeded the speed limit at 53 miles per hour.' I replied ' you fucking liar, you were parked by the shops.'

He just repeated his original statement, adding, 'hard luck.'

He gave me the ticket and walked away, smirking. Okay, he had got me for the other time, but I still hadn't met a copper that wasn't bent.

A few of us started going to the Embassy Club in Cheltenham. It was a small casino with all the usual games, my favourite being the craps, a game of dice. On Saturday nights, to liven the place up they usually had a stripper on. It was first time I had ever seen a stripper performing, she was at very close quarters and I found it very exciting. I was only earning about ten pounds a week and I set myself a limit of a pound as stake money. If I lost that, then I would give up. That gave me a minimum of eight tries on the craps table at half a crown a go. I rarely lost that pound and could usually play all evening, coming out around even or slightly up. One time I had what was a really big win for me, I came out twelve pounds up. Gambling never got the better of me though, that twelve pounds was probably the biggest win I have ever had. Although enjoying the thrill of winning, I could never get used to the disappointment of losing, so I decided not to become a gambling man.

I was walking around town one Saturday afternoon, idling the time away, when I bumped into Chunkie Kemmett. We talked for a while, then he said, 'do you fancy a meal'?

I said, 'yes, why'?

He said, 'we'll go down to the Gloucester rugby club and get something to eat.'

On the way, he explained that he did this occasionally and no one ever seemed to notice. The game had finished and rugby players traditionally have a meal afterwards. He told me we just had to wait until the players came out of the changing rooms to make their way to the clubhouse and join them. The Gloucester boys would think we were with the opposition and vice versa. We wandered into the clubhouse, sat down and were served a good meal, had a laugh and a joke with the teams, then wandered off. Nobody had taken any notice at all.

Back in town, I was going round with a gang of lad's. Some of them were shoplifting on a grand scale. I had indulged in a little shoplifting when I was a young boy, but this was too bad. They stole everything they could get their hands on. I didn't like it and had to stop meeting with them during the day. Brut aftershave was the fragrance that was the big thing at the time. If you weren't wearing Brut, you were nobody. It was the biggest thing on the shoplifting list. Shops had to make sure that it was locked away, they quickly learned that any Brut, even the sample bottle would disappear.

I was getting bored with all this and decided to join the Royal Marines. It was a decision that most of my friends met with incredulity, they said I must be mad, they couldn't believe it. I can hardly believe it myself, looking back. God knows what was going on in my head at the time I made that decision. I suppose I was just fed up with the aimlessness of my life and wanted to try something different.

Chapter 9
RM 26924

I went to the Royal Navy and Royal Marine recruiting office in Bristol, which was the closest one to Gloucester. I took the required academic and medical examinations and passed both with flying colours. The recruiting officer told me I had got the highest score in my English exam that he had so far encountered. During the medical examination, we went into a darkened room to test my eyes for colour blindness, night vision and general vision. The examiner was a Royal Navy officer, not a Marine. He said that I could take some of the tests while wearing my glasses, so that's what I did. My eyesight was tested as perfect. With all the tests completed I waited to find out if I would be accepted into the Royal Marines.

Christmas 1968 was getting near. I had left British Beef Co and had various odd jobs, but I was restless and didn't stay in any of them for very long. I was talking with Suresh one day, when he suggested that maybe we could get some work at the Post Office for the Christmas period. I asked my Dad if he could get us a job, which he did manage to do. He had been a postman for around thirteen years. For many of those years, he worked the nightshift at the sorting office in George Street. This was where Suresh and I were to work alongside him. We reported for work on the first night and were shown to a long workstation, full of small pigeon holes, where we were to be part of a row of temporary workers, taking letters from a sack and placing them into the relevant pigeon holes for delivery the next morning. I was split up from Suresh and was put next to a huge, fat man, who smelled so strongly of stale urine, I couldn't catch my breath. I stood it for an hour or so, but then I had had enough. I went over to my Dad and told him I couldn't work anywhere near that smelly old bastard. Dad said, sorry son, we'll move you somewhere else. He admitted that they had put me there, hoping I wouldn't complain. They had tried putting other men next to him, but they had all objected. I couldn't understand how they could employ such a man and expect others to work in close proximity.

Not being used to working nights, Suresh and I found it very hard to keep awake on that first night. We had been awake all day and were really struggling to keep our eyes open. We went to the canteen at lunchtime and collapsed into the big armchairs they had around the edges. When it was time to start back to work, a supervisor had to wake us up and herd us back into the sorting office. We were like zombies. The living dead.

Somehow, we survived the night and made it home to bed. I slept right through the day and the evening, getting up just in time to get back to work. I was okay that night, but Suresh was even worse than the previous night. I found out that he was trying to do a part time job during the day, as well as this job at night. It was never going to work. He made it through to lunchtime, when we again made our way to the canteen. This time I was alive enough to have something to eat, but Suresh collapsed into his favourite armchair and fell into a deep sleep. When it was time to go back to work, despite my best efforts, I was unable to rouse him. I left him there, curled up in the chair, partly covered by a large curtain that he had pulled around himself.

Some time later, the supervisor came to me and asked where Suresh was. I said I didn't know, maybe he was in the toilet. The supervisor went off in search of the sleeping beauty. Half an hour went by and the supervisor came back to me and said, 'I'm ever so sorry but I have had to send your friend home. I found him asleep in the canteen and he refused all my efforts to get him to return to work. I couldn't get him out of that chair, so I've told him to go home when he wakes up.'

So, on the second night, Suresh got the sack for sleeping on the job. I carried on working for the whole of the Christmas period. The money was okay and I quite enjoyed the experience. One night I went over the road to the Wellington for a pint with Dad and a few of his mates. It was the only time I ever sat and had a drink with my Dad in a pub. I got someone to take a photograph of us, to commemorate the occasion.

Dad wasn't looking too well, he looked very old, though he was only forty-nine. A few months later he was retired from the Post Office through ill health. He was suffering from thrombosis

Soon after that I got my enlistment date. I had only a few weeks left at home as a civilian.

On the tenth of February 1969 I reported to the Royal Marines training facility at Deal, on the Kent coast. I was inducted as RM 26924. Thirty of us were gathered together in a large room and left to get to know each other until it was time for our induction, which was done individually until we were all sworn in. As soon as we were finished with this process, Frank Brady who was from Northern Ireland asked the squad sergeant when he could go out to meet his girlfriend who was waiting outside the gates. Sergeant Watkins shouted him down, calling him an idiot and telling him to get in line. Our training had begun.

We formed up as a squad in four lines, which we would always do from now on. We went on a circuit of the camp to collect our kit. We doubled to the stores where everything was issued in quick time by a row of storemen who had no intention of making our lives easy. In this manner we got our full compliment of kit, except for dress uniforms, which we would be measured for, later. All the kit was stuffed into a bag, which by the time we had finished was stuffed to the limit and very heavy. We were told to get the kitbags onto our shoulders then double to the rooms, which were to be our homes for the next few months. There were ten men to a room, so 899 squad took up three rooms. Five beds and lockers down each side of the room. A large round aluminium rubbish bin, they called a gash bin sat in the middle of the highly polished parquet floor. The gash bin itself was also highly polished and looked like a flying saucer. In my room I was bunked next to Alfie Hammond, from Charlton in London. Paddy Brady was there, so were Ray Buck from Liverpool and Stuart McDonald from Fife in Scotland.

Our instructors were, Sergeant Watkins, Corporal Blatchford and Lieutenant Davis. They would be with us throughout our training and do most of the physical tasks that we were required to do. The first thing we had to do was get fit, the physical training was incredibly hard. We were given long runs, followed by periods of intense gym work. Sometimes these sessions were so intense that many of us were sick during the exercise, but it made no difference, we just kept going. While off duty on the camp, we had to march everywhere in pairs, even when we wanted to go to the NAAFI. Alfie Hammond was my best buddy, so we went everywhere together, on or off the camp.

Life was a constant round of physical exercise, marching and cleaning. It was very hard, but the life itself was not that different from boarding school, living closely with others of approximately the same age.

The difference was in the intensity of it all. Everything had to be done to perfection. Even then, sometimes it wasn't good enough, just so you didn't get too cocky. We were shown how to do everything in minute detail by either Sgt Watkins or Cpl Blatchford. They showed us how to iron our clothes, the Royal Marine way. How to mend our socks, how to clean our brasses, our rooms, polish the floors, clean the toilets and polish our boots, all the Royal Marine way, which we were told was the best way. The floors had to be polished to a shine unimaginable to a civilian, it took hours to do before an inspection, especially if we had recently come in from an exercise, covered in mud. The 'Heads' (toilet and shower block) had to be immaculate. Each squad took it in turns to be on general fatigues, which meant we had to take care of the shared facilities for a week, as well as our own rooms. Our squad corporal came and did a pre inspection and created a hell of a fuss if he found anything not up to scratch. The Officer came later followed by our squad NCO's. Lt Davis went through everything and although very strict, he wasn't usually as critical as our NCO's. Usually everything had been sorted out before he got there. One day though he surprised me, as to the lengths anyone would go to in the name of cleanliness. 899 squad had been on fatigues and we had to stand and watch while he inspected the toilets. He went into a cubicle, rolled up his sleeve and plunged his hand into the WC. He felt around the bend, brought his wet hand out, looked at it, put it to his nose and sniffed it, then asked for a towel to dry his hands. He didn't say anything. He just walked off. We had passed the inspection.

Weapon training was especially interesting. We were all given a 7.62 Self-Loading Rifle, which was to be our personal weapon. After some initial training to learn the workings of the weapon, it was off to the range to sight it in. The first thing to do was to get the SLR set up for my own eyesight. At a range of 25 yards, we were told to load five rounds and fire at the centre of a 'Figure Eleven, Charging Man target.' After the five rounds were fired, Cpl Bouchard, the weapons training instructor, proved the SLR empty. Proving means checking that a weapon is empty. When all weapons had been proved, we were sent to stand by our targets, for evaluation. The purpose of this exercise was to see where the group was printing so that Cpl Bouchard could adjust the sights to hit the centre of the target. The hope was that all recruits would be able to hit the target sufficiently well to make an assessment. This didn't prove to be the case. As I walked past some of the targets to get to mine, I couldn't help laughing. Some had hardly hit the target at all. Those who had were all over the place. The corporal was moving up the line cursing and swearing at each recruit in turn. When he got to me I was still sniggering.
He said, 'what are you sniggering at?'
'Nothing corporal' I replied.
He looked at my target and saw four holes in a group around the size of a fifty pence piece.
He said, 'that's pretty good, but where's the fifth shot.'
I said, 'It went through one of the other holes corporal.'

'Show me.' He said.

I showed him the very slight clip on the side of one of the holes. He just said, 'well done' and moved on to the next man, where he resumed his shouting of abuse, calling them a useless lot of bastards. Very soon I could tell I was going to get on well with Cpl Bouchard.

We had to learn to swim for great distances carrying large amounts of equipment. Like everything else, it was to be a gradual build up of proficiency. First time at the pool, the instructor said, good swimmers to one end and poor swimmers to the other end. I thought that if I went with the poor swimmers it would give me time to build up my stamina.

He shouted, 'everybody in the pool.'

Some jumped in, some lowered themselves in and some dived in. I dived in and after a couple of strokes, I came up on the other side of the pool. The instructor had seen it and shouted, 'YOU! Get up the other end.' So I was in the experienced class after all. First of all we swam round and round the pool for increasing lengths of time. Then we started swimming while wearing more and more kit. Starting with combat jacket and trousers, then adding boots, then packs, then stones in the pack to simulate a full kit, then the whole kit including an old rifle they kept especially for swimming with. It was very hard to keep afloat with all this kit on, let alone swim.

After a few weeks training, we were taken to the gym to play games against a squad that was further into their training than we were. We played a variety of games, including volleyball, football and some chase and contact games. We lost them all. We didn't even get near to winning any of them. It was a lesson that was very important. We had a lecture afterward, telling us that we were not expected to win anything. The extra training that the more advanced squad had, had increased their fitness and their confidence to such a degree, that we had never stood a chance. It would soon be our turn to play these games against a squad earlier in it's training than us and we would be expected to annihilate them, as we had been annihilated.

The runs got longer and longer, until we were easily doing 9 miles in full kit. Some had great difficulty with the runs, but all could do it in the end. We went out as a squad, doubling in close order. When we got out onto the open road, we went into open order. We doubled for twenty minutes, then marched single time for five minutes. We kept that up until we got back, close to the barracks, when we closed up again and put on a show as we went through the gates.

After a shower, Alfie and I went to the galley for dinner. Marine barracks are classed as ships, so nautical terms are used. We were going out after dinner and were dressed in civilian clothes. We were in the queue for our food when one of the cooks said to me, 'I like that tie you're wearing.' It was an old flower power tie, pretty nice really, but I had grown bored with it. I took it from around my neck and said, 'if you like it, it's yours.' He couldn't believe it, he thanked me profusely and said for me to take any food I wanted. As Alfie and I sat at a table, eating our dinner, I could see the cook showing the tie to his mates and nodding in my direction. It turned out to be one of the best moves I could have made. I got friendly with the cooks and eventually started a small business in the evenings, selling sandwiches around the barrack rooms. I also got the best of everything in the galley, especially later on when I missed breakfast and could go in through the back door and eat my breakfast in the kitchen.

The Reverend G P Thornley RN was the Navy Vicar for the Deal barracks. Geoff Thornley and I became friends very quickly. We just hit it off together. I was soon reading the lesson during the church services on Sundays. I had done it many times before at school, I even read the lesson in Gloucester Cathedral once. Although I have never been a religious person, it didn't seem to matter to Geoff. He never came on with a holy holy attitude, though there was never any doubt that he was a good and holy man. Our friendship has endured for nearly thirty years so far, although we rarely see each other these days, but we still keep in touch.

The post was handed out every morning at first assembly. We were ordered to form up as a squad, outside the barracks. Sergeant Watkins called out each name in turn, then handed any post to the persons concerned. I seemed to have something almost every day, mainly from girlfriends. One day he called my name, while waving a beautifully pink coloured envelope in the air. He said to everyone, while holding my letter to his nose. 'Look at this, a pink scented letter from America, what ever next.'
It was a letter from Patti Hughes, wishing that we could be together and wishing me luck. Shortly after this letter, Patti sent me a macramé belt that she had made for me, it was very sixties, I still have it. She also sent me a sweatshirt from New York City. It was the first sweatshirt I had ever seen. They were not yet available in England.

I was also writing to and receiving letters from Angie Talbot, maybe we would get back together. She said she missed me. I certainly missed her.

107

Soon we had our first leave. I was given a seven day pass and a travel warrant, to good old Gloucester. I was missing it too. Angie and I got together for that week, but I think we both knew it wasn't the same as it had been. I got the Lightning from under its covers and blasted around like a man possessed. Angie still didn't want to go on it. It was clear that we had no future together. I felt very sad when we parted but that's the way it goes.

During that leave I met with Suresh, he was taking photographs for the membership cards for a new club called The Swinging Plaice, in the Eastgate Market precinct. I sat with Suresh, at a table just inside the door, where every new member came over to have his or her picture taken. The club didn't last long, but at least Suresh got something out of it.

It wasn't much of a leave, I was almost glad to be going back to Deal. I took the train to Paddington, then the underground to Kings Cross, as I had done before without any problems. This time the train stopped in the tunnel for about three quarters of an hour. I knew I was going to be lucky to catch my connection to Deal. When I got to Kings Cross, I ran to the platform, but it was too late. The train had gone. I knew I would be in trouble if I was late back to barracks. I went to the information desk to find out when the next train was due. There was no other train to Deal that night, the next one only went as far as Dover. I had little choice but to take it, even though it would arrive at Dover at twenty past midnight, twenty minutes too late for my pass, with another twenty miles to go to Deal. When I arrived at Dover I walked out of the station to try to get a taxi to take me to Deal. I was in uniform, so it was pretty obvious where I was going. As I stood at the taxi rank, a Marine policeman came up to me and said. 'Hello Bootneck! Absent without leave'? I said, 'yes, how did you know.'
He said, 'me too. Were you on that poxy tube train, stopped in the tunnel'?
'Yes', I replied.
He said, 'Want to share a taxi?'
I was a bit worried by him being an RM policeman, but tried not to show it. I said, 'OK, why not'?
On the journey to Deal he said to me, 'have you got to hand your pass in to the guardroom'?
I said, 'no, it just has an expiry time on it.'
He said, 'mine too. The guards will know me so we'll double time, through the gates as if I have you under arrest. When we get round the corner from the guardhouse, we'll split up. You just disappear into your barrack room and I'll do the same. Okay'?

I said, 'Okay, it sounds like a good plan to me.'

It was a good plan and it worked like clockwork.

The next day, Alfie and Ray wanted to know how I had got into the camp without being arrested. When I told them, we all laughed our heads off. They said, you're the jammiest sod alive.

There was talk of a new uprising in Ireland. I asked Frank Brady what he thought of the IRA. He told me, there was no such thing as the IRA, it didn't exist. Shortly after this conversation, the first bombs went off and a war started that is still going on thirty years later. Frank went AWOL and I never saw him again. The IRA called it a war and set about killing our military and civilian personnel. Our politicians refused to call it a war and have continued to this day to allow the atrocities to continue.

We were soon back in training with a vengeance, it was getting tougher every day. The runs were getting longer and faster and the swimming was getting more and more arduous. Weapons training wasn't a problem and I looked forward to time on the range as a welcome relief to the more physical pursuits. We were shooting at up to 600 yards now. A far cry from the 25 yards we had started at. Sometimes during shooting practice, the instructors would decide it was time to test our shooting ability when we were exhausted. The range ran alongside the sea and there were chalk cliffs in one area. We were sent up the beach, over barbed wire, up the hill to the edge of the cliff were we were urged to hurl ourselves off the edge of a cliff which wasn't all that far off vertical. We had to slide down on our backs as fast as we could, digging our heels in very carefully to control the rate of descent. If you dug your heels in too strongly, you tumbled over, head first. If you didn't dig them in enough you came down too fast and ended in a heap at the bottom, too battered to run back along the beach, to the finish. After this we were required to hit a target with five rounds. It was difficult to steady your aim after this kind of exertion, but it could be done.

The range ran alongside the sea until it came to a cliff at the end where the target butts had been built into the cliff. The theory behind this type of range construction was that all stray rounds would either go into the cliff of into the sea. To ensure that we didn't shoot any boats that came round the point, one recruit was always sent around the back of the cliff where he could see any boats coming. His orders were to raise a red flag when it was clear to fire, but if he saw a boat coming he was supposed to lower the flag until the it had passed. The instructors always kept an eye on the flag, so they could give the order to cease firing in plenty of time. One day we were blazing away when an oil tanker came round the point. Everybody kept firing until the sergeant spotted it and called the cease fire. He went round to the other side of the cliff and found the recruit curled up asleep, amid all the noise, totally oblivious to what was going on around him. We could hear the shouting and balling from two hundred yards away. The sleepy marine spent the rest of the afternoon, doubling up and down the shingle beach with his rifle above his head, being constantly berated by a corporal.

899 squad went on a three-day exercise in a wood, in the middle of nowhere. We left Deal, riding in the back of a three ton lorry, arriving at our destination, a couple of bone shaking hours later. We disembarked from the lorry and were told to make ourselves at home for the next three days. We had been allowed only to bring with us, the minimum of regulation kit. Before we had left the barracks, the NCO's had searched our packs for anything that may have made life too easy. We had to exist as if we were in battle conditions. The weather was foul, it was the end of February and it was raining that cold winter rain that chills you to the bone.

Lt Davis briefed us that we were on our own and we could to take any action we saw fit. We could beg, borrow or steal anything to make our lives more comfortable. We were given enough rations to last three days, then the officers and NCO's got into their vehicles and left.

We split into small groups and chose places we thought would be both dry from any water running along the ground and would be easy to defend. We knew that it wasn't going to be as easy as we had been told. They weren't going to leave us alone for three days. We were going to be attacked at some time throughout the exercise.

We had a terrible time trying to get a fire going, with everything that could be used to start a fire, being sodden by the persistent rain. Alfie and I gave up after a while and decided to get on with making the bivouac that we would spend the next two nights, sleeping and trying to keep dry in. All we had with us to make this shelter with, was our poncho's and some string. We laced the two poncho's together as prescribed in the manual and made the bivouac up against a tree. We stuffed it from the open end with dead ferns and squashed them down to form a mattress, then threw some green ferns over it for camouflage. It looked good so Alfie and I crawled in to try it out, it was pretty snug. We would be all right in here.

The other lads in our group were still having very little success with the fire, so Alfie and I decided to explore the area. We hiked for a considerable distance through the woods, making sure we knew what bearing we were on, so we would be able to find our way back. We came upon a hut in a clearing and saw the instructor's vehicles parked at the front. We decided to creep in as close as we could for a recce. As we got close, we could see a large bunker full of sacks of coal, stacked in a row. We got to the bunker and picked up a full sack. It was a full one hundredweight sack and we were going to have difficulty getting it back to our base, but we knew it would make all the difference to our comfort.

We struggled through the woods for what seemed like an age before we got back to camp. When we emerged from the darkness struggling with this sack of coal, they all fell about laughing. They had managed to get the fire going but it was really feeble, all the wood was far too wet. We put the coal on and soon had a roaring fire. Someone found an old piece of corrugated tin plate and we constructed a roof for the fire to keep the rain off it. It was plain sailing now, we cooked our meal, made a brew of tea and spent a good old evening round the camp fire, telling silly stories and tales of drunkenness and bravado. We hid the rest of the coal so that we could use it when we needed it and to keep it away from prying eyes, especially if an officer turned up.

I woke up next morning, the rain had turned to snow. It was freezing, but we hadn't really noticed the cold while we were in the bivouac. Suddenly there was a commotion outside. The instructors had arrived and were shouting at everybody to fall in, in a clearing not far from our camp. We started rushing about, getting our kit together, although we had slept in full kit, including boots, with our rifles by our sides. We ran down to the clearing and fell in, as a squad.

I couldn't believe my eyes. The snow was falling quite heavily, we were wearing as much kit as we could, to keep warm and in front of us stood, our squad officer and two NCO's, stripped to the waist. Cpl Blatchford shouted, 'right you lot, get your tops off, were going for a run, to shake the cobwebs off.' So off came all our kit and we went off for our morning wake up run. Before long I was as warm as toast and we were soon back, dressed and told to go and make a brew.

We stoked up the fire, which we had kept going, with a bit more of our coal and soon the billy can of water was boiling. I was just making the tea when Lt Davis came to see how we were getting on. He looked around our camp, then came over to the fire for a warm. He saw the coal burning merrily and said, 'where did that coal come from?'

I said, 'we came across it sir.'

He said, ' I see.'

With that he smiled and walked away.

The officer and NCO's cleared off and left us to it again. We spent the day exploring the area and refining our bivouacs and cooking arrangements. We knew that anything could happen, at any time. So we had to be vigilant as well. Nothing happened all that day, so we retired to our makeshift beds with some trepidation. Something had to happen soon. In the early hours, I was woken by a terrific bang, quite close to our camp. We all leapt out of our bivouacs, rifles in hand, ready for battle. The dawn was just breaking, but it was still pretty dark. I could hear people shouting and running around, but couldn't see anything but flashes a short distance away. We decided to take cover and wait for something to come to us. The noise went on and on but never got any closer. We heard someone yelling for help, but ignored it. I later found out that one of the other camps had been attacked and one fool had run into the darkness and fell down an old pit and had been unable to climb out. Eventually the exercise was halted and we came out of hiding. No one had found us, we had fared much better than the ones who had been attacked and the ones who had made their way towards the action. They had all been caught out. We had made the right decision to wait where we were.

It was time to leave and get back to civilisation. Back in Deal we had a shower, got changed and made our way to the galley for some good food. I have to say, that all the food I ever ate at an RM establishment was always of a very high standard and with all this exercise, I was consuming vast amounts of it. Once fed, Alfie and I made our way into Deal to the local night club on the sea front. It was a small cellar club called The Dive Bar. It was aptly named, but it was the only place with some life to it in Deal, apart from the occasional camp dances. Marines often got into trouble with the locals at the Dive Bar. They seemed to resent Marines chatting up the local girls. There were often fights that spilled out onto the beach. This surprised me a little, because unless severely outnumbered, the marines always won. Shortly before I had arrived in Deal, a marine had been set upon by a number of local lads, a left on the beach, severely beaten. He was found the next morning, having died from his injuries. Because of this the marines were particularly belligerent at the time and some terrible fights ensued. No local lad was safe.

The camp dances were quite good, lots of girls came, which surprised me a bit. I would have thought that they wouldn't have wanted a man that they knew would be moving on soon, but they did. They were looking for casual affairs, as much as we were. At one of the dances, our room decided we would get on stage and play a tune. None of us played an instrument, but a little thing like that wasn't going to stop us. We formed a Gazoo band. A couple of gazoo's, one comb and paper and a bongo drum was all we needed to play Marmalade's ob-la-di ob-la-da. It was a rubbish song anyway and we made it worse, but everybody loved it. There were shouts of 'encore' from the audience. It was the only thing we knew, so we played it again to howls of laughter and rapturous applause. I thought the popular music scene was going through a bad patch at the moment. Thank God for the Heavy Progressive bands, which were coming to the fore.

Back on the range, it was time for the assessment of our night shooting skills. We went to the range, which was in total darkness. No light spilled from any local conurbations, it was pitch dark. We were let into the range hut for a briefing, where we were given ammunition and time to load magazines. Then we had to pick up a figure eleven target and carry it to the 25 yard range. That was a far enough distance to shoot in this kind of darkness. We put the targets in their holders and retired to the firing point, where the order was given to load a magazine of twenty rounds and make ready to fire. The technique was to look into the ground, to try to get some night vision. After a while you could make out the targets, but I had already sussed out a better way to do this. The targets were made of plywood and were reused many times with a new paper target pasted onto the board. I had chosen a target with plenty of old holes in it and I made sure I had my jacknife with me. A jacknife always had one of those spikes on it which are supposed to be for getting stones out of horse's hooves. This spike was about the same diameter as a 7.62 bullet. On the order to fire, I made sure I didn't hit the target at all. The next order was to recover the target and carry it back to the range hut for scoring. It took about five minutes to walk from the range to the hut and during that time I punched twenty good scoring holes in the target. Easy. I was a good shot, but why take unnecessary risks.

Part of the final test in the swimming pool was to dress in full battle order, climb to the top diving board and jump off. The theory was to hit the bottom of the pool, take off your rifle and pack while on the bottom, then spring to the surface and complete the test by swimming three lengths of the pool. It wasn't a big problem as long as everything came undone. The kit was so heavy that unless you managed to shed it you couldn't get to the surface. I got to the edge of the board, grasped the butt of my rifle with one hand and the foresight with the other and held it tight to stop the rifle coming up and hitting me under the chin when I hit the water. I jumped in, hit the bottom with a thump, pulled the sling of the rifle over my head, undid my webbing and discarded it. I bent my legs and pushed upwards, sucking in a big breath as soon as I broke the surface. I swam the required three lengths and got out. Nothing to it. Those who had completed the test, stood and watched the others, as their turn came. Some were nervous and took a little time to take the plunge. Some did it with no fuss at all, then came the show off. I have to admit, he was good at everything, but it could be irritating. He didn't walk to the edge of the board like everybody else. He ran from the back screaming, 'Geronimo' and leapt off the board. He had overdone it this time though, he jumped so high that the foresight of his rifle got caught in a polo net that had been hoisted to the ceiling to keep it out of the way. He had hold of the rifle by the butt and the foresight as we had been taught, but this caught him by surprise and the rifle came up and caught him by the neck. His rifle sight caught in the net and his neck caught between the rifle and the sling. Within seconds he started to go a funny colour. Suddenly there was a tearing sound and the net gave way. He hit the water with a mighty splash and crashed to the bottom of the pool. He was lying there with a small stream of bubbles coming from his mouth, when the instructor, shaking his head, put a long pole into the water and hooked his webbing. We grabbed the end of the pole and dragged him out. As we pulled him onto the side of the pool he was coughing and spluttering and spitting out water. Once we realised he was going to be all right we started to laugh until we were all rolling about, partly with relief and partly because it was such a funny sight, seeing him dangling from that net.

One of the shooting tests was a walk down from six hundred yards, to three hundred yards, two hundred, one hundred, fifty and twenty five. Five rounds to be fired at each distance. I was always amazed that they didn't seem to realise that these methods were wide open to cheating. As I said, I was a good shot but why take a chance. We were in a line, all shooting within the required time limit. I put the rifle to my shoulder, but I didn't shoot any of my rounds at six hundred yards, only a couple at three hundred, a couple at two hundred and a couple more at one hundred. When I got down to fifty yards I made sure I had twenty rounds in the magazine. I fired ten rounds from fifty yards and ten more from twenty five yards. My score was great.

Alfie, Ray and I were fooling around in our room one afternoon, when my glasses were knocked onto the floor and I fell off my bed, onto the glasses, breaking a lens. I only wore them for shooting so it wasn't a big problem, but I had to report it to an officer so that I could get them repaired.

The officer said, 'I didn't realise you wore glasses.'

I told him that I only wore them for shooting.

He asked me if any of the weapons training instructors had ever noticed.

I said, 'if they had, they had never mentioned it.'

Actually, they had noticed and made a joke about it, nicknaming me Joe 90.' To be fair, I don't know how anybody could have missed my thick black rimmed 'Buddy Holly' style glasses.

He told me that, as far as he knew GD Marines (general duty) were not allowed to wear glasses. I told him what had happened at the recruiting office and he said he would have to look into it, but it looked as if a mistake had been made.

Eventually I was sent to the Royal Navy Hospital Haslar, at Portsmouth, for tests. They tested my eyesight, then I went before a panel of officers. They told me that they were very sorry, but my eyesight failed to meet the required standard for the Royal Marines and I would be unable to remain in the service. They said my eyesight would be all right for the army or the navy, as they are allowed to wear glasses, but marines were not. I was given three options. I could transfer to another service, because it had been their error, I could remain in the marines, but only as a cook. Or I could take an honourable discharge.

There wasn't much to think about. I didn't want to be in any of the other services and to be honest, I was quite relieved that I was getting out.

I got back to Deal from my appointment with the medical board at Portsmouth, in the early evening. Just in time to get to the party being thrown to celebrate the end of training and our last evening in Deal. It had been arranged by our NCO's at a pub just out of town. It was the only time we had socialised with them. Their attitude towards us was completely different. Sgt Watkins told us that we were one of the best squads he had ever trained. You wouldn't have known it at times, to hear him bellowing what useless idiots we all were.

I said to him, 'I'll bet you say that to all the boys.'

But he said he meant it, we were very good. We had a real fun night, plenty to eat and drink. A night to remember.

We left Deal the next day for another week of leave, before the squad reported to Lympstone for advanced commando training. I already knew I would not be going with them. I was to report back to Deal to await my discharge. We all went our separate ways and I never saw any of them again, with the exception of Alfie Hammond, who I visited a few times in later years.

I went home for the week, got the Lightning out again and started doing the rounds of my mates, to find out what was happening. I came out of my house one afternoon, started the bike and set off down Fourth avenue. As I was accelerating away, a dog came running out of a house on my right. It ran after me, trying to bite my legs. Somehow it ran in front of the bike and I hit it with my front wheel. I went over the handlebars and landed in a heap on the road. Hughie MacPherson was in his garden and had seen what had happened. He came running down the road towards me, waving a shovel. The dog ran off just in time, before Hughie could get to it. He was really angry that it had caused the accident. We picked the bike up and assessed the damage. It wasn't much, the headlamp rim was bashed flat on one side and the chrome scraped off, but apart from that it was okay. I saw where the dog had come from and where it had gone, so I went to the house and knocked on the door. A man answered, asking what I wanted. I told him that his dog had just caused an accident, having knocked me off my bike. He was instantly aggressive, telling me that he didn't have a dog and that I should fuck off.
I said, 'look mate, I don't want any trouble. Pay for the damaged headlamp rim and I will say no more about it.' He didn't want to know, just repeating that I should fuck off.
I said, 'if I fuck off, I'll come back with the police.'
He said, 'I don't give a fuck who you come back with.'

I called the police and told them what had happened, so they sent a constable to see the man concerned. We went to the door and knocked again. The response was much the same as I had encountered an hour earlier, except that when he denied having a dog the policeman said, 'do you mind if we come in and have a look.'
The man didn't like it, but he let us in. The dog was lying in front of the fireplace, looking very ill.
The policeman said, 'that dog doesn't look well to me.'
The man said that the dog always looked like that.
The policeman asked if they could get the dog to stand up. They called it, but it wouldn't move. Then they tried to stand it up, but it fell back down again as soon as they let it go. It was obviously injured and in pain. The policeman had seen enough and said, 'I'm satisfied that this animal has been involved in the road traffic

accident described by Mr Ballinger and I will be making a report to that effect. I will also call the RSPCA to report that you are causing this animal unnecessary suffering, by neglecting it's injuries.'

At this point, the man said, 'I've already told you, it's nothing to do with me. The dog belongs to my wife.'

His wife had been standing in the corner of the room, saying nothing up to this point. I thought, how's that for a good relationship. Drop your wife in it when the going gets rough.

The policeman turned to the woman and said, 'is this correct madam, that the dog belongs to you?'

Hesitantly, she replied, 'yes.'

The policeman asked, 'have you a licence for this animal, madam?'

That was the last straw, she burst into tears and started blubbering away at what I took to be excuses, but the job was done and it was time for us to leave them to contemplate the court appearance that was sure to follow.

The dog had to be destroyed and some time later I saw the case in the Citizen. They had been fined on all three counts. Causing an accident, causing unnecessary suffering and no dog licence.

I was having trouble with a stiff neck for the next few days, so I thought I had better go to the accident unit, in Great Western Road to get it looked at. They X-rayed it but were unsure of the extent of the damage. They put me in a collar and told me to come back next week. I said I wouldn't be able to come back as I was due back at Deal on Monday. The doctor said, Oh no, you mustn't travel, just in case there is a problem. We will give you a sick certificate for a week. I rang Deal and told them I would be late back due to an accident. It wasn't a problem, I wouldn't have much to do there anyway. So I got an extra week at home out of it and there was no damage to my neck, it was just a strain.

When I got back to Deal, I was moved into a room with two other men who were waiting for a discharge. We were on light duties while in this room, it was very boring, with very little to do. But with new squads coming in, there was some money to be made. I was a wizard at bulling (spit and polishing) boots and could do a few pairs quickly during the day, when I had nothing better to do. I charged them a small fee for the service. I also had a key to the storeroom so that I could make tea for the Commanding officer and his secretary, at times throughout the day. In the storeroom was a radio, so I could lock myself in and keep out of sight for hours at a time. There was also a polishing machine. One of the worst jobs for a squad with an inspection due, was getting the floor shiny enough. I could polish the floor for them, with my machine, while they were out during the day. I charged them 2/6 each, that made twenty-five shilling a room. That wasn't bad seeing as I was only earning £9 a week. Five or six rooms, only took a couple of hours with my machine.

It took longer than I had expected for my discharge to come through, about a month from when the decision had been made. One day, a Captain came into the room and gave me some papers to sign and an itinerary to follow. I had to go from place to place all around the complex, handing in pieces of kit and signing different papers until suddenly, I was a civilian again. I had my severance pay and my last travel warrant, which I used to travel home to good old Gloucester.

Chapter 10
Theft

Back home again, it was spring of 1969, I had no job and didn't really want one. I wanted to have some fun before I got tied back down with a boring job. I have always found work to be a necessary evil and have never enjoyed it. I resolved to grow my hair long again and grow a beard. In other words, a low maintenance lifestyle. I got the Lightning out and rode a lot of miles, travelling anywhere the fancy took me. I signed on the dole and resisted all their attempts to place me in work. Signing on wasn't made so easy as it is today, I had to go to the employment exchange in Southgate Street, to register for work. Then I had to walk down Commercial Road to the dole office to sign on, before I could get any money. I had to sign on, every week at an allotted time and collect the money, in cash. If I was late, there was an inquest as to why I had been unable to attend when required. The staff were often rude and surly. I was never surprised when a row erupted between a claimant and a member of staff, as often happened. I was regularly called into the employment exchange, where they offered me all kinds of jobs, most which were totally unsuitable. One day my interviewer offered me a job as a bacon boner at Hilliers processed meat factory, in Nailsworth. I told him that I knew nothing about bacon boning. To which he replied that my record showed that I had worked at The British Beef Co. I agreed that I had indeed worked there, but I was a pen pusher, a clerk, not a bacon boner. I had never handled meat in my life and had no desire to do so. He wouldn't be put off that easily though. He said that I could learn.
I tried another tack and said, 'Nailsworth is twenty miles away, how am I supposed to get there, I don't have a car.'
He still wouldn't give up. I was amazed when he said, 'according to our records, you have a motorcycle.'
I looked the him straight in the eye and lied that as I was out of work, I had sold the bike to pay some debts. That did it, I had won this round, but it had been a hard fight.

It was hard living though, the money was only enough for a very poor existence. I went into town most days and hung around with Suresh and other old pals. We often sat for hours, in the Bon Marché café, with one cup of tea or sometimes a plate of chips with gravy over them. This was a good value meal, the gravy was thick and tasty. Some of the serving ladies objected to our requests for gravy, because there was no price for it without a meal We insisted it must be free,

119

because our plate of chips was a meal. We never had a problem when Ada was serving, she would ladle on as much as we wanted.

Sometimes I went to the college in Brunswick Road, I used the canteen for subsidised, students meals and then went to the common room for a rest in a nice easy chair and a free cup of tea. People got quite used to me being there and never seemed to notice that I never took any classes. I was relaxing in a chair one day, when I was engaged in conversation by some students, suddenly one of them asked what I was doing at the college. I replied with a joke that I was doing as little as possible. They all laughed and said, 'the same as the rest of us then.'

One evening I went to Kingsholm rugby ground to watch Gloucester play the Pennsylvanians, a team from the USA. It turned out to be a good fun game, with Gloucester winning by more than fifty points. But it was an eminently enjoyable evening. I came out of the ground, in a buoyant mood and went to where I had parked the Lightning, to make my way home. I had parked outside the Jockey, between two cars. My beloved Lightning was not there. Slightly stunned and not quite believing that it was gone, I thought perhaps I had parked farther down the road. I walked up and down Kingsholm Road two or three times before I admitted to myself that it had been stolen. Dejectedly, I walked to Bearland to report the theft. The policeman on the desk took the details of the bike and the circumstances of the theft, with little interest. I made my way from there, to the bus stop and made a miserable journey home to Tuffley.

All of a sudden, things didn't seem too great. I had no job, no money and now I had no transport. I wasn't very happy.

My brother Gordon had become friendly with Phil Large, who was to become another lifelong friend. They were running the Sound City mobile disco, travelling all around the area playing their records and having fun doing it. I started going with them, in Phil's old Bedford van. They were doing village halls, skittle alleys, church halls, pubs, clubs, school dances, private parties, anywhere they could get a booking. They were good at it too, they were very entertaining DJ's. I was immensely proud of Gordon's flair for it. He was very popular wherever he went. I had some great night's out by going along with them. In return, I kept order when it was necessary. One night, we were at a church hall in Belgrave Road. A young lad was really playing up, making everybody nervous. Eventually he went too far and smashed a window. I grabbed him by the scruff of the neck and the seat of his trousers and threw him out. He stood outside, cursing and threatening that he would return with his mates, who would give me a good hiding. I just told him to bugger off. Half an hour later, he was back with the man he thought was going to do it for him. I smiled as they walked towards me and said hello John. It was John Myatt, an old friend. The lad's jaw dropped, it was obvious that there would be no fight between John and me. John asked me what had gone on and I told him. He turned to the lad and cuffed him round the head, telling him to clear off home and stop causing trouble. John was a real hard case, but a very nice man. He was a member of the Scorpions motorcycle gang, as was I. We didn't fight among ourselves, but we would fight anyone else. But at the moment, I was a biker without a bike.

Gordon and Phil were both on the dole, while they were doing these disco's and it was a constant worry that someone from the dole office would be at one of the gigs. Phil didn't seem to care much, which he proved when he took a booking to do a party at Cedar House, the new Social Security office, in Spa Road. It had just been built and the top floor was not yet in use, so they decided to have a staff party up there. There was an incredible amount of food laid on, which we helped ourselves to, as a perk of the job. I was constantly broke and any free food was always welcome. There was so much at this party, that we decided to take some home, to carry on the party and to eat the next day. We kept going up to the tables, filling a plate and returning to behind the record decks, where we transferred the food into LP record cases which we had emptied and quietly taken the records down to the van. We filled up a couple of cases with sandwiches, chicken legs, vol au vents and cakes then carried them down to the van. It was enough to keep us fed for days. Nobody noticed the missing food, or the fact that Gordon and Phil were claiming benefit.

One night we were at Quedgeley Village Hall, where Sound City had been booked for the local Friday night hop. It wasn't a great night, so I decided to wander off, down to the Plough for an hour. I was walking down the Bristol Road, when I was surprised by my Dad pulling up alongside me. He got out and told me he had just read the Citizen and there was a small piece about someone having been fined £40 at Gloucester magistrate's court for the theft of my bike. It was the first I had heard of it.
Dad said, 'come on, I'll take you to the police station.' We went to reception at Bearland and enquired what had happened.
The constable made some enquiries and said, 'oh yes, the bike has been here for some time. Didn't anybody inform you?'
'You won't be able to have it tonight, it's in one of the garages, round the back of the station. You'll have to come back tomorrow.'

We went off home and although I was annoyed by the incompetence of the police, in not telling me the bike had been recovered, I was also elated to think I would be getting it back tomorrow.

I made my way to Bearland, the next morning, full of anticipation. I would soon be back on the road. A policeman took me to a garage, undid the lock and lifted the up and over door.

I said, 'it's not here!'

The policeman looked at his clipboard and said, 'it must be here, this is the right garage, according to my sheet. Let's have a look around.'

This was only a small domestic sized concrete garage, you couldn't hide a large motorcycle in it. Then, over in a far corner I saw it, behind some junk. All that was left of my Lightning was a frame and an engine.

I turned to the copper and said, 'how am I supposed to ride that home? He wasn't at all interested, he said, it's not my problem mate.'

I said, 'you're all a bunch of tossers. First you don't tell me that it's here, I have to read about it in the paper. Then you tell me to collect it, without telling me that it's just a bag of bits. What's the matter with you pratts.'

He said, there's no need for that attitude.

I just said, 'bollocks you fucking wanker and walked away.'

This bloke, Ken something, I have forgotten his full name, had stolen my bike, stripped everything off it and had only been fined £40. He had made a profit. Where's the justice in that? I vaguely knew this Ken, I had occasionally ridden with him along with others. He had a BSA Thunderbolt, the model lower in specification to mine. Apparently he had been jealous that my Lightning could always beat his Thunderbolt, so he had stolen it, with the intention of hotting up his own bike, using the parts from mine.

I went back to Bearland the next day, with a friend who had a van. This time, the detective who had been on the case, came with me to open the garage. As we put the sorrowful few parts of what had been my pride and joy, into the van, the detective told me that the bike had been found at the Golden Valley motorcycle club at Barbers Bridge, near Newent. I could hardly believe it, the Golden Valley club members were always thought of as the goody goody bikers. It was us, The Scorpions who were the archetypal rebel bikers.

The detective said, 'when are you going to sort this out then?'

I asked him what he meant.

The detective smiled and said, 'I know what I would do and I think I know what you'll do.' I assured him that there would be nothing like that going on.

Dejectedly, I looked at the small pile of parts, gathered together, in the shed at the back of our prefab. I went to my insurers and started the usual rigmarole. Fortunately I had been insured, but it didn't lessen the pain and annoyance I felt about the theft.

Roger Haines turned up and sympathised over the state of the bike, we both stood there looking at it, shaking our heads, not knowing what to say to each other, except for growling things like, 'the bastard,'
I was building up to an all pervading, powerful rage. It had taken a few days to find out where Ken lived, but now I knew. I asked Roger to take me there in his car. When we got to Ken's house in Cotteswold Road, I went to the front door and knocked gently. Ken answered the door, but as soon as he saw who it was, he tried to close it again as fast as he could. He wasn't fast enough though. In a fraction of a second I had grasped him by the throat with my left hand and pulled him through the door, into the garden. I hit him with my right hand, which tore him from my grasp and knocked him to the ground. As he hit the ground, I started kicking his head in. The red mist had come over me and I wanted to hurt him severely. As I was kicking him, I could hear him saying something like, if I stopped hitting him, he had some parts I could have. I couldn't believe my ears, he was offering some of my own bike back. I stopped hitting him and dragged him to his feet.
I said, 'show me!'
He took Roger and me to the shed at the back of the house and to my amazement, it was full of bike parts. It was obvious where most of it must have come from. I found my own headlight and a few other small parts, plus some exhaust pipes that were better than mine had been. We loaded it all into the car and left Ken to lick his wounds.

Barbers Bridge was to be the next target, I was furious that they could allow such a thing to happen at their club. The club house was an old red brick British rail station, that had been closed down during the Dr Beeching cuts a few years previous. Even the track had been taken up. My bike had been found in one of the old station outbuildings that now belonged to the club. I knew that they must have seen what had been going on.

A few days later, I asked Hughie MacPherson to take me to there. It was early on a Saturday evening. I knew there would be club members there. Hughie was a bit dubious about going into a biker club to start trouble, with the odds liable to be stacked heavily against us. I told him not to worry, I would handle it. I didn't care how many were in there, after all, I had my sledge hammer and they didn't. We pulled up outside the club, I could see immediately that there was a good few of them inside. I got out of the car with my sledge hammer in hand and crashed through the door, screaming like a maniac. BASTAAAAARDS, I shouted, at the top of my voice. I brought the hammer down onto a table that had people sitting around it. It smashed to pieces, scattering the bikers in all directions. I was attacking anything that came into my field of view, which was very narrow, due to the fact that the red mist had descended again. As I was attacking the fireplace, I could see that everybody had pressed themselves against the walls, shuffling backwards and forwards trying to keep out of the way of the swinging sledge hammer.

I heard someone shouting, 'stop him! Stop him!'
But who was going to do it?
I heard Hughie say, 'I can't stop him.'
Then I heard someone shout, 'it was us who shopped Ken to the police.'

That did it. I stopped what I was doing and said, 'what was that?'
Someone repeated what I thought I had heard. They said, they had found out what Ken had been doing and had reported it to the police. That bastard copper had led me to believe that the Golden Valley club had been partly to blame. I suddenly felt very sheepish about all the damage I had done.
I said, 'sorry lads, turned and left.' Nobody ever mentioned it again.

Now that the fate of my bike was known, the insurance company sent their assessor to look at what was left of it. He made his offer which would be enough to get it back on the road, but not enough to make it the same as it had been before the theft. It would never be the same again. To keep the cost down, I ordered the parts from Nettleton Motorcycles with the intention of doing the work myself. I took all of the bits into my bedroom and started to put the bike back together. Once I had got all of the parts together, it took me about a week to finish the assembly. I put some petrol into the tank and fired her up. The high level exhaust pipes had no silencers on them, just small mutes pushed inside and secured with a small screw. The noise in that small bedroom was tremendous and the room soon started to fill with exhaust gas. I opened the window to let the gas out so that I could continue to rev the engine, to enable me to warm it up to tune the carbs. Just then, I heard a knock on the door, it was Roger Haines calling to see if I needed any help. Roger was great at setting the ignition timing and tuning the carbs, so I asked him to take over.

He said, 'we'll have to get it outside first, we're going to die if we stay in here.'
I said, 'okay, open the door for me.'
Roger opened the front door and I blasted out of the bedroom, along the hall and out through the door, down the two steps, into the front garden. Roger was rolling about laughing, he said he'd never seen anything like it.

It seemed quite logical to me that I would do the rebuild in the bedroom, I needed electricity so that I could work into the night and I needed it to be dry, so that I didn't have to worry about the rain. The small shed, out the back, was too small to work in and had no power, so the bedroom had to be my temporary workshop.

Everybody knew Roger's reputation as a tuner and he was often asked to help out with setting carbs. One afternoon, I went with him to a prefab in Podsmead, where someone had asked Roger to set up a fuel injector on a Triumph.
Roger looked and the injector and said, 'I had one of these but it was so dangerous, I got rid of it.'
The major fault was, that if the fuel tap was left on, fuel leaked through the injector, some dripping out of the back and some running into the engine, gradually filling it up. Roger asked the owner, if the timing had been set correctly and was assured that it had been. He turned the petrol on and kicked the engine over. It let out a small bang, through the injector.
Roger asked again, 'are you sure this timing is right?'
The answer for the second time was yes, it was definitely okay. Roger kicked the bike over again and this time the bike started and sounded fine. During this starting procedure, some fuel had leaked from the back of the injector, but it wasn't a problem. Suddenly there was a bang and a flame shot out of the injector, igniting the leaked fuel, erupting in a ball of flame. It was such a shock and so powerful, that Roger and I, ran around the side of the house, in case the bike blew up and to get away from the fire,. The owner of the bike was in a panic, but he was much more interested in putting the fire out than we were. He started running in and out of the house throwing water onto the fire. His mum was in the kitchen filling buckets for him to throw over the bike. We were still peering around the corner of the house, with just our heads showing. He shouted for us to come and help him put the fire out. We told him he was doing all right and to carry on. He got it out after a few minutes but there was a considerable amount of damage done in that short time. There would be no need for any more tuning to this bike for a while. Roger advised him to throw the injector away, before the bike blew up completely.

I had got the bike together just in time to ride to the Bath Blues festival. I had been looking forward to it for ages, it was the first festival I had ever been to and the line up was very impressive. Bands that would become legends played, one after the other, at this one day venue at the recreation ground in Bath. Fleetwood Mac, John Mayall, Ten Years After, Led Zeppelin, The Nice, Keef Hartley, Chicken Shack, to name but a few, all introduced by the very young DJ, John Peel. There were about twenty big name acts playing back to back for about twelve hours, all for eighteen shillings and sixpence. It was worth going just to see Led Zeppelin, they were the most outstanding band I have ever seen. The other band which made a huge impression on me was Ten Years After, who also gave a wonderful performance at Woodstock. I still listen to their music today, almost thirty years on.

That summer I spent a lot of time just hanging around town with friends, it seemed quite strange because dad was doing the same and we often met. He was still doing some part time taxi work and some part time coach driving, but since his retirement through ill health, he had a lot of time on his hands. He had two friends of around his own age, which was only fifty, very young to have to retire. They could invariably be found together, sitting at a table in the Cadena café, a place mum had often taken Gordon and me, when we were children. Mum had bought me my first knickerbocker glory in the Cadena. It was a very large, rather dark, but quite splendid old café, the lighting always seemed to me to make everything brown. Dark brown floor, brown paint, brown furniture, brown place, but warm and friendly with neat waitresses, dressed with white aprons and hats.

As the summer started to change into autumn, I decided that it was time to get a job to get some money together. I bought a Citizen and went into Eastgate Market to get a cup of tea at Peter Fahey's tea stall and to sit and check the vacancies in the paper. Hughie MacPherson was working in the market at W T Johns butchers and he came over for a cup of coffee. We talked and went through the ads together, I didn't have a lot of experience in anything so I didn't find much that I thought would be suitable. Hughie pointed to an ad for a capstan operator at Bound and Topham engineering works, in Hempstead Lane.
I said, 'I don't even know what a capstan is, Hughie.'
He said, 'it doesn't matter, you'll be able to do it, go for it.'
He had more faith than I did, but I went for the job and to my surprise, they gave it to me. I was shown what to do and Hughie had been right, I soon got to grips with it. I was working the capstan, turning out stainless steel balls, which fitted inside valves. Soon I was earning bonus on the job, the boss told me that I was the fastest man they had ever had on that machine. I was earning more money than I had ever earned before. I was making ten shillings an hour, plus tuppence a ball over a certain amount. I had never worked in a factory environment and found the regime

quite difficult to live with. I had been there a few months when one day I had to go out during the lunch hour and I knew time would be tight. We were allowed three minutes to wash our hands before lunch, but my machine was on a cycle so I didn't go to the washbasin. I kept my coat next to my machine and I put it on so that when the machine stopped, I could press the off button and rush out without washing my hands if there wasn't time before one o clock. Everybody else had gone to the washbasin and I was the only one left in the workshop, when the foreman came up to me and said, 'what are you doing with your coat on?'

I answered that I was in a hurry to get out as soon as the bell went. He started to tear me off a strip and told me to get my coat back off.

I said, 'hang on a minute, I'm the only one working, there's nobody else in the shop. Why are you bollocking me?'

He was totally unreasonable about it and the more I argued, the nastier he got.

He said, 'get your coat off or you can go to see Mr Topham.'

I grabbed him by the throat and squeezed till he went a funny colour. Some of the others had come back into the workshop and witnessed what had happened and were shouting 'go on, fill the bastard in.'

I threw him to the floor and walked out of the factory, got on the bike and went off to do what I had intended to do. When I returned, I went back to my machine as if nothing had happened. Before long, Mr Topham sent for me. I went to his office not worried if I got the sack. He asked me what had happened and I told him.

He just said, 'don't do it again, you can go back to work.'

The foreman never had a go at me again.

I worked there for a few months but became increasingly bored with standing next to a machine for ten hours a day. I started to have more and more time off, sometimes telling them that I was sick, sometimes not telling them anything at all. The two weeks coming up to Christmas, I just didn't bother to turn up. They had organised a Christmas party at the Fleece hotel, in Westgate Street. I hadn't been at work for two weeks, but I turned up at the party, anyway. Mr Topham came over to me and said, 'I thought you had left.' I replied that I hadn't, but I might as well. I told him that I would call in, some time after the Christmas break, for my P45 and any money owing to me. I had a good night at the party and used the occasion to say goodbye to some of the friends I had made while I worked there.

Christmas 1969 came and went. There was no sense of occasion about it for me. Christmas is very much a time for sharing, a family thing. I was very distant from my family, feeling very alone. Aunty Ina invited Dad, Gordon and I, for Christmas dinner, with her, Hugh and Uncle Den. We were made very welcome and had a nice day, but I knew I would never do it again. I was feeling more and more isolated. I felt that I needed no one to survive, but did I want to survive? I wasn't sure.

I have an old black and white photograph of that Christmas day. When I look at it, I can't believe that my dad is only fifty years old. He looked seventy and not well at that.

Chapter 11
Adventure

January 1970 was cold and depressing. Not much was happening, it was too cold to work up much enthusiasm for anything. January gave way to February and the cold got even worse. One cold dark evening, I was in the Market bar with Phil Large, sitting at a table just passing the time. We were idly talking of what we wished we were doing and where we wished we were going, to get away from the winter. Phil said, why don't we go somewhere. I said, 'okay, lets pack some things and go to try to find the sun.' I had never been abroad and had no conception of what it would be like or where the sun would be, but I had been told that the South of France would be warm and sunny. I thought, how far can it be. France is only just across the channel. We went into Gloucester, bought some lightweight sleeping bags from Millets, packed our things into a rucksack, strapped it and Phil's guitar onto the rack on the back of the bike and we were ready for our adventure.

Late one night we set off for Dover, to catch the ferry to Boulogne first thing in the morning. The cold was intense, so I was wearing as many clothes as I could get on, under my Parka jacket. I was wearing my old Union Jack crash helmet, which I only wore when the weather was bad. I have always hated wearing a crash helmet, but when it was cold, it kept my head warm. Phil was similarly attired, but nothing was going to keep out this kind of cold. We travelled up the A40 towards London, through Oxford. When we got to High Wycombe, I was so cold I couldn't feel anything, I was going to have to stop. I saw a parade of shops on my left and decided to pull off the road. I couldn't move my legs to put them down to hold us up, so I very gently stopped next to a wall, so that we could fall against it without having to move. Phil got off, then I slowly got my legs to move off the footrests and managed to get off. We crouched down next to the engine, trying to warm ourselves by the heat of the engine. After about ten minutes, it cooled so we got going again. We made it to London and took the South Circular Road, where we found an all night café. We stopped for a welcome cup of tea, which warmed us up no end. Despite the cold, I was excited at the prospect of the forthcoming journey into the unknown.

We arrived at Dover in the morning, in plenty of time to catch the ferry, but first we had to go to the RAC office to get an international driving license. I had to go into a photo booth to get a passport size photo, to stick on the license. I had been riding all night and didn't look too clean, together with long hair and a beard, that photo made me look like a Bahder Mienhoff terrorist on a bad day. It didn't matter though, it was good enough. We were soon on the ferry and into uncharted territory. It was a cold but bright sunny day and the trip was pretty good apart from the pangs of seasickness. On the boat we met some French motorcyclists who were on their way home after a rally in England, we told them we were going in search of the sun and they wished us luck.

The ferry docked in Boulogne, we rode down the gangway into the cobbled street, looking for the road to Paris. We took what we thought was the right road, but after a few miles I was having doubts. The road looked a bit small and quiet for the main road to Paris. Up ahead I saw a small moped going in the same direction as us so I pulled alongside it and shouted across to the middle aged, lady rider, 'Ou est le route de Paris', my French was pretty crap, but she understood. She shook her head and shouted, 'Non, le route de Paris' and turned and started pointing back the way we had come. The problem was, she was pointing backwards so intently that she wasn't looking where she was going. She went off the road and down a ditch at the side of the road. I stopped the bike, turned around and went back to see if she was all right. As we got to where she had fallen, her head appeared out of the ditch with bits of grass and debris sticking out of her hair. It looked so funny, but we couldn't laugh. We helped her and her moped out of the ditch, apologising profusely for distracting her, but she assured us that she was all right and that it was her own fault. I felt so bad about it, but as soon as we were out of her sight, we couldn't help laughing, until tears were rolling down our cheeks.

We retraced our route, back into Boulogne. As soon as we got to the main road, I saw where we had gone wrong, I followed the sign and we were on our way to Paris. It was a fine bright day and our spirits were high. We had only been travelling for a few minutes, when the two French lads we had met on the ferry came past. They flagged us down and said, 'if we were going to Paris, we could follow them. They were riding an old 1950's BMW which to my amazement, kept up a terrific speed on the autoroute. They had to stop once or twice, to top up with oil, because the engine was worn out, but it still went like the clappers.

Soon we were riding through Paris, following Marc through the rush hour traffic. He was a Parisian and knew his way around very well. It was quite something to be travelling through Paris so surely and swiftly. Marc told us to follow him to his home in Chantilly, where we could stop for a rest. When we arrived at Marc's home, we found it to be his family's home. We went in and were introduced to

Marc's mother and father, his brother and sister and his grandfather. They all lived together in a huge grey stone house with beautiful wrought iron balconies and railings. We were made welcome and invited to stay for dinner, which we gratefully accepted. We all sat around a large table and ate a terrific French meal of things I had never had before, there was crab in scallop shells, a superb soup, lots of bread and absolutely gorgeous coffee. I had never had real French bread or French coffee before and I found in it, something I would always love.

As we sat around the table, talking about our intended trip to the sun, Marc told us that he didn't live in this house at the moment. He was living in a flat in Clermont Ferrand, in the Massif Central. He was an engineer and had been able to defer his National service with the army, by moving to Clermont, to work in a factory which made military aircraft. He had to be back in Clermont by the next morning, for work and we were welcome to follow him and stay in his flat until we went on with our trip. It would take around four hours in the saddle to reach Clermont, so at about ten o clock we got ready to leave. When we went to the bikes, to my horror I saw that the Lightning had sustained a puncture. The back tire was as flat as a pancake. Marc made his apologies but said he had to leave, to make sure he got back in time, but he gave us his address and a map to help us find him and told us to be sure to stop when we got there.

Marc's brother volunteered to take me to an all night garage, where he said I would be able to get my puncture repaired. I got the back wheel out and put in his car. It was an old Citroen 2CV which he started and had to wait a few minutes for it to warm up before it had enough power to pull away. Once we got going, we were soon rattling along the old cobbled streets at what seemed a breakneck speed, cornering at crazy angles, but he seemed quite casual about it so I didn't worry.

We arrived at a small backstreet garage, with just one old man working there. He seemed glad that we had turned up, for the company as much as for the business. Marc's brother explained that we needed the puncture repaired and the old man said it would not be a problem, he would get on with it immediately. But first we must have a Cognac with him. We sat in his office, where he produced a small glass for each of us and a large bottle of Cognac. He poured us a tot each and said 'salut,' downing the Cognac in one swallow. He went into the workshop to start on the puncture, telling us to stay in the office, in the warm. A short time later he reappeared and said he had found the puncture by immersing the tube in water, but would have to let it dry before he could put the glue on, so we had better have another glass of Cognac while we waited. So he poured us another one and went through the same ritual as the last time, then went back into the workshop. A few minutes later he was back again. He said he had put the glue on, but had to wait a few minutes for it to become tacky so we might as well have another drink. By this time I was starting to feel the effects of the Cognac, I wasn't used to it. He went back into the workshop to stick the patch on the tube, then came back again, saying he had to wait for it to stick before he put it back on the wheel, so we better have another drink. I was as pissed as a fart by now and was giggling about the whole situation. Finally he went back into the workshop and a short time later, reappeared with my wheel, duly repaired. He said, we couldn't leave just yet, we'd better have a coffee to sober us up a bit. He got his coffee machine going and made each of us a superb cup of espresso, which we sat and drank with him. When I asked him the cost of the repair, I almost burst out laughing when he charged the equivalent of about five shillings. We had been there about two hours and drunk more Cognac than you could buy for five shillings.

We got back into the car and made the return journey to Chantilly. It was even more hair raising than the first journey, obviously I wasn't the only one feeling the effect of the Cognac.

When we got there, it had been decided that seeing as it was so late, we would stay the night and move on, the next morning. Early next morning, I was woken by Marc's sister wanting to say goodbye. She was leaving for work and wanted to give us a kiss and wish us well, it was a lovely moment. We got out of bed and made ready to leave. Marc's mum made us a huge bowl of café au lait and gave us some bread to dip into it. She said that this was a traditional breakfast in France. After we had eaten, we loaded our things onto the bike and after giving them our heartfelt thanks, we were on the road again.

We followed Marc's instructions and took a leisurely run south. The weather was still pretty good, cold but clear and blue. After about three hours, we stopped to get something out of our rucksack. When we opened it, on the top we found a tin of fruit, with a ten franc note attached to it with an elastic band. What a wonderful family and what a welcome to France.

We arrived in Clermont Ferrand during late afternoon and followed Marc's instructions, going through to the south side of Clermont, to the small suburb called Royat. As we came to the main road through Royat, we heard cheering and saw Marc and some friends leaning over a balcony. They had been keeping an eye out for us. They ran down to greet us and showed me where to park the bike round the back of the large apartment building. It was only a small one bedroom flat, but it had a small kitchen and a toilet, so it was quite a nice little place. Marc invited us to stay as long as we liked. I was overwhelmed by his generosity.

That night Marc suggested that we go out for a meal in a cheap self service restaurant he knew. We got on the bikes and went to the restaurant, it was unlike anything I have ever encountered, before or since. It was a bit like a factory canteen. We went along the counter, picking what we fancied. Phil saw a steak and couldn't believe how cheap it was,
'that's for me', he said.
It was uncooked, so the chef picked it up and dropped it into boiling fat. To my astonishment, it was no sooner in the fat than it was out again. It was still raw as far as I was concerned, but Marc said that was how it was eaten. Phil didn't seem to mind either, he is much more of a carnivore than I am. I was glad I had stuck with egg and chips. Phil was tucking into it with gusto, he said it was different to the steak he had at home. Marc waited a few minutes then asked Phil if he knew what kind of steak it was.
Phil said, 'no, what is it? Sirloin? Rump? What are you all laughing at?' Marc said, 'I wasn't asking what cut it was, I was asking if you knew what animal it came from, it's not beef, it's horse steak.'
Phil started spluttering that he didn't believe it, but from his face, we all knew that he did. He just didn't want to.

After the meal we went back to the flat to get some sleep. We had to use our sleeping bags, on a blow up mattress on the floor. When Marc got up for work Phil and I jumped into the warm bed for a couple of hours. We got up about mid morning and went to explore Clermont. It was quite a place, at the base of a mountain. There was a famous Grand Prix motor racing circuit there and a large casino, high up on the lower slope of the mountain. It was very different to Gloucester.

Marc took us everywhere, he introduced us to a large circle of friends and over the next few weeks we became a part of their social scene. We had nothing but kindness from everyone we met, except one. A group of us went to a tenpin bowling alley for an evening out. As we stood at one end of the bar, which must have been twenty feet long, the owner stood at the other end and pointed at me and Phil, followed by a hand gesture which obviously meant, go away. He was saying something which I couldn't understand, so I asked Marc what the bar owner was saying. Marc told me that the man was just saying, he wouldn't serve us and that we should leave immediately. I pleaded with the man to allow us to stay, but he became very agitated and started shouting that he would call the police. I was getting pretty annoyed myself and started shouting that he was an asshole and if he wanted trouble he could have it. At that, he picked up the phone and started dialling the police. Instantly the place erupted in a flurry of activity, everybody was rushing for the door.

Marc grabbed my arm and said, 'let's go.'

I said, 'why? We haven't done anything.'

He replied that the police in France were not like the police in England. French police were paid for by local businesses and if we were there when they arrived we would be arrested on the bar owners word that we were troublemakers. Also they would be just a likely to wade in with batons and ask questions later, that's why the whole place was emptying. We were the last to leave, I looked around and in just a few minutes the place had emptied. I took some satisfaction from the fact that he would make no more profit tonight.

Phil and I were living mainly on bread and pate, with yoghurt for desert. Money was really tight. Phil played his guitar and sang sometimes, but we were getting nearer to destitution, every day. We were in the local café with our new friends one evening, when Marc picked up my helmet and said to them,

'Cliff and Phil will have to leave soon, because they are running out of money. If you would like them to stay, put some money into the helmet.' They all threw money in and despite our protests, they said they were glad to do it, we were their friends and they enjoyed having us around. They saw us as English hippies, we were outrageous in our looks and dress compared to them.

Marc gave us the collection and said, 'now you can stay.'

We saw a poster announcing that Mickey Baker, a legendary American bluesman would be appearing at the local casino. Phil and I wanted to go to see him, but Marc said it would be far too expensive for any of us to go there. The casino was only for well off people. Undeterred, we turned up at the door, carrying Phil's Guitar and told the doormen we were friends of Mickey's from America. They wouldn't let us in at first, but we managed to sweet talk them. They showed us backstage, where we literally bumped into Mickey, as he was coming down some steps at the back of the stage.

We said, 'Hi Mickey, how are you doing?'

He replied, 'Hi guys, hey you English?'

The doorman didn't speak English and it sure looked like we were friends, with all the smiling and handshaking going on, so, satisfied that we had been telling the truth, he turned and left.

We sat at a table with Mickey and his wife, chatting about what we were doing travelling in France and about Phil's prowess with the guitar. Mickey said, 'I'll get you a spot, if you want one. Would you like to play with the house band, with my band, or on your own?'

It turned out that the band that was backing Mickey was the same band that regularly backed Ray Charles, so Phil asked if he could play with them. And so it was arranged, in between the house band's and Mickey's spot, Phil would go on and do his stuff.

This casino was a new experience for us, the waiters were all dressed in dark suits and were carrying silver champagne buckets to and from the tables. The people seated around the tables were even more impressive, dressed up to the nines. There was some serious money sitting here. I wondered how they would react to Phil. It was likely that we were the first long haired hippies, they had ever seen in the flesh.

The house band came on and started their set. We couldn't stop ourselves laughing. It wasn't that their musicianship was in question, they actually played quite well. They were wearing black trousers and orange jackets that looked like they had been made out of a carpet. They had Beatle style haircuts that had been the fashion in England eight or nine years previous. No one would be seen dead looking like that in 1969. The funniest thing though, was that they played all English songs and it soon became obvious to us that none of them actually spoke English. They must have learned the songs by listening to the records, because a lot of the words they used, only sounded like the real words. It was very odd, but not surprising as the whole world was listening to English records and taking note of what was happening in England throughout the whole of the 60's.

Then it was time for Phil to take the stage. He took centre stage, in front of the band and started to play. He played some Led Zeppelin numbers, finishing with The Lemon Song. He was playing a great set, singing

Squeeze me baby, till the juice runs down my leg,
Squeeze me baby, till the juice runs down my leg,
The way you squeeze my lemon,
I swear I'm gonna fall right out of bed.

Phil was brilliant, he went down a storm.

The audience started chanting, 'Vive l'anglais, Vive l'anglais', then they started throwing money onto the floor in front of the stage. I realised this was a good opportunity to raise some cash, so I took off the black sombrero I was wearing and went round the audience. We made a good sum that night, enough to keep us going a bit longer. It was a great night too, a really memorable experience. We stayed on to watch Mickey play his set, he was very impressive. I now have a couple of his albums in my collection. He was a great blues guitarist and a very nice man.

There had been a local radio presenter in the audience and he came up to us and introduced himself. He invited us back to his apartment for a drink. What he really wanted though, was to talk to us about the British music scene. He wanted to know first hand, what was happening in England. He also had a Pink Floyd album, which had some lyrics that he couldn't decipher and he wanted us to explain them to him. His English was very good, but some of the words he asked about, even we couldn't catch, so he had no chance. His English was much better than our French that's for sure. Phil's philosophy was to speak English, very slowly, hoping they would understand. If they didn't understand, Phil increased the volume and decreased the speed of his speech. He did this two or three times, then if they still didn't understand, he gave up. We didn't have any such problems with this radio presenter, he said he had been very impressed with Phil and spoke about trying to get him onto the radio. Phil said maybe, but we didn't know how much longer we would be here.

We were sitting in a large café with Marc and some friends, when a family came in and sat down a few tables away from us. As soon as they sat down, I noticed people starting to move away. Marc said come on, we must move, so we got up and moved to the other end of the café. It was very strange, the family were at one end of the café and everyone else had moved to the other end. I asked Marc what was going on. He just said, Germans, as if that would be explanation enough.
I said, 'what about it?'
Marc explained that people in this region would have nothing to do with Germans because of things that had happened during the German occupation in the Second World War. The atmosphere could be cut with a knife, but the Germans didn't take any notice, they had their drinks without hurrying and then left. When they had gone, things returned to normal, people started talking again and spread out around the whole café.

The weather in Clermont was growing worse. A huge quantity of snow fell one evening and I was worried that we would be stuck there. When we got up, around lunch time the next day, all the roads had been cleared and traffic was moving normally. We kept checking the weather forecasts and were disappointed to hear that we were in the grip of one of the worst winters for years. When I heard that it was snowing in Rome, I said to Phil, 'I've had enough of this, I'm going to make a dash for home.' Phil wanted to keep going south, but we were desperately short of money and common sense said we should get back to where we once belonged.

We took a ride high up into the mountains, above the snow line. It was so beautiful up there, but the decision had been made, we would leave the next day. We told Marc that we were leaving and again he tried to persuade us to stay. His hospitality knew no bounds and we were very grateful to him, but we told him we had to go.

Next morning, the weather had turned really nasty, but we loaded the bike and got ready to leave. As I kicked the bike over, the sole fell right off my shoe, it had rotted away. I knew my shoes were rough, but didn't expect them to give up quite so badly. I went back to the flat and found an old pair of gym shoes, that belonged to Marc. I left him a note explaining what had happened, then we were on the road again. It was raining steadily, a cold rain that soaked through every layer of clothing, right through to the skin. We rode for a couple of hours, in the pouring rain, before we came upon a small village café. We stopped and went in, hoping to be able to get a warm. Sure enough, there was a roaring coal fire. The lady who owned the cafe, fussed around us like we were her long lost sons. She made us take off our wet clothes and put them on chair backs in front of the fire. As we sat and drank our coffee, I started looking at the photographs hanging all around the walls. The pictures were all of rugby teams and suddenly I spotted a picture of the Cherry and Whites. I asked the old lady about the picture and she told us that her son played rugby for a top French team and had played at Kingsholm. These pictures were all of the places he had played. We stayed for about an hour, chatting with this lovely lady, before deciding to head off for Paris. She kissed us on both cheeks and bade us au revoir, then stood in the doorway and waved us off, as we rode away.

Night fell and I was picking up speed, going through the quiet little villages at seventy or eighty miles an hour. The rain had stopped and I wanted to get to Paris before we stopped again. I was thundering through a small village, when I saw a policeman standing in the middle of the road, waving his torch. He obviously wanted to me to stop, but at this speed I had no chance.

I sped past him, shouting back to Phil, 'shall I keep going or what Phil?' Phil shouted back, 'Stop! French police have got guns and I'm on the back,' so I heaved on the brakes and stopped a long way from the policeman. I had to turn round and go back slowly towards him. When we stopped, the policeman asked if I knew what the speed limit was. I acted completely ignorant, saying I understood no French at all.

Then in perfect English, the policeman said, 'are on holiday?'

I replied, 'yes, we are on our way home, we have had a wonderful time in France.'

He said, 'okay but keep your speed down through the villages.'

He pointed to thirty miles an hour on my speedometer and said, 'keep to that speed and you will be all right. Have a good journey.' I thanked him and set off again for Paris. I'd, had to come to France to find a decent copper.

Late that night we arrived back in Paris. It was late enough for the traffic to be light, making it easy to find our way through. We wouldn't be able to get a ferry from Boulogne, until next morning, so we were in no hurry to get there. We trundled along, looking for a café, to have a rest, waste a little time and of course, get a drink. Travelling along a wide boulevard, we spotted two café's on opposite corners. As I turned the corner, we saw that there was a riot going on in one of the café's, so I crossed the road and stopped outside the other one. We went in and ordered two coffees, then sat looking out of the window at what was happening across the road. The fight was getting worse, we could see people getting hit with chairs, bottles and anything else that came to hand. Then we heard the police sirens. Two corrugated tin Black Maria's, screeched to a halt outside the café and disgorged it's contents of long baton wielding Gendarmerie. I soon realised why Marc had been so keen to get out of the bowling alley, back in Clermont. These police didn't ask questions, they waded straight in, beating everyone within striking range. They were felling people with well practised professionalism and dragging them into the street, throwing them into the Black Maria. In just a few minutes, the riot was over, the police had cleared the café and when they drove off, there was no sign of anyone left on that side of the street.

With the entertainment over, we got up to leave, going to the bar to pay the bill. The barman told us that the bill had been taken care of. I asked who had paid it and the barman pointed to a young man sitting at a table in the corner of the café. When we went over to thank him for his generosity, he asked us if we needed somewhere to stay for the night. I told him, we were heading for Boulogne, but were in no hurry and would be glad to take him up on his offer.

He told us that he lived nearby and we could follow him to his apartment. Only a few hundred yards from the café, he turned through some gigantic iron gates, into a large courtyard with high buildings on all four sides. It was pitch dark and for the first time on our journey, a feeling of apprehension swept over us. The place had an air of menace about it. Phil looked up and saw what he thought was someone watching us from high up on one of the buildings.

I was unpacking the rucksack from the bike, when Phil whispered to me, 'I don't like it, there's something wrong here, let's get out of it.'

I said, 'no, it's all right, it's just the darkness making it frightening.'

Phil was adamant that he was going to leave, but in the end I managed to persuade him to come up to the apartment. I had a huge hunting knife in the rucksack and for the first time, I got it out and stuck it inside my coat. I said to Phil, 'be on your guard as we go up the stairs and into the apartment, any trouble and we'll cut and run.'

When we got into the apartment, we sat around a table chatting with the young man, but could not shift the feeling of unease we both felt. He showed us into a bedroom, where we settled down for the night. Phil wanted the knife, so that he could keep it close to him while he slept, but I wouldn't give it to him. It was so dark in the room that I couldn't see my watch, even though it had a luminous face. I lay there for hours without getting a wink of sleep. Phil was the same, we would have been better staying on the road, we were paranoid about this place. Suddenly a scraping sound started outside. We couldn't make out what it was, but it increased the fear factor considerably. We lay there for hour after hour, with more and more dire thoughts going through our heads.

Eventually I said, 'I can't stay here any more, I don't care what time it is, I'm getting out of here.'

We got up and opened the curtains. To our astonishment, it was broad daylight, these were the most efficient blackout curtains I had ever come across. We looked down into the courtyard and immediately realised what the scraping noises had been. The refuse collectors had been to empty the large number of bins kept in the middle of the courtyard. We looked around and realised that the menacing face we had seen looking at us from high up on the building had been nothing more than a chimney pot with two holes in it, looking like eyes. Where the light that had shone through the holes had come from I have no idea, but it had certainly scared us. In the daylight, this place made me think of the Bastille, in darkness in had scared us half to death. Even now we knew that our fears had been unfounded, we still couldn't get out of there fast enough. We loaded the bike and left, breathing a sigh of relief and laughing as we rode down the road, relieved that we had survived the night.

A couple of hours later we arrived in Boulogne with a little time to spare before we caught the ferry. We were so short of money that we went into a boulangerie and asked them to sell us half a loaf of bread. We didn't have enough francs for a whole loaf. They were reluctant at first, but then had pity on us and gave us the bread. I had kept a few pounds, so that when we got to England, I would have enough money for petrol to get us home and to buy some good old English food.

We disembarked in Dover and was very surprised that the customs waved us right on through without having to stop. I think if I had been a customs officer I would have stopped us. Not that we had any money to buy anything worth smuggling. I went straight to a garage and filled the tank, then found a café and settled down to a good meal of egg, chips and beans, bread and butter and a cup of tea. Heaven! The best meal I'd had for ages. Then it was time for the long ride home. A ride that was largely uneventful, except that at Oxford, Phil shouted to me that one of his footrests had fallen off. I shouted back that we wouldn't be able to find it in the dark, so he would have to wedge his foot on top of the silencer. He had to keep moving his foot around because the sole of his shoe kept starting to melt, but never mind, we would be home soon.

It was about two o clock in the morning as I turned onto the Barnwood bypass, I saw a police car coming round the roundabout. I saw him look at us and turn to follow us. My Lightning, EFH 618C was a local registration so the police knew we would be from Gloucester.
I said to Phil, 'here we go, now I know were home.'
The patrol car followed us along Eastern Avenue, when finally he decided to stop us. We got off the bike, taking the opportunity to stand up and loosen up a bit. Two policemen got out of the car and approached us.
I said, 'what's the problem?'
One of the policemen said, 'I've stopped you because you're dangerous.'
I said, 'what are you on about?'
He continued, 'you're dangerous because you can't possibly control that bike properly with all that luggage strapped to the back.'
I smiled and said, 'that's what you think is it? How do you think we've managed to stay on it for the last two thousand miles then?'
He said, 'oh yeah, where have you been to do two thousand miles?'

I reached into the top pocket of my Parka and took out my documents. Passport, international driving license, green card insurance, test certificate and log book. I had taken everything with me, in case of unforeseen problems.

I held them up and said, 'look at this lot. We've been touring Europe, more than two thousand miles, then you stop me two miles from home and tell me I can't control the bike. You tosser! Why don't you piss off and harass somebody else?'

As the conversation unfolded, the other copper could obviously see the funny side of it and kept urging his colleague to get back in the car and leave it. When I called the first copper a tosser, the other one burst out laughing and said, 'come on let's go, before it gets even sillier.'

The first copper was a right asshole, but even he could see he was on a loser, so they got back into the car and cleared off.

As I was getting back on the bike, I looked down at the rear footrest that Phil thought had fallen off. It was still there, it had just come loose and folded down. Phil had just ridden fifty miles with his foot balanced on top of the exhaust, when in two minutes, I could have put the footrest right. I did it now anyway and Phil had a comfortable last mile home. I dropped him off in Beaufort Road then went home.

I went into the house which was in darkness, I don't know if anyone was home. I just went straight to bed. Next day I saw dad sitting in the living room, we grunted at each other as I went through the room and out of the door. I don't think he even knew I had been away.

The adventure was over, but it had been fun.

A Gloucester Fan

Mum and Dad at a Ball in the fifties.
I think it was at The Guildhall

Barclays Bank in Southgate Street 1969

1950. Aunty Ethel and me, taking the air in Hillfield Gardens

Left:
Mum and Gran, at our front door in Sweetbriar Sreet.

Right:
Opposite view from our front door, note Tartaglia's ice cream van in the background.
Circa 1954

Left:
1950. Me sitting in the back yard of our house in Sweetbriar Street

Right:
1960. Ten years later, playing cricket in front of our house in Underhill Road, Matson.

Dad's cars outside our Prefab at Tuffley

Looking down The Oxebode from Kings Square

"THE BEAT SCENE"

BIG BEAT SHOW – Every Wednesday

LISTEN OR DANCE — 8.0 p.m. to 11.0 p.m.

THIS IS OUR OCTOBER PROGRAMME

OCTOBER 5th—

UNIT FOUR PLUS TWO
(Decca)   (" Concrete and Clay ")

ADMISSION 6/6

OCTOBER 12th—

JENNY WREN AND THE OUTLOOK
(Fontana)

MARK ROMAN AND THE JAVELINS
(Decca)

ADMISSION 5/-

OCTOBER 19th—

SONNY CHILDE AND THE EXPLOSIVE T.N.T.
(Sam Cooke's Nephew and 10 Piece Group)

ADMISSION 5/-

OCTOBER 26th—

SOUNDS INCORPORATED
(E.M.I.)

ADMISSION 6/6

PLUS EVERY WEEK—

Star Supporting Groups and
"THE RAY NELSON RECORD SHOW"
at
The Stonehouse Church Hall

★ XMAS WEEK — YOUR COMPLETE PROGRAMME ★

Thursday, 16th Dec. 7.30.
TOP LINE LONDON GROUP

Friday, 17th Dec. 7.30 p.m. 2/6

DISCOTHEQUE AT THE MOON
plus ALAN WALKER GROUP
Only 7 more days to go !

Saturday, 18th Dec. 7.30. 5/-
HELLIONS *plus the ADVOCATES*

Sunday, 19th Dec. 7.30 p.m. 2/6.

DISCOTHEQUE AT THE MOON
Getting warmer.

Thursday, 23rd Dec. 7.30. 2/6.
XMAS SPECIAL DISCOTHEQUE
Pre warm up for tomorrow.

EDDIE, BILL
and JOHN, and
EVERYONE
AT THE
MOON WISH
ONE AND ALL
A MERRY
XMAS AND A
HAPPY
NEW YEAR

XMAS EVE Party
7.30 p.m. UNTIL UNCONSCIOUS ! 7/6

featuring the sensational

JOHN MAYALL
plus great Xmas Show
Prizes, Surprises, and Special Guests.
Make sure you dont miss this party

XMAS DAY   -   MOON CLOSED

Xmas Sunday, 26th Dec. 3/6.

RECORDS PARTY NIGHT
Special surprises guests, records,
and boobies given away.

BOXING DAY BONANZA
Monday, 27th Dec. 7.30. 5/-.
ALAN WALKER GROUP and the Advocates

Christmas 1966 at the Blue Moon

Thursday, 30th Dec. 7.30 p.m. 2/6.
DISCOTHEQUE AT THE MOON
Recovering from Xmas! and getting
ready for tomorrow's gas !!

Friday, 31st Dec. 7.30 to 1 a.m.

NEW YEAR'S EVE PARTY
featuring that great attraction and
group from London —

JOHN LEE and the GROUNDHOGS
plus full supporting new year's show,
prizes, etc., in fact one great rave up !

Saturday, 1st JANUARY, 1966. 5/-.
Start the new year at the Moon with
another top line group.

Sunday, 2nd Jan. 7.30. 2/6.
DISCOTHEQUE AT THE MOON
Back to normal !! Whew, wot a week !!!

XMAS at the BLUE MOON
170 High Street,
Cheltenham 55114
Eddie Norman - Bill Reid.

Thursday, 9th Dec. 7.30 p.m. 7/6.

SPENCER DAVIS *plus*
The Hellions ---- A great night !!

Friday, 10th Dec. 7.30 p.m. 2/6.
DISCOTHEQUE AT THE MOON
plus Alan Walker group.
Only 14 more days !!

Saturday, 11th Dec. 7.30 p.m. 6/-.

DOWNLINERS SECT

Sunday, 12th Dec. 7.30 p.m. 2/6.
DISCOTHEQUE AT THE MOON

Corner of The Bon Marche and Kings Square

Looking from Kings Square across the car park to The Regal.
On the billboard, the live acts appearing soon are The Kinks,
The Tremeloes, The Herd and Gene Pittney.
The Regal was Gloucester's
premier live venue.

Mods in Kings Square

Ada Mathews. Star of The Bon Marche

Gloucester Supporters enjoying a day at Twickenham

Lots of happy Gloucester Boys at Twickenham

ROCK 'N' ROLL
TOP POPS
TRADITIONAL

290

Hon. Secretary: Mr. R. Boyce

"FORTY-ONE CLUB"

NEW PILOT INN, SOUTHGATE STREET,
GLOUCESTER

EVERY MONDAY AND THURSDAY EVENING

8 p.m.—10 p.m.

THE MANAGEMENT RESERVES THE RIGHT TO REFUSE ADMISSION

MEMBER _M. Johns._   HI-FI
STEREO SOUND

THE LIBRARY

MEMBERS CARD

RULES
----

1. This card is not transferable and will only be issued to persons of 18 years and over upon satisfactory proof of age.

2. No admission to The Library will be permitted without presentation of this card and it must be produced at any time during the holder's visit if required by the manager or other authorised persons.

3. At the sole discretion of the management members may be permitted to invite one or more guests at certain sessions provided that both guests and members sign the register and produce such proof of age as may be required.

4. The Library is covered by licence to permit a limited number of persons per session. The management must therefore reserve the right to allow or refuse admission to members and/or their guests in accordance with the regulations. Admission may be refused to patrons who in the opinion of the management, are unsuitably attired.

5. The management is responsible under licensing law for the good conduct of these premises and may, if it sees fit, refuse to allow patrons to remain on the premises and withdraw membership if deemed necessary where behaviour is likely to be prejudicial to the running of the establishment.

6. The charge for this card is 7/6 and it is valid until 31st December, 1968. It must be produced for renewal upon the holder's first visit after that date.

7. Admission charges per session are :—

    Members   2/6 each
    Guests   3/6 each

Membership No...42..

THE LIBRARY
NEW INN LANE
GLOUCESTER

MEMBERS CARD

Valid until 31st December, 1968

Issued to

Roy Cambridge.

*I have read and agree to abide to
the Rules printed opposite, and declare
that I am over 18 years of age.*

Signed   R Cambridge

Date   30 - Oct - 1967

Rights of Admission Reserved

Dave Lee Travis at Tracy's nightclub

Edwin Starr also at Tracy's

Chapter 12

The End and The Beginning

Life went on at 98 Fourth Avenue, I seemed to be getting on with dad, better than I ever had. We seemed to have accepted each other for what we were and were better off for it. Now that I was twenty, perhaps he had started to see me as an adult. I was bringing a constant succession of girls home. If dad was home, I just said hello as we went through to my room. One day he said, 'my God, I thought I'd had some women, but I've done nothing compared to you.'
He laughed and said, if you've ever got more than you can handle, put a word in for me.
I think I had won a kind of admiration from him. He had always been a ladies man and he could identify with my love of women. He was fifty years old and still had girlfriends of all ages, ranging from his own age to an age closer to mine.

I needed to get some money so Phil and I started doing a few odd jobs for anyone who would hire us. We got a decorating job at a music shop in Barton Street. When the owner went out at lunchtimes, we got some of the instruments out and set about making some music. There was a drum kit set up in the window on which I banged out some kind of beat while Phil played a guitar. You could hear us half way down the street. Included in the job, the owner wanted us to replace a small pane of glass in an upstairs window. Neither of us had any glazing experience but we said we could do it. I didn't have a tape measure so I got a piece of string and tied a knot in it. I pushed the knot into one corner of the window and held the string at right angles to the knot, cutting it to the correct length. I went off the Gloucester Glass in Russell Street and presented the glasscutter with my piece of string. He rolled about laughing and said, 'I've seen it all now, that's the first time I've ever had a piece of string brought in.' Nonetheless he cut the glass to the piece of string and it fitted perfectly. I got in a bit of a mess with the putty but it looked all right in the end.

I couldn't make enough money with these odd jobs so I decided that it was time to get another full time job. I put my respectable head on and managed to land the position of Chief clerk at the FMC Meat Company. I worked there for about three months, it was easy work and the money wasn't bad. I thought I had cracked it, but I was unprepared for what was to happen next.

One cold night at the end of April, I was sitting on the settee in front of the fire in our living room. Dad was sitting next to me in his favourite chair. We were watching something on the television, when suddenly dad slumped forward, holding his head in his hands. I was very alarmed and asked him what was wrong. His reply shook me to the core.

He said, 'I'm going to die son.'

I said, 'no you're not! I'll go and call the doctor.'

He pleaded with me not to leave him, because he would be dead by the time I got back and he didn't want to die alone.

I told him I had to go for the doctor and wouldn't be long. I helped him to the settee and laid him down, then ran to the phone box in Sixth Avenue and called his doctor. I told the doctor what had happened and asked if I should call an ambulance. He said no, he would come straight out. When he arrived, he made an examination then asked me how much dad had had to drink.

I went mad and said, 'he's had a stroke or something you fucking idiot. Fuck you! I'm going to call an ambulance.'

I ran back to the phone box and dialled 999. I should have done that in the first place. I should have known better than to trust a GP, Mum had died through the incompetence of her GP. Whether the doctors at the hospital would be any better I had no idea, but surely they couldn't be any worse. The ambulance took us to the Royal Hospital in Southgate street, where they made Dad comfortable, then told me to go home and come back the next day when they would be able to tell me more, but Dad was not in immediate danger.

Dad had a taxi outside the house. He was still working part time for Thomas taxis and he had a contract job to do the next day. I rang Mr Thomas to tell him that Dad had had a stroke and he would have to arrange to have the car collected. All that miserable old bastard said was, 'he's not going to do the job then, that's bloody inconvenient.' I put the phone down.

The next day, Gordon and Aunty Ina wanted to go the hospital to see how Dad was. All three of us couldn't get on the bike, so I took Dad's car. I had no license but I had learned to drive by having the odd drive in friend's cars.

Dad was very ill, he had had a cerebral haemorrhage. He had been a lifelong smoker and it had given him high blood pressure, due to hardening of the arteries.

The doctor told us that Dad's condition was serious and that we shouldn't hold out too much hope for his recovery. I was devastated. We had never been that close, but he was my Dad and I loved him for all his faults.

I rang FMC where I worked and told them I needed some time off, due to Dad's condition, which they agreed to. I went to Matson to collect Aunty Ethel, to take her to see Dad. I had never seen her so down, the man she had brought up as her own son was now in hospital, fighting for his life. It was so hard for her. He was in danger of dying at fifty years old and she was eighty-four and in good health. It was so difficult to reconcile.

I continued to visit him and he seemed to be making progress. After a few days with very little change, I got to the hospital and found Dad sitting up in bed as if nothing had happened. He said, 'hello son, that was a close one, I thought I was going to die, but I'm feeling much better today.' My spirits were uplifted. I could hardly believe my ears when he said he realised he should have taught me to drive, in case of emergencies, just like this. He said he would make sure I passed my test, when he came out of hospital. He had always said, he would never let me drive his beloved car.

As I left the ward, I saw the doctor who had been treating Dad. I remarked to him, what a miraculous recovery Dad had made.
The doctor took me aside and said gently, 'don't build up your hopes, he is still very ill.'
I asked him what he meant, because Dad looked so good.
The doctor made some more rather sympathetic noises, until I bluntly asked him, 'are you telling me Dad is going to die?'
He said, 'yes, I think so.'
I thanked the doctor and rushed from the building, unable to hold back the flood of tears.

A week had passed, so I rang in to work and told them I would need another week off. They didn't like it but I told them I could do nothing about it.

A few days later, Dad had his fifty-first birthday. He was still looking well and was talking about coming home. I started to think the doctor had been wrong, but he had been so definite. I thought, a doctor wouldn't say what he had, unless he had been sure. But I still couldn't believe it, or perhaps it was because I didn't want to believe it.

A few more days passed and I walked into the ward, to be met by a dramatic change. Dad looked really ill and was talking in Arabic. He had been in North Africa during the war, but I had never heard him speak any of the language, or even of his experiences. I was shocked at how small he looked, overnight he seemed to have shrunk to skin and bone. When I left the hospital that night, I knew that it was only a matter of time.

The next morning, a policeman came to the door. He told me that he had received a message from the hospital, for me to go there immediately. I got on the bike and raced to the hospital as fast as I could. I went into the ward and straight to Dad's bed, which had been curtained off. The shock was even greater than before. There was almost nothing left of him, he had wasted away to almost nothing. His breathing was very shallow and laboured. I stayed with him until suddenly, he stopped breathing. I turned to the nurse and said, 'is that it'? At the instant she said no, Dad started to breathe again. This went on for about half an hour, when he stopped breathing again, but this time I knew it was different. I sat there for a few minutes, knowing he was gone. I got up and walked away, I had to get out of there and be alone for a while.

I went to Aunty Ethel and broke the news to her. I think, in some ways it was harder for her than it was for me. Dad had been the apple of her eye, before I came along, when I think she saw me as a little version of him. I think she was right too. I can see him in me, in lots of ways, some good and some not so good.

I rang work again and told them I would be off for another week. They told me to come back or lose the job. I told them, they could stick the job up their ass. That was the end of FMC as far as I was concerned.

The next day, I had to go to the register office in Montpellier, at the end of Spa Road, to register Dad's death. It was very hard to have to go into an office and give Dad's details to the registrar, so soon after what is a great personal tragedy.

Then I went to the Co-op funeral directors to organise the funeral. Dad had enough insurance to cover the cost of the funeral plus about eight hundred pounds which was to be split between Gordon and me.

A lot of people came to the funeral, many were relatives that I had never met, some were old girlfriends and some were his old mates. Five years after Mum had been cremated at Coney Hill crematorium, we were back there to pay our last respects to dad. After the short service, Dad's ashes were scattered to the winds, in the same area that Mum's had been scattered. Both of my parents were gone, I would have no one to fall back on. Whatever happened from now on, there would be no safety net, it would all be down to me. Dad had always paid the household bills, now I had to come to terms with the harsh reality of running my own home.

Dad had worked part time, both for Cathedral coaches and Thomas Taxis. He had always had the habit of not taking his wages until they had built up to a good amount, so that he could buy something special. As far as I know, he had never had a bank account and used this method as a form of saving. He had often bought a car this way. Dad had been doing quite a bit of work for Cathedral and for Bill Thomas, so it was a good bet that he had some money owing. I went to Rowley Chandler of Cathedral Coaches and asked him for the money he owed dad, but he said there was none due. He said that had recently paid Dad up to date. I didn't believe it and was very angry, but there was nothing I could do. I went next, to see Bill Thomas to ask him for Dad's money. His answer was the same, that there was nothing owed. To make matters worse, he was even more abusive than he had been the last time I had spoken to him. I had not forgotten his attitude when I had told him that Dad had been taken ill.

Bill Thomas said threateningly that he didn't owe anything and that I should bugger off and not come back.

Almost before he stopped speaking, I stuck the nut on him. I got him right on the bridge of his nose. He staggered back, with blood pouring from his nose. He was stunned and made no move to retaliate. I think that was a good move on his part, as I may have injured him severely if he had tried to take me on. The mood I was in, I could easily have given him a beating.

I looked at him standing in his doorway, whimpering and holding his nose.

I said, 'you're not telling me to bugger off now, are you Bill? I hope it's broke, you fucking bastard.'

Then I turned and walked away.

I applied to the council to have the tenancy of our prefab transferred to me so that Gordon and I could continue living at our family home. They agreed to the transfer and gave me a new rent book. I soon realised how expensive it was, paying all the bills, the rent, the electric and the gas, as well as having to buy all of the groceries. I knew I would have to find another job, pretty quickly. I hadn't really needed to work before, but now it was a necessity if I was to be able to live to a reasonable standard.

I got a job as a meat porter, back where I had been an office junior four years before. Fred Brain gave me the job, back at Weddel's in Longsmith Street. I was loading and unloading lorries and stacking frozen New Zealand lambs in the cold stores. It wasn't a bad job, we worked from early in the mornings, but finished early in the afternoons. I liked that because it meant I could get out and about on the Lightning on nice sunny days.

I had not been home long on one of these days, when there was a knock on the door. I looked out of the window and saw Bobby Grant smiling beautifully. It immediately raised my spirits just to see her. She said she had come to make sure I was all right and to see if I needed cheering up. We went out for a ride on the Lightning, ending up at the Stagecoach Inn at Newport along the Bristol Road. We talked about old times, because I hadn't seen her for a couple of years. When it was time to go she said, 'let's go back to your place.' I was really surprised, because throughout the years we had been friends, we had never been lovers. We had a wonderful night together, even though we both knew that we always be friends and would ultimately go our own ways. We repeated these wonderful evenings for a few weeks, then decided that it was time to end it. We went back to just being the friends we knew we would always be. Bobby is one of the greatest women I have been privileged to know. I rarely see her now because she no longer lives in Gloucester. She met a man and chose the life of a traveller, which I'm sure suits her free spirit.

One afternoon, I went to see my friends, Hughie and Diana. Hughie was home alone, Diana was out with Gillian and Carol. Hughie and I were sitting talking when Diana and the kids came in through the back door. Carol saw me sitting on the settee and ran towards me, arms outstretched and shouting excitedly, Uncle Cliff!
She jumped onto my lap for a cuddle, but as she did so, her knees caught me full in the balls. It was instant agony and brought tears to my eyes. The pain soon went away though and everything was back to normal so I thought no more of it until the next morning. I got up to go to work and my balls were aching terribly. I went to work but couldn't do much, the aching was getting worse. After work I met my cousin Hugh and told him about the pain I was in and that my balls were swollen.
He said, 'let's have a look.'
With some embarrassment, I pulled my trousers down and showed him. As soon as he saw the size of them, about the size of a grapefruit.
He said, 'I'd get down the hospital if I were you.'

I said I'd think about it.

That evening I went to the Talbot, in Southgate Street, where a lot of my pals hung out. It was often full of Scorpions, the old biker gang. It was my regular watering hole for years. Roger Haines was in there, so I related my sad story to him, he also advised me to go to the hospital. He said he'd come with me, so off we went to the casualty which had moved to Great Western Road. It was no different then to now. Even though there were hardly any people waiting to be seen, you still had to wait for hours. Nothing ever seemed to be happening, until suddenly everybody would be dealt with very quickly. The pain was getting worse, I think I had left it a bit too long, but I had been hoping it would clear up on it's own. I kept going to the nurse asking how much longer I was likely to have to wait, but couldn't get a sensible answer. It's no wonder they get problems with violence when they treat people in that manner. Eventually I was getting very aggravated and started shouting that if somebody didn't do something soon, I would start smashing the place up. A sister came out to see what the noise was about. She told me to sit down and be quiet, that I would be seen in due course.

I had had enough by now so I turned to her and said, 'I am in terrible pain here, I keep saying it but nobody is taking any notice. If a doctor doesn't see me in the next five minutes, I'm going to start causing pain to other people and you're the first one I'm going to look for. Get moving, I'm counting down.'

A few minutes later, a doctor turned up. I was called into a cubicle and he asked me what was wrong. By his attitude, I could tell that he had been told that I was a troublemaker, but as soon as he saw the extent of my problem, his attitude changed to one of concern. He said that I should have been seen straight away and told the sister so.

He told me I would have to be admitted into hospital for them to deal with it, but the ward I would have to go to was in Southgate Street. He asked if I needed an ambulance, but I said no, Roger would take me. The hospital in Southgate Street was just a few doors down from the Talbot so we went there first. It was just before closing time, so Roger parked in the back yard and we went in for a quick one. I walked from there to the hospital and booked in. This time they had been waiting for me, they asked me what had taken so long for me to get there, so I told them I'd had to arrange to get my car home. I was still driving Dad's car, even though I didn't have a license.

A bed had been made ready for me. It was about 11pm, so the rest of the patients were asleep. I got into bed and waited for someone to come to see me. Soon a very pretty, lady doctor arrived and told me she would be dealing with my problem and that she wanted to have a look. I was very embarrassed, I had never been in hospital before and certainly had never had to deal with a personal problem with a woman. She was very professional though, she told me that a blood vessel had burst in my scrotum and that it was filling with blood, squeezing my testicles. It was like someone squeezing constantly, without a let up. She told me that a few days rest and a course of injections would put me right. The next morning I saw that I was in a ward full of old men, all with urinary problems, like prostrate trouble, but thankfully the doctor had been right and after three days I was discharged from there, back to normal.

I went to a party at Diana MacPherson's parent's house, in Coney Hill Road. They are a lovely family, George Golding being the patriarch. The Golding's have all been good friends to me over the years and have been closer than many families are. I always enjoy seeing them on any occasion, but on this occasion I made a date with Diana's sister Dot. I was planning to go to the Bath blues festival and Dot said she wanted to go too, so I told her I would get the tickets. We saw each other for a few weeks, before we went our separate ways. I told her I would get in touch again nearer the date of the festival, we could still go together.

One evening I went to Longlevens youth club to meet Dave Bull and Dick Spackman. While there I met two girls, a few years younger than me. Two girls, one who would turn out to be the biggest ever influence on my life, the other would become a lifelong friend. They were Lynn Scarrott and Cathy Murphy aka Spud. I made a lot of friends at that club who would stand the test of time, Paul Colley aka "Jack" being one of the most notable.

A few days later I was riding around Kings Square when I spotted Lynn and Cath standing there. I stopped for a chat, then offered Cath a lift home on the bike. She jumped on and I took her to Pirton Corner, where I dropped her off, so she could walk the short distance to her home. I think she was a bit worried about her Dad seeing her turn up on my bike.

Gloucester carnival was due on Saturday, it was a really big occasion then. All of the big stores put floats in, all trying to out do each other. It was a spectacle well worth seeing then. My bike had metamorphosed into a chopper style with ape hanger handlebars and exhausts which pointed high up into the air. I had also changed and was looking more and more outrageous. The crowds had formed to watch the carnival procession and I managed to get to the head of it. I was wearing a shaggy waistcoat that had the colours of a piebald horse, blue jeans, sandals and a Nazi helmet. I took the bike slowly along Parkend Road, waving to the crowd. As I got almost to the turning with Park Road, there on crowd control duty was the Special Constable who I owed a debt to. I accelerated away and turned up Arthur Street where I parked the bike. When I got back to Parkend Road, the procession was in full swing, passing slowly by. The copper had his back to the crowd, watching the procession pass. He was wearing a flat cap, not the traditional helmet. He had made two big mistakes. One, he had set me up for something I hadn't done and two, he had no protection for his head. I managed to get behind him, the crowd was about four or five deep, but that was as close as I needed to get. I took off my Nazi helmet, grabbed it by the rim and swung it, with great force, over the heads of the people in front of me, catching him just off centre of the top of his head. He went down like he had been pole axed, I was already walking quietly away, no hurry, nobody realised exactly what had happened, I could see the fuss mounting but I was well away. I looked back and thought, I've let you off lightly mate, you deserved worse than that, but I'll call it quits. I saw him many times after that and could never resist a little smile. He never knew that it was me, but every time we were close up, I would point my finger at him and smile, while gently nodding my head.

Roger Haines and I decided to take a trip to Weston super Mare one weekend, we took Dad's old Austin Cambridge which I was still using without a license. We had a good day out, just wandering around, enjoying the sights. On the way home, I opened the car up, to see what it would do. Roger, who was more used to cars than I was, cautioned me against it, he said it's not like your bike, if you push this car too hard it will blow up. I was just about to argue, when there was an almighty bang from the engine. I pulled onto the hard shoulder and lifted the bonnet. I couldn't see anything wrong, but the clattering was horrendous.

I said, Oh well, I reckon it's knackered so we might as well keep going. I got off the motorway at the Patchway interchange at Bristol. As I took the A38 I saw Dave Coughlin and his girlfriend hitchhiking. I stopped and picked them up. I told them that it might be a slow trip or that we might not make it at all but they were welcome to come along with us. We kept going at about twenty miles an hour all the way back to Gloucester. The clattering continued unabated and the engine was boiling, with great clouds of steam coming from beneath the bonnet. I dropped Dave off, then Roger and I made our way home to Tuffley. I parked the car off the road, relieved that we had made it. The engine was completely knackered, it had broken a con rod which had thrashed around, beating the engine to death from the inside. It would never run again. Dave Keveren came and diagnosed the problem for me. I couldn't afford to have it repaired, so I sold it to him as it was. I had only used it occasionally anyway. I was much happier riding the Lightning.

The weekend of the Bath Blues Festival came. They had changed the venue from last year and expanded it to a two-day event. Gordon and Phil had left in the old Bedford van, on Friday afternoon, to make sure they got to the site in good time. Woodstock had been the biggest music festival ever and it was expected, a large crowd would attend this one. The era of the big festival was just starting. I picked Dot up on Saturday morning, the 26th June 1970. We set off on the Lightning, going through Bath towards the old army camp, which was now called the Bath and West showground at Shepton Mallet. A few miles from Shepton Mallet the traffic came to a standstill. I was glad we were on the bike, because it soon became impossible for anyone in a car to move. We threaded our way through the traffic until we got to the festival site. People were abandoning their vehicles and walking, making the traffic problems even worse, but we got there easily, parked up and walked into the showground and picked a spot on the ground where we had a good view not far from the stage. We would stay in this spot for the next two days. It soon became obvious that this festival was going to be bigger than anyone had ever expected. The music was supposed to start at midday, but there were so many people trying to get there that even the bands couldn't get through the traffic. When the music was due to start, somebody came on stage and told that there were no band's there yet but they were trying to organise some helicopters. There was a massive sound system set up, so when no one had turned up, Donovan who had been in the crowd, went on stage and asked if we wanted him to do a few songs until someone else got there. We all shouted, YES!

Donovan started singing his hit songs of a few years previous. He was on for so long I think he sang everything he knew, but still no one else had arrived. He said he would keep going if we wanted him to and we all shouted YES! so he started all over again. He was a real star, keeping us entertained, I admired him for that. Eventually a band arrived and the festival started, with non-stop music for the next thirty-six hours.

People kept flooding in, it was soon clear that this was going to be something special. It turned out that this festival was to be the biggest festival ever held on mainland Britain, with nearly a quarter of a million people packing into the site. I was glad that I had got here reasonably early, because Dot and I had a place not too far from the stage. At least we were close enough to see the artists performing. As I looked behind me, as far as the eye could see, there was a sea of people, rising up a slope, away in the distance. It was an awesome spectacle. The organisers had set up large video screen on either side of the stage, something that was in it's infancy then, but they were very effective, if only during the hours of darkness. They were essential for the people who were a long way off, but for us they were a bonus. Johnny Winter, an albino blues and rock guitar player from Texas came on late that night, he gave the most impressive performance I have ever seen in my life. I could see him on the stage and I could see him close up, on the screens. His music, combined with the energetic stage act, just blew me away. Of all the big names performing this weekend, Johnny was the tops for me. I have been buying his music ever since. On the first day, as well as Johnny Winter and Donovan, we were treated to performances by Fat Harry, Keef Hartley, Maynard Ferguson's Big Band, Fairport Convention, Colloseum, It's a Beautiful Day, Steppenwolf and Pink Floyd. On the Sunday, John Mayall's Bluesbreakers did the early morning shift followed by Canned Heat, who were brilliant, Joe Jammer, Frank Zappa and the Mothers of Invention, Santana, Flock, a fantastic set by Led Zeppelin, Hot Tuna, Country Joe, Jefferson Airplane, The Byrds and finally Dr John. The Moody Blues were supposed to appear but didn't do so. Apparently because of the risk of electrocution due to a downpour of rain we suffered. Still, it was great value at £2/10/- each I paid for the tickets.

The sheer size of the audience had caught everyone by surprise, estimated to have been in excess of 200,000, consequently all the facilities were woefully inadequate. The toilets couldn't cope and anyone, like me, who hadn't brought their own food was going to go hungry. There was a van selling chips, not far from where we were sitting and though the queue was perhaps a hundred yards long, I decided that I would go to try to get us something. I stood in the queue for hours, making my way inexorably towards the hatch at the back of the van. All the time I was in the queue, there were entrepreneurs walking up and down, openly selling acid as if it were sweets. They were slowly traversing the queue shouting 'acid, get your acid here, acid mate'? It was easier to buy drugs than it was to buy food, that's for sure.

At last there was only one more person between me and the food.
Then I heard the man say, 'sorry mate, that's the lot, I've run out of everything, there's nothing left.'
The guy in front of me bowed his head and walked away, looking really dejected. I knew how he felt, I was absolutely starving. I had spotted a large pile of scrumps, you know, the bits of crunchy batter that are left after frying the fish, piled up on

the far end of the fryer. I moved forward and asked him if I could have a couple of bags of those.

He said, 'sure, I didn't think anybody would eat them.'

I said, when you're as hungry as I am, you'll eat anything.'

Anyway, what's wrong with a good bag of scrumps? A bit oily, but so what, they kept us going. I really enjoyed them.

We left the showground on Sunday afternoon, hoping that we would be able to find something to eat and drink soon. We stopped at a pub not far from the site, but it was heaving with people and they had next to nothing left. It wasn't worth staying. We went into Shepton Mallet, but it was as if a plague of locusts had descended on it. All of the food shops were closed and looking through the windows we could see that they had sold out of everything. We gave up and decided that we might as well break for home. We had attended an historic event which was ultimately to lead to the founding of the Glastonbury festival

Shortly after the Bath festival came the Isle of Wight festival. Some of my friends were going and Dave Bull asked me if I wanted to ride along with him. It is one of my biggest regrets that I was too lazy to make the trip and missed out on what was to be the greatest festival of them all. I missed out on some great performances by legendary artists, not least, the last performance by Jimi Hendrix and one of the last by Jim Morrison of The Doors. How could I have missed such an event? Dave had an accident on the way to the Isle of Wight and came back with his forks bent right back like bananas, but he had still made it there and back.

Dad's insurance money paid out, it wasn't much but it gave Gordon and me a couple of hundred pounds each and it was more than I had ever had at any one time. I gave up my job and decided to enjoy myself. I bought a new leather biker jacket from Mcad and Tomkinson's and I still have it.

Paul Hayes came to the house one afternoon to ask if I wanted to go to H and L motorcycles in Stroud. They were Triumph agents and Paul wanted to get some parts for his Thunderbird. We got there okay, but on the way back, just outside Stonehouse, Paul's bike started to misfire, eventually expiring altogether. Paul diagnosed a stripped timing gear so there was no way we were going to be able to repair it on the side of the road. We were in the middle of nowhere, nothing but fields. We looked around us and spotted an old harrow, out in the middle of one of the fields. On investigation, we found that we could get a piece of chain off the harrow and planned to use it to tow Paul home. If anyone has ever tried to tow a motorcycle with another motorcycle, they will now how bad it is, but to do it with a chain makes it ten times worse. We tied it to Paul's forks and to the back of the Lightning and set off. Every time we tried to slow down then speed up or go round a corner, it snatched and almost pulled us both off. It was a journey of only a few miles to Matson, but it was probably the worst journey I have ever made.

About this time, I fell out with my brother Gordon. I don't think he had come to terms with the fact that I was not going to provide everything, the way Dad had. He complained to me that there was no orange squash in the house so I offered him the money to go to get some. He said that he wasn't going to get it and that I should go. We had a row and I told him that anything he wanted in future, he would have to provide for himself. He said he was fed up with living here and was going to move out, which he promptly did. He got a flat somewhere and for a while I didn't know where he had gone.

I can never remember the door at 98 Fourth Avenue being locked. I never even gave it a thought, we just came and went as we pleased. I often came home to find one of more of my friends sitting in the living room, waiting for me. There was next to nothing in the house worth stealing and although some things disappeared, I never had a problem with it. Mostly my friends were honest. Sometimes they would turn up with some grass and we would put some music on and sit around getting stoned. I had an old record deck, which stood on blocks of wood and an amplifier with no case. All the electrics were exposed, sometimes it would stop working, but I found that if I put my hand under the deck and waggled the wires, it would start up again. I frequently got an electric shock from it, but I kept it going like that for months until I got an old broken down radiogram and put my old amp into it. I wired it to the huge speaker in the middle of the radiogram and to another across the other side of the room. My first stereo and what a sound it had, with it's big bass speaker.

I started going out more often with Cath, but we had a problem. Her Dad was very strict over her timekeeping and I was very undisciplined over everything. Some of the places I went, never got going until after Cath should have been home. We often went to the Ship at Brimscombe, on a Saturday night. A lot of my old gang, 'The Scorpions', went there, sometimes we rode over, en masse, sometimes we all packed into cars, but it was always a good night out.

By the time we got back to Churchdown from Brimscombe, it was way past Cath's curfew. When I took her home late, she wouldn't let me come to the door, in case her Dad was there. The next time I called for her, he made a point of telling me to watch my step. Yeah! Like I was worried. I had no fear of anybody and no respect for anybody's rules but my own.

I was living alone, I had little contact with any family I had left, I was living life at a furious pace, riding fast and dangerously, I expected to die violently at any moment and I didn't care.

I could tell I was sinking lower and lower, so one night I came home from The Ship, sat alone in the dark for a while and decided to take a trip to Scotland to see my Aunty May and cousins Jenny and Vic. It was something like two-o clock in the morning so I went to Westgate filling station for fuel. They were the only all night garage then. Once my tank was full, I carried on along St Oswalds Road and saw the lights on in the British Beef building, so I turned in. They often worked all night and I knew I would be all right for a cup of tea and something to eat to set me up for the journey. When I got there I went up to the mess room and found the guys all sitting around playing cards and drinking tea. Nothing had changed since I worked here a few years ago, but they were a good crowd and they made me welcome. There was always food here so I cooked a piece of steak, a few sausages and a couple of eggs and ate it followed by a cup of tea. We had a good laugh as men do in these kind of situations, told a few silly stories, a few harmless lies, all being exaggerated out of all proportion about good times past. It was the best laugh I had had for ages and it boosted my spirits no end. I thanked them for their hospitality, bade them farewell, kicked the bike into life and roared off into night, feeling pretty good for the journey ahead.

Chapter 13
Battles

Six hours later, I arrived in the City of Edinburgh, a city I had visited many times with Mum and Dad. This time I was alone. I parked the bike and walked along Princes Street, to Scott Monument. As a boy I had climbed the 287 steps inside the monument that led to the top. I stood by it and looked up at the Castle, thinking of the good times we'd had here as a family. I didn't stop for long, I got back on the bike and took the coast road out of Edinburgh, through Portobello and Musselburgh, to Tranent. I knocked on the door of 164 Northfield and waited for an answer, but there was no one home. I had never even thought that they might not be here. I got back on the bike and rode the short distance to Granny Wilson's house, in Harkness Crescent. Again I knocked on the door, but this time I had more success. Aunty May came to the door, they were all here, visiting gran. It was lovely to see them, they were very surprised to see me there, but greeted me with genuine affection. I had long ago made my peace with gran, she had forgiven me my childhood indiscretions and we were now on the best of terms.

We went back to Aunty May's where she gave me some food, let me shower and made up a bed in the spare room. I stayed for a couple of days, just hanging around doing nothing, when she said to me, 'come on, let's get on that bike of yours and I'll show you some of the countryside.'
I was taken by surprise that she would want to take the risk of riding with me, but she was adamant. She produced a pair of goggles from somewhere, put on an overcoat and a pair of boots and said, 'let's go.'

Off we went, to Haddington, then on into the Lammermuir Hills. We climbed higher and higher into the hills, passing Camelshiel Castle then dropping down to the small town of Duns. On through Greenlaw, Gordon, Melrose and Galashiels, before getting to Lauder and climbing back into the hills and heading for Tranent. It was a fine day out, we both enjoyed it immensely. I don't think I had ever seen Aunty May so full of fun as that day.

Soon it was time for me to go home. I took the A1 coast road out of Tranent, travelling east through Berwick on Tweed, down to Newcastle on Tyne. I took a slow run home, down the M1, travelling for some eight or nine hours. That's a long time in the saddle.

It was dark when I pulled up outside the prefab. I had been away for a week, but again I hadn't bothered about locking the door. I went in, switched a light on, put the kettle on for a cup of tea, looked around, nothing had changed. I don't think anyone had been there, if they had I couldn't tell. I had my tea then collapsed into bed to sleep the sleep of the damned. I was exhausted after my journey.

A gang of us got on our bikes and went to a dance at Minchinhampton village hall, where a favourite band of mine were playing. The Arthur Hinge Speed Band played wild progressive rock and had an incredible stage act. I had two friends in the band, Mickey Clarke, a fine drummer and Mick 'Wanger' Wainright, the singer and terrific front man. During the wild stage act, a strobe light would start flashing, then Wanger would start cranking the handle of an air raid siren. As the noise of it built up, he lifted it of the stage so the inertia of the thing started swinging it round and round as Wanger held on to the handle. He moved around the stage with the siren wailing and flailing around, bouncing it onto the stage then high up into the air, over and over again. It was obviously a big heavy thing by the way it almost took over control of Wanger's tall slim body, but it was a very exciting performance. To add to the drama, they played a number which culminated in smashing the tubes in some old TV sets causing them to explode. What a band, they were great. Mickey lives in Spain now and Wanger lives in California. Making music is still part of both their lives. On this night, Dick Spackman offered to sell me his girlfriend for the night, it was just a bit of fun but she didn't appreciate it at all. We had a fair bit to drink and as usual when we went to one of these country venues, the local lads took exception to our invasion. Once we realised that trouble was brewing we pre-empted it by banding together in a show of strength in front of the stage and directing a bit of menace towards them. Fortunately they realised that it would be a bad move to upset us and the situation relaxed. We had a good night out and left without any trouble.

Cath's mum and dad went away for a few days, giving us a free weekend when we wouldn't have to worry about getting home. There was a pop festival on, in Tewkesbury and it had been decided that the Scorpions were going to make a night of it. We all met at the Union in Westgate Street and rode en masse to Tewkesbury. We parked the bikes, then went on a pub crawl before deciding how to get into the festival without tickets and more importantly, without paying. We moved down Barton Street, going from pub to pub. We were a bit noisy, but the atmosphere was good humoured. By the time we got to the Bell hotel, opposite the Abbey, we were all well oiled and having a laugh. The barroom was long and narrow with a door at either end and a row of tables and chairs along the wall opposite. We were sitting at one end, drinking and talking when a gang of local bikers came in and settled at the other end of the bar. They started shouting disparaging remarks at us which prompted a spirited response. These lads obviously didn't appreciate who they were trying to take the piss out of. It went on for a while, without too much to worry about, but then the landlord decided to throw us out. We were the strangers, therefore we would have to go.

He started shouting, 'right you lot, you've had enough, get out.'

I said 'Yeah, okay man, we'll drink up and move on.'

He said, 'No you won't, you'll get out now.'

Some of us tried to reason with him, telling him that we would be gone in a few more minutes, but he had come round the bar and was getting aggressive. He wouldn't listen to anything we said and it was obvious that trouble was imminent. We weren't going to be thrown out of anywhere, by anybody, let alone this landlord and a few bar staff. The bar was packed and he would probably be able to count on some of the regulars, plus the local bikers, but twenty Scorpions were always going to win.

The landlord got even more aggressive, he had a bottle in his hand and was threatening to use it if we didn't go immediately. He upped the stakes for the last time, making a move to hit Dick Spackman, who was sitting next to me. Before he could connect, I jumped up and hit him over the head with my pint mug, then all hell let loose. By choosing confrontation, he had made a big mistake. Now that the fighting had started, there would be no quarter asked or given. People who wanted nothing to do with it, started to try to get out of the two doors. Those who wanted to fight, waded in with great ferocity, it was like a scene from a wild west saloon. Furniture was flying in all directions, wrecking the optics and all the mirrors and general paraphernalia behind the bar. A chair went through the top of the jukebox, silencing it without ceremony. Our opponents had by now realised what they had let loose and apart from the ones unconscious on the floor, had all taken refuge behind the bar and had resorted to trying to keep us at bay by throwing bottles at us. Honour had been satisfied so we started to retreat through both of the doors. I saw Cath going out of the far door and continued to keep our opponents heads down while the retreat was made. I was the last man standing on my side of the bar. Looking at the unconscious bodies, I could see that there was none of ours among them, so I turned to go out of the door. As I turned, I was hit on the back of the head by a bottle. It stunned me for a few seconds, followed by a rage which took over all reason. I ran back into the room, jumped onto the bar and kicked the landlord in the face, knocking him flat. I ran up and down the bar, wrecking anything left and showering it down onto the rest of them, who were cowering down as low as they could go. I jumped back off the bar and headed for the door, with more success this time.

When I got outside, I couldn't see anybody, I didn't know which way they had gone. I walked along the side of the river and found the gang standing by a large boat. When I got there, they were discussing whether they could take the boat with all of us aboard, to the other side of the river where the festival was. After due consideration, it was decided that we would all probably be swept away, so we would have to find another way in.

We made our way back up to the main street, where the police had finally arrived and were looking for us. They came up to us, in a threatening manner, but it soon became obvious to them that we weren't going to be intimidated, especially when the dog handler pushed his luck and John Myatt punched the dog on the head, putting the dog and his handler right off. They decided to assert their authority by telling us to quieten down and make our way directly to the festival, then they left.

When we got to the festival entrance, it was decided that all the tactics talked, about ways of getting in, were for nothing. The mood the Scorpions were now in, who was going to stop them from just walking in. No one with any sense. I was covered in blood from the blow I had taken from the bottle. Tony Hawker kept looking at it and advised me to go to the hospital, so I bade them farewell and Cath and I took off for casualty department in Gloucester. The blood had run down my back and covered my furry waistcoat. I looked like an old Viking warrior just come from a battle. A couple more of the gang came strolling in, with minor injuries requiring stitches, I heard a nurse say, it looks like the greasers have been fighting tonight, let's get rid of them as quick as we can. We were dealt with quickly, the only time I have had quick service there. We left the hospital and went home to bed.

The lads who made it to the festival had a rare old night. I was sorry to have missed it, I had wanted to give Cath a good night out, but hey! That's life, things don't always go according to plan.

Tom Murphy, Cath's dad was getting ever more protective of his daughter. I don't think he liked the way things were going, so when one night I called for her, he refused to allow her to come out with me. There followed a violent encounter, which ended with me leaving without Cath and the police being called to the scene.

That night, Roger Haines and I, went to The Ship at Brimscombe. There were a lot of Scorpions there that night and they were having a good time, but the events of earlier that evening were weighing heavily on my mind. The local lads were taking even more exception than was usual, to the Gloucester boys, making free with the local girls. The atmosphere became very tense. We had been there many times without incident, so I think some of the local hard cases saw this as a sign of weakness. Nothing could have been further from the truth.

I don't know what started it, but suddenly there was an eruption and a mass brawl started, unleashing a level of violence undreamed of by these country boys. Once they realised the seriousness of their situation, they started to try to escape by any means available to them. Some started jumping out of the windows, the problem was, the windows on one side of the building, were directly above the canal. Some of them must have been scared to death, because for quite a few, falling ten feet into an icy cold canal was the preferred option to taking their chances with us.

We soon drove all the locals out of the club, then followed them out into the street, where they had regrouped on the opposite side of the road. Again they made a mistake. Someone threw a rock at us, but we were standing at the club entrance, many still holding on to their drinks. Almost as soon as the rock had been thrown, an avalanche of beer mugs and bottles started raining down on them. By this time, we were laughing and enjoying the battle. Most of our opponents had made off, leaving only a few hardy souls left, so we suddenly ran at them, covering the few feet that was between us so quickly, they only just managed to turn and run, before we got to them. That was the end of it, so we decided that it was time to go. The battle had only lasted a few minutes but had been fierce and decisive. The Scorpions were a powerful force to be reckoned with.

We left the scene and made our way home. A few minutes after Roger had dropped me off, Tony Hawker and Paul Mulhern arrived, Paul with his girlfriend and Tony with a girl he had brought from Brimscombe. They asked if they could stay the night and I said it was okay. I went to bed and left them to their own devices.

A few hours later I was woken up by one of the girls getting into bed with me. I turned to her and asked what was going on, I didn't even know who she was, or anything about her. She said, Tony had left, saying he was going to get some cigarettes, but as time wore on it had become obvious that he was not going to return. She had been left, with only the settee to lie on and nothing to cover herself with, to keep warm. She said she was freezing and I could see she was shivering with cold, so I told her to get in and make herself comfortable. I turned over and went back to sleep.

Half way through the next morning, I was woken up again. This time the shock was far worse. Cath had fallen out with her dad over the events of the previous night and had come to see me. She came into the bedroom and saw me lying there with a girl I didn't even know. Cath stood at the foot of the bed, looking really disappointed, then she started crying. The girl I was in bed with asked sleepily, 'who is this?'
I replied, 'she's my girlfriend, it's time you went' and gave her a push out of the bed to help her on her way. Then I had the difficult task of trying to explain the truth to Cath. I don't know if she ever really believed me, but we managed to smooth things over.

Soon after, Cath moved in with me and we became a couple. I enjoyed her company and had a greater affection for her than I had ever felt for a girl before. I suppose that we had begun what was to become a long lasting, loving relationship.

Chapter 14
Poor But Happy

It was great to have Cath living with me. She soon set about turning what was a typical scruffy bachelor pad, into a more acceptable home. There had only been men in this house since mum died and since I had been living alone, it had got even worse. Housework was pretty low on my list of priorities, but Cath was different, she wanted everything to be clean and tidy. We even did some decorating, my first efforts, perhaps not to everyone's taste with blue ceiling and orange walls, but it was freshly painted. I could not remember the prefab ever being decorated before.

I was doing some day work, labouring for my cousin Hugh, who was a plasterer. I went on many jobs with him but it was only occasional work and I knew it was time I looked for another job. We went to a house in Vauxhall Terrace to replace a bedroom ceiling, re-plaster the stairs and the front living room. The house was rented by an old lady and the landlord had put off doing any repairs until it was absolutely essential. Some bits of the ceiling had fallen on the lady during the night and it had become dangerous for her to sleep there, so we had been called in to sort it out. We went into the bedroom and took a look at the job, Hugh got a sweeping brush and started to prod the ceiling to find out how bad it was. He prodded it a couple of times, then wished he hadn't, he shouted for me to get out of the room. I went outside the door and looked back to see Hugh with the head of the brush on the ceiling trying to hold up a huge bulge that had appeared. He made his way towards the door, keeping the brush up on the ceiling, the bulge getting bigger and bigger as he moved towards me. Suddenly it started to go and Hugh made a dash for the door, slamming it shut as soon as he was through. We could hear all kinds of banging and crashing behind the door, it was obvious that it wasn't going to take us long to get that plaster down. When we thought it was safe. We opened the door, but couldn't see anything for the cloud of dust swirling about, so we closed it back up and went to look at the other parts of the house that needed doing. Hugh decided that he would start to prepare the living room, leaving me to knock the old plaster off the stairs. They were the old fashioned kind of stairs, hidden behind a door, leading off the kitchen. I set up a pair of stepladders and some planks, so that I could get to the top of the walls, to start hacking the plaster off. After a few minutes chipping away with a lump hammer and bolster chisel, the whole lot came away with another great rumble. I dodged most of it as it came crashing down. I had closed the door at the bottom of the stairs, so as to keep the dust contained. I looked down from the plank I was standing on, halfway up the stairs and saw that the rubble had half filled the stairway. I stepped off the plank, straight onto the rubble, bent down and opened the door leading to the kitchen. The rubble started to rumble and shift through the doorway, into the kitchen. This time I was standing on top of it and had to jump into the kitchen and move quickly out of it's way. I went into the front room where Hugh was working, listening to the radio. He hadn't heard a thing.

I said, 'haven't you finished this little job yet? I've done the stairs.'

I started laughing and told him to come and take a look. That house was so dangerous, it's a wonder the poor old lady wasn't killed. In a few days, we had it all spruced up and ready for her to move back in. It took almost as long to get rid of the dust we had created as it did to do the job.

Christmas came and we were invited to Hughie and Diana's for Christmas day. It was a great day with them and Gillian and Carol. We played with the girls and their toys and Diana cooked a wonderful dinner, which we all enjoyed immensely. In the evening we had a few drinks, Cath had some sherry and when that ran out Hughie produced some bottles of Pony (something similar to Babycham) which Cath tried and said she liked. She was not used to drinking in any quantity and got drunk for the first time in her life. She started to go to sleep, so I put her to bed and we stayed the night at Hughie's. Cath would never have made the couple of hundred yards between our houses.

1971 dawned, soon I would be twenty one, I already had the key to the door, even if I never knew where it was. I got a job at Graham Reeves, builders merchants, as a warehouseman, back on the plumbing and heating, as I had been at Western Trading, five years earlier. I liked it there, they seemed to be a good firm, Jim the foreman was a nice man and it was easy going.

On a freezing cold January morning about two weeks after I had started, I was on my way to work at about a quarter to eight, when disaster struck. I was riding the Lightning along Southern Avenue, following a line of cars. As I went over the railway bridge, into Cole Avenue, the road split into three lanes. I looked down the road and pulled into the middle lane. As I did so, a sports car did the same, coming in the other direction. He saw me and started to weave about, I think he panicked. I tried to swerve in front of the car I was passing, but as I did so, the sports car hit my right leg. I flew off the bike and over the top of the car. Things went into slow motion. As I flew through the air, I thought, this is like Superman flying. Then I hit the ground and started bouncing over and over, ending up on my back, sliding down the road with the back of my head banging on the tarmac, over and over again. I saw a shower of sparks flying past me, still in slow motion. I realised that I had been flying faster than the Lightning and it was just coming past me. I came to a halt, lying in the middle of the road. I lay there thinking, well, this is it, I knew it wouldn't be long before I would die and now is the time and it was easier than I thought it would be. There was no pain, I felt nothing, I was just sinking into unconsciousness. All of this must have happened in seconds, because no one had yet got to me, but it felt like for ever.

All of a sudden, things came back to real time and I saw a car whiz past my head, almost taking it off. I realised that I was lying in the middle of the road and some cars weren't even slowing down. I saw people running towards me, trying to stop the cars from running me over. I tried to move and realised I couldn't get up, so I dragged myself as quickly as I could, to the verge at the side of the road. All of this before the first person reached me, offering to help. I was pretty groggy, but now it was starting to hurt. I could see that my leg was in a pretty bad way, my foot was at a crazy angle and the bone stuck straight out of the front of my leg. My trousers reminded me of those worn by Robinson Crusoe in an old film I'd seen. They were all ripped to shreds at the bottom with my bare legs sticking out. I had been wearing brown Chelsea boots and I could see my foot sticking out of the bottom of the boot, where the sole had been ripped off. I lay in the road thinking, that's a good pair of boots gone and my favourite old Parka jacket. Somebody covered me over with a coat, as I had started to shiver. The man covering me with the coat started saying he was sorry but it wasn't his fault. I realised it had been him that had hit me and I had a fit of rage. I threw his coat into the road and told him to fuck off.

The next person I saw looking over me was one of the lorry drivers from Graham Reeves, he was also a biker friend and he asked me if I wanted the bike taken home. I thanked him and said yes.

The ambulance arrived and the paramedics started to see to my injuries. I had no idea how good or bad it was going to be. I could see the leg was bad, but I couldn't see or feel much else. They put me into the ambulance and we sped off towards the hospital, lights flashing and two tone horns wailing. I asked the ambulance man how bad it was, he replied that my leg was broken.
I said, 'I know it's broken, I can see the end of the bone sticking out, I'm asking how bad it is.'

He tried to keep the conversation light and kept smiling, rather inanely I thought. I got nothing out of him, except that they would be able to sort it out when we got to the hospital. To make matters worse, he asked me if it was hurting. When I told him that it was agony, he said they had a new type of gas on board that would ease the pain, but he was sorry he was unable to give me any as he hadn't been on the training course.

I said, 'you fucking idiot! What are you telling me that for?'

He tried to calm me down, but I found it increasingly irritating and in between my groans, I kept mumbling things like, 'fucking pratt,' so eventually he gave up and we finished the rest of the journey in silence.

When we arrived at the casualty department in Great Western Road, I was removed from the ambulance and wheeled into a room. The medic's were very impressive at this stage. It was just like you see on the television, when everyone springs into action. They started cutting my clothes off, administering injections and asking me questions. I was surrounded by people and everything seemed to be happening at lightning speed. They asked me if I knew my blood type and I answered, 'yes, it's **A Negative**.'

I heard one of the doctors groan and say, 'I don't expect we've got any of that, better give him some plasma.'

I thought to myself, that's handy, they haven't got any of my blood type, maybe I'm going to die after all. I asked them to get a message to Cath, telling her not to worry.

They wheeled me away, into a cubicle and I don't remember much else until I came round from the anaesthetic used to perform the operation to plate and pin the bones in my leg. Apparently, I had been at the hospital from around eight thirty until four o'clock before they could start the operation. It had taken that long to get the blood they needed from another area.

It was dark when I started to come round. I awoke in a side ward with two beds in it. An old man who I later found out was an Irishman named Dennis Mahoney was in the other bed. A nurse came into the room and I asked if I could have a drink of water. My mouth was so dry from the anaesthetic, I could have drunk a gallon of water, but the nurse said it was too soon after recovery and she would give me some water, later. When she had gone, I looked around the room and saw, only a few feet away, there was a small washbasin. I started to try to shuffle up in the bed so that I could hang over the side and get a hand on the basin. It was a real struggle but I managed to get a hand on it and ease myself just that little bit further until I

183

was on the verge of falling out. I managed to turn on the tap and by hanging on to the other side of the bed, I could get a few drops of water in my cupped hand and take a very small drink. I continued to do this until I was absolutely exhausted and collapsed back into a deep sleep. I awoke again, I had no idea what the time was except that it was still pitch dark and the old man was still sleeping. The pain was starting to come now, I was greater agony now than I had been at any time. A nurse came in and gave me an injection and I slipped back to sleep. The next time I woke up, it was morning and people were fussing around, Dennis was having his breakfast and the nurses were coming in and out asking how I was. I wasn't feeling too bad considering.

I lifted up the bedclothes and took a look at the leg encased in plaster of paris. The front of the plaster was stained brown from dried blood, it didn't look too good, but nobody seemed too concerned, so I assumed that the operation must have gone all right.

Cath came in to see me as soon as they would let her in. She was beside herself with worry, they hadn't told her very much. She was a young girl and they hadn't treated her very well, she may have been young but she was the only one I wanted to be here with me. I was delighted to see her and had a very strong feeling of the love I had for her when I saw her come into the room. For the first of many hundreds of times over the years, I looked at her face and thought how lucky I was to have her. I still look at her today and think the same things as I thought then. I knew that whatever happened, I would be able to count on her, she was and still is my best friend.

Aunty Ethel would have to be told that I was in hospital but there was time for that and I didn't want to worry her. It wasn't long ago that she had seen dad die and I didn't want to hurt her any more.

After a couple of days, they decided to cut a large trapdoor in the plastercast, so they could take a look at the wound where the bone had come through and where they had cut to insert the plates. When they opened it up, it looked horrible. The area where the bone had come out had gone green and smelled terrible. The nurse said it was nothing to worry about and cleaned it up every few hours. It didn't look very good to me.

After a few days, at least I was starting to feel okay. Cath was coming to see me every day and some days I had a lot of visitors. It was nice in the side ward, the nurses didn't worry about how many visitors were in the room. I shared some of my visitors with Dennis, in the next bed, so if the nurses did complain, I could still have twice as many as normally allowed.

I wasn't getting on very well with the hospital food, by the time it got to us in the very end side ward, it was often cold. Cath started to bring in all sorts of things. There was a chip shop in London Road so Cath went there and brought back chicken and chips, it was manna from heaven.

I was getting slowly better and things weren't too bad, but it was no place to be for your twenty first birthday. Cath turned up with a few of my friends, some sandwiches and a birthday cake and we had a small party. Old Dennis Mohoney really enjoyed all the company, he had no family in Gloucester and had few visitors, mainly from the catholic church of St Peters. He was a lovely old man and we tried to involve him in everything we did.

During the second week of my stay in hospital, they tried to move me out of the side ward into the main ward, but I told them that I would rather stay where I was. I had got used to being there and didn't like the thought of the loss of privacy. I hoped I wouldn't be there much longer anyway. In the end they left me alone.

I had been in bed for about two weeks, when a nurse brought me a pair of crutches. She said, as soon as I could use them, I could go home. I got out of bed and set off very tentatively towards the main ward. By the time I got to the end of the ward and back, I was absolutely exhausted. I told the nurse I would be ready to go home the next day. She said she would tell the consultant that I was ready.

Mr Merryweather, the consultant surgeon, came on his rounds, looked at my leg through the trapdoor in the plaster, checked the state of the wound and decided that I could go home once the plaster had been replaced with a new one. The old cast not only had this hole cut in it, but was a disgusting looking thing, coloured brown with dried blood.

Cath came in and I told her that I was ready to come home. She went off and contacted Hughie MacPherson who came and collected me as quickly as he could. Was I glad to get out of there? As we drove away I experienced a feeling of great relief. I thought it must be like getting out of prison. I felt free again.

When we got home, Cath told me to go into the back bedroom. I went in and had a real shock. The Lightning was in there, my friend Roger Haines had been coming in the evenings and had repaired the damage. It was ready to ride, if only I could.

The clothes I had been wearing when I'd had the accident, were returned by the hospital, all stuffed into a large plastic bag. My trousers and boots were only fit for the dustbin and my helmet which I had only been wearing because of the cold weather, had been bashed in at the back and was all but useless. My trusty old Parka jacket had stood up well to the experience. The only thing wrong with it was the elbows had been worn away. Cath got a couple of leather patches and sewed them on for me, making it as good as new.

It was great to be home again, Cath was making it a nicer place to live all the time. She was working, earning around six pounds a week and I was getting state sickness benefit of around three pounds a week. Almost all of my money went on paying the rent. By the time Cath bought some food and kept some money aside to pay her bus fares to work, we were pretty near destitute. I couldn't get out of the house yet, I wasn't good enough on the crutches for long trips, so I asked Cath to get in touch with the Department of Social Security to see if I could get any help. The answer was an emphatic no, they weren't interested at all. Because Cath and I weren't married, they wouldn't even talk to her about it.

As soon as I was able, I caught the bus into town, then hobbled down to Cedar House in Spa Road to ask for some assistance. After a long wait, sitting in some pain on a hard chair, too worn out from the journey to move around much, I eventually got an interview. They treated me as if I was rubbish and gave me nothing. I went home and waited for Cath to get home from work. I told her we were in trouble and I had no idea how we were going to survive. She said not to worry, we'd manage somehow.

I had been at home for a couple of weeks, when on a Saturday night, Cath told me she was going to her mother's and would not be home until late. I was sitting alone, when Roger Haines came in and asked me if I wanted to go out for the evening. I said no, I hadn't been out on an evening since I came out of hospital. I really didn't feel much like it. He kept on, telling me to go and put some good clothes on and come out and have some fun. In the end, I gave in and agreed to go as long as we weren't too long as I wasn't really up to it. I had no idea where we were going, but Roger said he had to call in to the Longford Inn before we went on somewhere. When we got to the Longford, Roger told me to wait in the car. He got out and disappeared round the back, where the skittle alley was. I waited for a while and started to think there was something wrong. I waited and waited, still he didn't come back so by now I was getting worried. I got out of the car and hobbled in the direction Roger had gone. I hoped he wasn't doing something he shouldn't have been doing because there was no way I was going to make a quick get away. I got to the door of the skittle alley and found it open, but all in darkness. I thought, good god, Roger's robbing the place. I stuck my head through the door and all hell let loose. The lights came on and all my friends and family were there, shouting and singing happy birthday. It was such a shock that for a second, I nearly turned and tried to run. While Cath had been busy keeping my spirits up while I was lying in my hospital bed, Gordon and Wendy had secretly organised a belated birthday party for me and I nearly hadn't gone. I had a wonderful night and it was lovely to be among so many friends. It was the last good night out we were to have for quite a time.

The full impact of not being able to get any benefit, above the small amount of statutory sick pay had not yet fully hit us. Things gradually got worse and I started selling anything I had that had any value at all.

It was mid winter and bitterly cold. The cheapest form of heating was an old paraffin stove. We could light it and site it in the middle of the room. We could sit around it and use it to boil a kettle for a cup of tea at the same time. We had slot meters for the gas, electricity and television, so we often had to make a choice which meter to put any money in. We would usually choose the television, because we could sit in the dark with only the light from the screen but at least we had some entertainment. We didn't always need the gas, because we could use the top of the paraffin heater unless we had a meal to cook, which wasn't every day, even though Cath did her best to bring something home every day. When we had nothing at all, we went to Hughie and Diana's house and sat with them in the evenings.

I sat at home during the day, unable to do very much. It was still painful to move around during the first few weeks. I had no money to do anything anyway, so anyone who came to see me, I asked if they could get me any leftover balls of wool from anywhere. I started to crochet a blanket, to try to keep myself occupied and hopefully end up with something useful at the end. I sat in my chair for hours on end for weeks crocheting this blanket and it turned out okay. I still have it today.

Cath and I went back to the hospital to visit Dennis Mahoney. As we were coming out, a nurse called to me and said that a friend of mine was in one of the side wards.

He was another biker who had had an accident. I went in and saw someone lying in the bed. I looked but didn't know who it was. I said sorry, I don't recognise him and turned to leave. As I turned, a very weak voice said 'hello Cliff.'
It was so weak I hardly heard it, but as soon as I did, a shock of realisation went through me. I knew immediately who it was, but his face was so swollen I hadn't recognised him. It was Phil Coopey, a fellow Scorpion. I left after a few minutes, with tears in my eyes, he looked so bad I didn't know how he could survive, but survive he did and made a full recovery. Like me he still rides a motorcycle almost thirty years later.

It was a bad year for us as bikers, there had been a lot of accidents and then came the worst of all. Harry Gay and John Westbury were killed when they hit a bus, while travelling back to Gloucester from the motorcycle races at Staverton. Harry was twenty one, the same age as me and John was only seventeen. It was a tragedy that hit everyone hard. We had all had spills and we knew that sometimes we lived close to the edge, but we were unprepared for this. In the next few years, more of my friends were to die on the roads. It brings tears to my eyes still, just thinking about it.

As the weeks went by, I started to be able to move about a bit easier. There was no way I would be able to ride the Lightning, but I had an old Cotton 250cc two stroke twin. It was small and light and much easier to handle than the Lightning. The only problem was that if I didn't get the balance over to the left when I had to stop, I couldn't take any weight on the right leg so I had to fall off. I soon got used to it though and didn't fall off very often after the first week. I couldn't start it either, so I always had to wait until someone came to help, either kicking it over, or giving me a push start. Cath got quite good at pushing it while I sat aboard and got it going. Once started I could wait for Cath to get on and we could go visiting, or shopping when we could afford it. I also needed the passenger to carry my crutches which I needed to walk when we got to our destination.

Chris Marchant became my most regular companion on the little Cotton. We used to go round the lanes to Haresfield, to visit his relations or sometimes a drink in the Beacon. Chris had to pay though because I had no money for beer or for petrol. We went all around the country lanes and only fell off a few times. We were coming over Stroud Road hill one afternoon, when I heard a loud whistling sound. I turned to Chris and said, 'what's that noise, Chris'? He started laughing and I could hear a tune playing. I couldn't make out what it was until I saw him with his fingers over the holes in my walking stick. I had traded my crutches for an aluminium adjustable walking stick and the wind was blowing through the holes making a high pitched sound. Chris got quite good at playing tunes on it as we rode along.

Dido Vance also became a regular visitor, we sat for hours in the evenings, talking, listening to rock and roll records, or playing cribbage. The two of us playing cribbage drove Cath mad, for some reason she couldn't stand all the reckoning up. Fifteen two, fifteen four and one for his hat, but Dido was a good friend to both of us, another friendship which has stood the test of time.

Before I had been involved in the accident, along with Hughie MacPherson, I had been a regular darts player at the Union public house in Westgate Street. They had organised a darts team outing, by coach to the Webbington country club near Taunton. It was going to be a nice change to get out to a club with some entertainment and I always enjoyed going anywhere with Hughie.

The drive down was largely uneventful, but soon after our arrival, the serious drinking started. The entertainment consisted of some exotic dancers, who went down well. Then came the top of the bill, the singer Tony Christie. He was very impressive, his stage act and his voice was very powerful. All too soon, it was time to leave. On the coach for the return journey, there was even more beer being consumed and many were much the worse for wear. One who had definitely had too much and was unable to control himself was Ron Watkins. There was an inoffensive young man sitting in the seat opposite mine and I couldn't help hearing Ron giving him a hard time from the seat in front. Ron fancied himself, but the way he was terrorising this person was inexcusable. It was bullying of the worst kind. The man was trembling with fear and looked as if he was going to burst into tears at any moment. Even though I still had my leg in plaster I couldn't let this go on. I said, 'give it a rest Ron.' He told me quite aggressively to mind my own business. I said I'm making my business, leave the lad alone.
Ron turned nasty at that and said, 'keep your nose out or I'll have you next.'
Instantly he made the threat I launched myself across the seat at him. It took him by surprise and he started to go backwards. Some of the other passengers grabbed him and told him to shut up and sit down or they'd all join in and give him the kicking he deserved. He sat down, moaning and grumbling but kept himself to himself for the rest of the trip.

Ron Watkins still holds a grudge over that incident and whenever I went into the Union after that, it was obvious that I was not welcome. Ron's mother, Peggy Watkins was the landlady of The Union and when she retired, Ron took it over.

The Union is now called The Taylor's House. Now Ron himself has retired and to the very end, he didn't like me going in there. I can't understand why anyone should take such an attitude, especially as all I did was stop him making an idiot of himself by beating up a defenceless person while under the influence of alcohol. Still, it's right what they say, 'there's nowt so queer as folk.'

I spent much more time in Southgate Street at the Talbot Inn, with Roger Haines. The landlord, old Jim Price, although a miserable old bastard was usually very easy going. It was a proper biker pub and we never gave Jim any trouble. We used the lounge at the back of the pub, which was a pretty rough room, but had a football table and a pinball machine. We could sit in there and talk or play the machines without being disturbed. Roger was working for Bell Fruit slot machines at the time and used to get hold of lots of tokens that would go in the pinball machine. Jim was constantly complaining about these tokens but he never knew where they came from.

The ceiling in that back room was coloured dirty brown from the effect of smoking over the years. It also had hundreds of silver paper cups of all sizes stuck to it, some of them were up there for all the years I was a regular. Most of these cups were made by taking the silver paper out of cigarette packets, splitting the tissue from the silver paper, making a trophy shaped cup and filling the base with the tissue, made soggy by chewing it, then throwing it up as hard as you could. They hit the ceiling with a splat and stuck there. Some people brought custom made cups of all sizes and hurled them up, just to add a bit of variety. They must have made them from kitchen foil and filled the bases with toilet tissue.

I came out of the back room one evening and went up to the bar. There was an old wino sitting on a bar stool trying to mind his own business, but he was getting a hard time from two young men who had had too much to drink. The wino was clearly terrified by what was happening which was too ridiculous for words. One of the men was accusing him of leering at his girlfriend. The old wino wouldn't look them in the eye, he just kept mumbling his innocence while looking down at the floor. I stood there waiting to be served, listening to this, getting very annoyed. I called to the nasty one of the two, to pack it in. That didn't work, he just told me to shut the fuck up. I smiled and turned back to the bar, continuing to listen. A few moments later, this same man went to punch the old wino, but I was ready for him. I hit him a mighty blow across the head with my walking stick. As he went back, I hit him a few more times but I couldn't move very fast with the plaster on my leg. He composed himself and along with his mate, started to come towards me. As they

190

did so, Jim Price got his solid rubber mangle roller from under the bar and said to them, 'one more step and I'll bash your brains out, fuck off out of my pub.'

It was then that one of them said something that turned out to be very funny. He said, 'we'll come back and sort you out. We'll come back with the Scorpions and do this place.'

I started laughing and asked, 'you know the Scorpions do you?'

I pointed to the lounge doorway and said, 'who do you think they are?' They looked behind them and saw about a dozen bikers ready to rip their heads off.

I said, 'I don't know who you think you know, but they are Scorpions so you'd better get out while you've still got the chance.'

They took my advice and left very quickly.

A few nights later, the least offensive of the two, came back into the pub. He came straight up to me and apologised for the trouble he and his friend had caused. They had had too much to drink and had let it get the better of them. I accepted his apology and held no grudge. The threat to bring the Scorpions in, to sort us out had apparently come from the fact that they worked with one of us and had heard of our exploits, so they thought they could scare me by threatening to return with them.

In August another friend died. Roger Lane was riding down the A38 near Thornbury, when he was in collision with a Jaguar travelling in the opposite direction. He was thrown from his bike and was killed instantly. How much worse could this year get?

At home, things took another turn for the worse but my troubles paled into insignificance, compared to the death toll that was climbing. The council had found out that Gordon had left and Cath had moved in. They sent a man round to tell us we would have to leave the prefab as the tenancy depended on my brother living there as well. I tried to explain the situation but they were having none of it. The man was extremely officious and I asked him to leave. He kept trying to get me to sign a letter agreeing that I had broken the tenancy agreement. I refused, but he kept coming back at all times of the day and night, harassing us and making our lives a misery. After weeks of harassment I'd had enough of it. I grabbed him by the throat and told him that if I saw him again I would squeeze the life out of him. I let him go and as he ran off up the path, he turned his head and shouted that he would come back with the police. I was so angry that I think, if I could have gone after him I would have given him a real battering. I had gotten to hate the sight and sound of him. Becoming homeless was the last thing I wanted to have to worry about what with the problems we already had. However tight money had become, I always made sure that the rent was paid. I had never missed a payment and they had no need to hound me like they did.

After a couple of months of wearing the plastercast, I was relieved to be able to have it cut off. When my leg was revealed, I looked at it and couldn't believe how small and withered it was compared to the other one. It was so weak that I had a terrible limp that I couldn't shake off. It was obviously going to be a long job getting back to full strength. But at least now that the plaster was off, I felt that I was making some progress. I could also see that the leg was never going to be the same again. There was a terrific scar all the way from just below the knee to just above the ankle. There was also a large lump at the front where the muscle had been moved. The stitch marks were huge and unsightly and I was sure I had only got the common man's job. They certainly hadn't tried to make a very nice job of it.

I had to try to walk about as much as I could, to build up some strength in the withered muscles. I still couldn't walk properly without the walking stick but I kept at it as much as I could. Financially, things were gradually getting even worse. It got to a stage where in the dead of night, I started to go over the fence, into the garden next door to steal some vegetables. Only enough to keep us going when we had nothing else. Mr Hooper was a brilliant gardener and he grew all kinds of stuff. Sometimes I would dig a few potatoes without disturbing the plant, I'm sure he must have thought that the yield must have been very poor from some of his plants. Sometimes I would take a cabbage, or a few carrots, anything I thought there was plenty of and he wouldn't miss. It kept us from starving at times.

I continued selling anything I had that was of any value. I sold my BSA Airsporter rifle, some of my record collection, anything anyone would buy. The only thing I wanted to try to keep was the Lightning. It was still in the bedroom, untaxed and with no MOT or insurance. I still couldn't ride it anyway so it was best left where it was.

As time went on, we were able to get about on the little Cotton. We often visited our friends Jeff and Pauline Aston, who lived in a lovely old farm cottage in Sandhurst. The only problem was, when we on our way home at night, the lights on the Cotton were so dim that in the pitch darkness out in the country, I couldn't see the road. There was a bit of a dilemma in that the faster the bike went, the brighter the lights were, but I couldn't go fast because the road was so narrow and twisty. Every so often I had to pull in the clutch and rev the engine to catch a glimpse of which way the road turned. On one occasion we left Sandhurst in the early hours of the morning. As we went along Southgate Street, I slowed down and let the engine tick over as we passed the hospital. I wanted to make as little noise as I could so as not to disturb anyone. Halfway past the hospital a policeman stepped out into the road and stopped us.

He said, you haven't got your lights on.

I revved the bike and the lights came up, I said, 'yes I have, what's that then?'

He could see that I hadn't touched anything except the throttle.

He said, 'that can't be right, can it?'

I said, 'yes, of course it's right, that's the way these bikes are. It's pretty crap I know, but that's how they work. The reason the lights went out was because I was coasting on very low revs to keep the noise to a minimum.' He said, 'okay, on your way, I only stopped you because I was bored anyway.'

Not long after that, I had another experience with the police. There was a knock on the door one evening, so I looked out of the window to see a sergeant and a constable standing at the door. I opened the window and asked what they wanted. The sergeant asked me if I was Mr Ballinger and I answered that I was. He told me that I had dumped a van down at the garages in Seventh Avenue and I must move it or face prosecution. I told him I didn't have a van. He told me that there was no doubt that the van was mine and not to argue, just get it moved. I didn't care much for his attitude, especially as he was wrong.

I said, 'are you some kind of pratt? I've just told you I didn't have a van. I've never had a van. I don't possess a license to drive a van and I've no desire to drive a van, so why don't you fuck off.'

At this point he realised that he must have made a mistake. He asked me again who I was, only this time he added, you are Mr Gordon Ballinger?

I said, 'no I'm not Gordon.'

He said, 'well let me speak to him then.'

I said, 'he's not here, he doesn't live here any more.'

He then asked me for Gordon's address, but since we had fallen out, I had no idea what his address was, not that I would have told this asshole anyway.

I just said, 'I don't know where he lives.'

He came back with, 'you're aiding and abetting him.'

I couldn't help laughing when he said that. I turned to Roger Haines and the others in the room and said, 'did you hear that?'

They said yes, they had heard it and were also laughing. I looked behind the sergeant at the constable and could see that he was having trouble stopping himself laughing as well.

I don't think the sergeant had realised that I had a room full of people listening to this nonsense, because as soon as he heard them, he decided to back off.
He went off up the path looking decidedly sheepish, with our laughter ringing in his ears, knowing he had made a right fool of himself in front of the constable.

Things were getting desperate, I had nothing left worth selling except the bikes. I didn't want to sell either of them as the Lightning was my pride and joy and the Cotton was our lifeline to the outside world. Without it we would be unable to go anywhere.

To their credit, Graham Reeves said they would keep my job open as long as it took for me to get fit enough to return. The problem was that it was a manual job and my leg was gaining strength very slowly. If I didn't get some money before long I was in danger of starving to death. I got dressed up and went off around the industrial areas, limping with the aid of my walking stick from company to company, looking for an office job or anything I could do sitting down. The search was fruitless, I felt very dejected for a while but just had to carry on. I tried the DSS again, but it was a waste of time, they wouldn't help us at all. Cath was a rock through all this, just as she is today. Things would have been much harder for me without her. She kept my spirits up whatever happened. We were desperately poor but we were happy and things could only get better. We loved each other so what could go wrong?

By December, I was getting much stronger. Before the accident, we had been regulars at the rock n roll dances, held on Friday nights at 'The Bell' public house in Stroud. Hughie MacPherson asked us if we wanted to go with him on Friday the 3rd December. We went with him and Diana and had a really good evening. When it was time to leave, Hughie being a very gregarious person had asked a load of people back to his house to keep the evening going. We got there and went in to wait for everyone else to arrive. We waited and waited but nobody else turned up. We were getting worried, when Ian, Hughie's brother came in and said that there had been an accident of some sort, near the bridge over the motorway on the Stroud Road at Brookthorpe. The reason they had been so long getting here, was that they had been diverted through the lanes because the road was completely blocked. We waited a bit longer and some still hadn't arrived so Hughie decided to go out and see what had happened. He came back later and told us that three of the lads from the Forest had been killed on their way here, Geoff Milner, Steve Twynning and John Lee. Two other people, Dennis Bowyer, his wife Eileen and their dog had also been killed in this terrible accident. Five people killed in a horrendous crash at a place that was known for the dangerous condition of the road. They had probably been going too fast, so when they came off the bridge, back on to the normal road surface, they would have felt a big bump where the two surfaces met. It was a horrible place and I had felt that bump many times. They had lost control and ploughed into the car coming in the opposite direction.

Geoff had the most striking blue eyes I have ever seen on a man and in my minds eye I can still see him.

The death toll for this year had reached six, plus two poor people who were unknown to us.

I was hoping that 1972 would be a better year. January started off better, it was just short of a year since my accident by the time I was fit enough to go back to work. It had been a serious injury which still gives me trouble on occasions, but as soon as I got back to work, things started to look up. Fortunately, although it had been very bad financially, there had been no way that we could get into debt by borrowing. The credit card boom had not yet arrived, so apart from paying the rent, which we did religiously, the only other things we had to pay for, gas, electricity and television were by meter, so no debts had built up. We hadn't any other bills such as we have today, like insurance or pension plans. I was never worried about being burgled, there was nothing worth stealing, except for the gas and electricity meters, but I never thought of that. Only if the house had gone up in flames, would we have been really destitute.

From the time I drew my first pay packet, we started getting back to normal. We could afford to buy the food we wanted and Mr Hooper's garden was safe again.

Chapter 15
Tug of War

When I started back to work, a large number of the people I had worked with, were no longer there. While I had been off, about a dozen workers had been sacked for stealing. I had only been back a short time when the police returned the stolen property to Graham Reeves. We had to unload the goods to put them back into stock. I was amazed by the amount of stuff being returned. It came in about three lorry loads, all this having been stolen over a short period of time and had probably gone on for years previously.

During my second week back, I climbed up a stack of stillages and looked into one to see if it contained what I was looking for. It didn't so I jumped down, but as I jumped, the ring on the third finger of my left hand, caught on a spike on top of the stillage so instead of hitting the ground I was suspended a few feet up, hanging by the ring on my finger. I reached up and grabbed the top of the stillage and pulled myself up so I could get a foot back on the top of the one below to enable me to release my finger. I jumped down, this time without incident. I looked at the finger which was already beginning to swell. It looked bad, it was cut almost all the way round and was swelling so fast that I could hardly see the ring. I thought, January isn't being a very good month for me lately. I almost killed myself last year, now I've almost cut my finger off. I'm an Aquarian, this isn't supposed to be happening, This is the dawning of the age of Aquarius.

I was taken to the hospital where they cut the ring off , stitched the finger up and told me to take a couple of weeks off work. There was no chance of me doing that. They did a good job with the finger but I wasn't going to take their advice and take time off work. I had to make some money.

Cath and I were in bed one freezing cold night during that winter, when we both heard a noise outside. Our two dogs, Tina and Wimpy, started to bark furiously, running around the house barking towards where the noise had come from. There were some blackberry bushes at one side of the house and we were used to them scraping the wall during bad weather, but this was different. There was a ripping sound as if someone had caught their clothes on the thorns, then a voice cursing as he tried to free himself. The dogs were beside themselves, I had never seen them so agitated. I leapt out of bed and opened the front door, letting the dogs out. One went one way and one went the other, barking like mad. I put some clothes on and followed them out. They were still running to and fro, searching but finding nothing. There had been a fresh fall of snow that evening and though I looked all around the house, there was no evidence of anyone ever being there. The only prints in the snow belonged to Tina, Wimpy and me. It was a very strange experience that we still talk about.

I still had the same black and white television that dad had rented from Atkinson's in Whitfield Street. It had a slot meter on the back that took two shilling pieces. When the agent came to empty the meter, he took the rental and gave me back the excess, so there was a little money to spare. That television often went wrong as they tended to do in those days. One day it did so I reported the fault and waited for an engineer to call. We had no telephone then, so I had to use the phone box in Sixth Avenue. After a couple of days I walked to the phone box and called again, but still no engineer came. I got on the Bike and rode to Atkinson's shop to tell them that I wasn't very happy. They apologised and promised to send someone as soon as possible. I could do no more so I left the shop. As I was riding down Stroud Road, I passed an Atkinson's service van going in the opposite direction. I braked hard and did a quick turn, speeding after him. Before he got to St Barnabas roundabout, I had overtaken him and flagged him down. I told him the story and that I wanted him to follow me to my house. He wasn't very keen, but I insisted. When we got to the house, he went behind the television and started work on it. He took the back off and was delving around inside it, when there was a terrific bang and a blue flash. I looked at him and he was standing in the corner, trembling, with his hair standing on end. He had obviously had a fair old electric shock because he couldn't even speak properly, he sounded very strange indeed, his voice was all quivery. He did manage to say that he wouldn't be able to fix it and that he had to go. I tried to get him to take the set with him but he was too far gone to get any sense out of him, so I had to let him go. I thought, well that plan didn't work, I'll have to go to plan B. I carried this huge television outside and bungeed it to the back seat of the bike. It was so big I could hardly get on the bike myself, I was going to have great difficulty riding with this huge lump pushing me in the back. I was almost sitting on the tank, but I made it back to the shop. They looked out in astonishment as I pulled up at the door with their television on my back seat. I told them to fix it while I waited or give me another set. They said they couldn't let me take a set on the back of the bike. I said, that's okay, you can deliver it, I'll stay here, in the shop until a van comes in and I'll lead him to my house. They tried to get rid of me but I wouldn't go. I told them that I hoped a van came in before closing time or they would have to lock me in. They got the message and organised a replacement to be delivered immediately. I never did get that old set back.

One evening, Cath and I were sitting watching the television, when we heard a commotion at the back door. Diana MacPherson came rushing in, obviously very distressed. Things had not been going well between her and Hughie and they were on the verge of divorce. This was a cause of great concern for me as they were two of my very best friends and I wished the best for both of them. When Diana calmed down enough to speak, she told me that they had had a row and Hughie was after her with an axe. I couldn't believe it, Hughie was a lot of things but he wasn't violent. I said that I would walk down to her house to see Hughie and find out what was going on. Diana begged me not to go, in case he had gone mad and wouldn't listen to reason. I still couldn't believe it and told her not to worry. When I got to the house, I went round the back and found the door open. I went in and called to Hughie. He answered, come on in, I'm in the hall. I went through the living room, into the hall and found him on his knees hitting some nails into the toilet doorframe with the back of an axe. One of the things Hughie wasn't, was a DIY man with a box full of tools. He didn't even have a hammer.
I said, 'hello mate, what's up then?'
He said rather dejectedly, 'look what I've done to this door, I was having a row with Diana and she locked herself in the toilet and wouldn't come out. I lost my temper and put my shoulder behind the door and broke the frame. When I got in there, she had climbed out of the window and disappeared.'
I told him that Diana was at my house, convinced that he was trying to get her with the axe.
He said, 'I wondered what was wrong with her when she ran off up the street. I came out of the house to go into the shed to get something to mend the door. As I came out of the shed, Diana was coming from round the back. I thought she was coming back into the house, but when she saw me she shrieked, turned and ran off, so I just came in to get on with the job, figuring that she would come back when she calmed down.'
We had a laugh over it but wasn't very funny for Diana.

Jerry Lee Lewis, one of my all time favourite rock and roll idols, came to the Regal in April. We had tickets for the second performance and the buzz of anticipation was high. There were small gatherings of Teddy boys all around St Aldate Street. It was like a scene direct from the 1950's. It was a bit worrying though, the word going round was that the early performance had been crap. People were saying that Jerry Lee was going through a country music phase and wouldn't play rock and roll. We heard that he had played in Southampton prior to coming to Gloucester and had disappointed his fans there.

The show started with a pretty weak band called Country Fever and we hoped that this wasn't an omen about what was to follow. Then came Liz Christian, another country singer. Again it was a pretty uninspired performance, we wanted rock and roll. More precisely, we wanted Jerry Lee Lewis hammering out his particular brand of rock and roll. Next came someone called James Royal. Unfortunately for him, we had had enough by now and wanted 'The Killer' himself. The audience soon started chanting 'off, off, off.' The poor man never stood a chance.

Then, on sauntered a bearded, cigar smoking, very relaxed looking Jerry Lee Lewis. He walked up to the piano and opened with a pounding 'Mean Woman Blues.' The audience erupted with appreciation, but our delight was short lived, Jerry continued the set with what seemed like an endless collection of country and western songs that nobody wanted to hear. We started shouting at him to play 'rock and roll', more and more people started shouting, louder and louder, until suddenly he seemed to realise that he had got it seriously wrong. He asked us what we wanted to hear, so we started shouting out our favourite songs. He blasted straight into 'Great Balls Of Fire' then continued to hammer out all the classics like 'High School Confidential', 'Chantilly Lace' and 'Whole Lotta Shakin Goin On.' The show was really rocking now and when Jerry threw his stool out of the way, I couldn't stop myself. I jumped up and ran to the stage, leaped up onto it and grabbed Jerry by the hand. He looked a bit startled just for a second, but I said to him, 'I'm one of your greatest fans, keep on rocking.' He smiled and thanked me, looking instantly relaxed again. A lot more Ted's had by now got onto the stage and we helped Jerry up on to the piano where he continued to give a brilliant performance. The whole house was rocking and dancing in the aisles, Jerry Lee responded to the attention, like the great showman that he is and gave us a show that no one who was there would ever forget. We went home that night knowing we had seen a rock and roll legend at his best. The tickets had cost £1-75 each, that's what I call good value.

We had been talking with my cousin Hugh about a holiday he was planning. He wanted to hire a cruiser on the Norfolk Broads. He was a nautical type and loved the life on the water. It was a perfect holiday for him. He asked Cath and I, if we would like to go with him and his girlfriend Lynn Gribble. We didn't think we would be able to afford it but Aunty Ina told us that if we saved a little, every week from now to the time of the holiday, which gave us a few months, we would be able to do it. It wasn't an unreasonable amount so we decided to go for it. Every week we gave the money to Aunty Ina for safe keeping so that we couldn't be tempted by it and soon Cath and I had enough to pay for our first holiday together and have a little spending money. It was the first holiday I had ever had that wasn't spent visiting relatives.

We set off for Norfolk in Hugh's Austin 7, loaded with the four of us and our luggage. We were in high spirits in anticipation of our adventure. The old Austin had trouble making the hills and when we got to the hill from Andoversford, out on the Stow road, it became obvious that it wasn't going to make it. Hugh turned the car around and headed back for home. Lynn had a Ford Popular which stood a much better chance of getting us there, so we transferred our luggage and set off for a second time. This time, slowly but surely we got there. A few hours later we arrived at the boatyard to pick up the Chelsea Bridge, a traditional thirty foot, four berth cruiser. After a short introduction to the boat we were on our way into the broads for what turned out to be one of the most memorable holidays we have ever had. The days were warm and long, it was so relaxing, so far away from our normal lives at home. It was just what we needed.

Soon after returning from this holiday, I got a new job at Mead and Tomkinson's motorcycle shop in Westgate Street. I was working in the stores and serving on the parts counter. Working with motorcycles was a dream job for me but as usual, the reality doesn't live up to the dream. I enjoyed working there but it had it's drawbacks as any job has. I didn't like working Saturdays and dealing with the public in a retail situation wasn't my cup of tea. Mr Mead had dozens of valuable vintage and classic bikes, hidden away from general view. Every chance I got I would go up onto the balcony where they were kept and walk around looking at them. That building in Westgate Street was huge and the amount of old bikes and spares hidden away was phenomenal.

One night I was with the Scorpions in the cellar bar at the back of the Dirty Duck, in Ladybellegate Street. We were having a good night out, but it was a bit rowdy in there and for a change, it wasn't us making the noise. There were some lads in there I didn't know who were making a general nuisance of themselves, but making sure they kept away from us. Suddenly one of them started a fight, he was punching some unfortunate lad who was being driven backwards by the force of the attack. They came past me in a flurry of punches swinging from all angles and ended up with the lad who was being attacked falling backwards onto a bench with his assailant on top of him, punching him in the face. We had all moved out of the way as they had come barging through, but I was closest to the action and had been knocked aside. I turned and grabbed the assailant by the collar dragging him off his victim, saying as I did so, 'that's enough mate, give it a rest.' He jumped to his feet and as he turned, he swung a vicious punch at my face which I only just managed to avoid. As the punch came in, I just managed to lean backwards enough to make it miss, but it caught the corner of my glasses and whipped them clean off my face. The lads must have been ready for something to happen because the response was so fast that even though I had been standing directly in front of my attacker, there were so many Scorpions laying into him that I couldn't get through the crush to get at him. In a few seconds it was all over, someone came up to me and handed me my glasses, thankfully undamaged. I looked down at this pathetic, beaten body lying on the floor, none of his mates had come to his aid, they had realised that discretion was the better part of valour. We were in a pretty buoyant mood but that didn't mean we were any the less dangerous when necessary. One of the bouncers came through the crowd to see what had been going on. He also lived by that same motto about discretion, he wasn't going to upset us, even if it had been our fault, which this time it wasn't. Anyway, it was much easier to throw out the weaker strangers and leave us alone. The bouncer helped him up and as they started to move past us, I said to the lad, 'that was the biggest mistake you've ever made, wasn't it'? He didn't answer, I don't think he could, he was so battered.

We came out of The Dirty Duck and made our way down Eastgate Street to the Sun Wah Chinese restaurant. The first few of us went in but Pete, the owner, didn't want the whole gang in so as soon as we sat down he went to the door and locked it, then drew the curtains so no one could see in. When the rest of the lads arrived, Pete stood behind the locked door, shouting 'we are closed.' Try as they might he wouldn't let them in. We were in though so Pete came to our table and told us he wouldn't serve us until we paid what we owed him from last time when we had done a runner. We pleaded with him to serve us, so he asked to see the money first. He took what he estimated we owed him from last time then took some more and said he would bring us food to the value of what he had taken. He brought out a good meal and we all enjoyed it immensely. We often did a runner, but we never gave Pete any trouble and we always paid in the end. He never called the police to us even though we were pretty rowdy at times. Sitting opposite us, was Chummy and a man he had picked up in the pub across the road. We were all a bit worse for drink and started to give them a hard time. Chummy kept telling us to shut up or we would spoil it. We couldn't believe that the stranger hadn't realised that Chummy was a man, but he hadn't. As we kept making these loud comments it dawned on him. I've never seen anybody look more embarrassed.

I had the Lightning back on the road now and I had also picked up an old Triumph Tiger Cub that I was using to have some fun on. I sprayed it with fluorescent pink paint that glowed in the dark. I could abuse it without having to worry about damaging it. I rode it around for a while until Brian Jones, a friend of mine said he had a 1953 Triumph Thunderbird in his garage and he would like to do a deal with me for the Cub. The Thunderbird wasn't running but I was still interested so I went to his house to see it. When he opened the garage I saw this nice looking bike and couldn't believe that he wanted to get rid of it. It had a sidecar on it but I could soon get that off. He said he had never been able to get it going properly and was fed up with it. I had a look at it and immediately realised that the valve timing wasn't set correctly, I reset it and had the bike running like a dream within half an hour. The deal was done, I handed over twenty quid and the Cub and prepared to ride home on the Thunderbird. Brian was going to follow me home in his car, to get the logbook for the Cub. It was a good job he did because I had never ridden a bike with a sidecar, especially one so badly set up as this. A mile or so up the road I stopped and said to Brian, 'I can't ride this, it's horrendous.' Brian said, I'll ride it home for you, you take my car. I didn't have a licence to drive a car, but I could drive better than I could ride that bike. As soon as I got it home, I took the sidecar off and tried it again. It rode beautifully, it wasn't fast but it was very smooth, I enjoyed riding it no end. I started riding it to work in preference to the Lightning, although I still rode the Lightning for fun, there was no comparison in performance.

I left Mead and Tomkinson's after only a few months and started a new job at Dowty Hydraulic Units at Arle Court in Cheltenham. I worked for a short time in the general stores, then I was put in charge of a bonded store specifically for a product for the Eaton Yale Corporation of America. The store was kept locked at all times except when taking things in and out, I locked myself in while I was working and answered a doorbell when anyone wanted me. I worked closely in association with Ray Lock, the planner and Dave Toomey, the progress chaser on the project and soon got to know a great deal about it. One day Dave rang the bell to come in, he had one of the trolleys we used, to make up the kits of parts needed to assemble the finished product. These trolleys had two wheels at one end and a ball hitch on the other end which could be connected to a handle with two small wheels on it, allowing the work movers to wheel them around the factory. They would leave the trolleys where they were needed and take the handles away with them, like small articulated vehicles. It was unusual to see Dave with one of these trolleys as it wasn't part of his job. I opened the doors for him to wheel the trolley through and went back to my desk. I could see him pushing the trolley backwards through the door when all of a sudden I heard a bang. The trolley came flying through the doorway followed by Dave falling flat on his face. Just as he looked up, the handle of the trolley came loose and hit Dave square on the forehead almost knocking him out. It was like something out of a comedy sketch and I couldn't help laughing even as I was trying to help him. He had pushed up against a large platform that had been stood on its edge up against the wall opposite the doorway, which had slowly fallen over hitting him on the back of legs, throwing him forward and trapping his legs under it. I don't know how, but I managed to lift the platform off his legs to give him some relief, then went to raise the alarm. He was taken to the company sick bay and then to the hospital where he was found to have a slight fracture in one of his bones. It was clear he was going to be off work for some time.

I told them that if they put another storeman in to cover my job, I would do the progress chasing job until Dave came back. They took me up on the offer and immediately increased my wages to the correct rate for the job. I took to it like a duck to water and enjoyed it more than any other job I had done before. Some weeks later I was told that Dave had decided not to return and the job was mine if I wanted it.

Things were starting to look up, I was feeling pretty good about life. After a shaky start, this hadn't been such a bad year. Cath and I were getting on really well, I think we were made for each other. I asked her to marry me and she said yes. We were going to a Christmas party with some friends and family at the Rorty Crankle Club at the Tudor Arms in Slimbridge, so we chose a ring for Cath and decided to announce our engagement at the club. It was a lovely evening, one I will always remember.

1973 dawned and things were still going well, except for the continual harassment from the council to get me out of the prefab. It had been like a nagging pain for more than a year, but I hadn't done anything wrong so they were having difficulty making me do something I didn't want to do. They told us we would have to move into a one bedroom flat, but I just kept telling them to bugger off. They threatened us with eviction but they couldn't frighten me, I just told them to bugger off some more, but louder.

Talking to Wanger Wainwright one day, he told me that his new band '9.30 FLY' were playing in Hay on Wye and asked me to come along. He said it would be a good gig. I hadn't seen them for a while so decided to make the trip. Cath, myself and Wendy Pyart went, in Wendy's Mini. The weather was abominable, the rain was so bad, we were starting to worry whether we would make it or not, but make it we did. When we got there, we told the doorman we were with the band and were shown into the dressing room. Wanger, his wife Barbara, Lyn Oakey, Gary Charman and Mickey Clark, they were all there, larger than life. It was the Glam rock era and they certainly looked the part, all made up and wearing shiny clothes. We had a good laugh and soon it was time for the performance. We went out front and waited for the band to come on. Dramatically, all the lights went out, the curtains opened to a totally dark stage, then suddenly the lights came on and the band made a powerful start. Even at the volume they were playing, they were all but drowned out by screaming teenagers, I could hardly believe the reception they got, it was like the Beatles had come on. They played a brilliant set and I could see why they were so popular. I thought maybe they would go all the way to the top but it wasn't to be. They certainly had the talent. They made an album which is now a very valuable collectors item. It is one of my regrets that I didn't get one. I went into HMV to buy one but they had sold out, I tried to order one but it never came. I now have it on CD but it's not like having the original.

Phil Large and his girlfriend Ruth, decided to do some travelling. They asked if we would look after some of their belongings while they were gone. It was no problem to us so we told them to leave anything they wanted. Phil turned up with his old van filled with the disco gear and a few household bits and pieces. He told us to use anything we wanted, while they were away. He set up the disco gear in the front room so we could keep it warm. It had two huge speaker cabinets, a two hundred watt amplifier and twin decks. The power was phenomenal, the neighbours were going to suffer now. When I turned up the volume, the ornaments vibrated off the sideboard. They left a lampshade, a big faceted globe, which I fell in love with, but best of all, Phil left one of his paintings which I thought was the most interesting painting I had ever seen. When they returned for their stuff, that was the thing I missed the most.

I was still working at Dowty's and getting on well. The job was challenging but very enjoyable. I was on the canteen complaints committee, representing my fellow workers and had got to know many senior employees with whom Cath and I started to meet socially. A long way from the Biker image in a very short space of time. I decided that it was about time I took my driving test in a car.

Things were going well, but I was about to press the self destruct button. I had never committed to anything in my life and I was being torn apart by the thought of getting married. There was a tug of war going on in my head and I didn't know which side was going to win. Eventually, I told Cath that we had to split. She couldn't understand what had gone wrong and was really upset. I couldn't understand what had gone wrong either, but I couldn't help myself. I felt trapped and I had to be alone again. Our friend, Roy Mayo had a car and was kind enough to help Cath with her belongings and take her home to her parents.

A few weeks after we had split up, I put in for my driving test. I went to a driving school for a trial lesson and the instructor said, 'I'm not going to get rich out of you am I'? He advised me to apply for my test immediately. I told him I'd already applied and that the test was scheduled for two weeks later. I had two more lessons, then had the car for my test which I passed without incident. I had arranged to buy a Ford Thames van from Cath's dad, so I went to the house and did the deal for £40. I drove away in my first legal car, or more accurately van. That little Thames van had a three speed gearbox with a column change and windscreen wipers that went slower as the van went faster, they ran off the vacuum of the engine. Who designs features like that? Anyway I drove the van to work during the day and still rode bikes at night.

I swapped the old Thunderbird for a BSA A10 Chopper, with my friend Zip Jordan. I felt real cool riding it and knew that this was the way the Lightning would ultimately go. I had seen Easy Rider and was trying to get closer to the ideal, which was a Harley Davidson, but that was to be a long time coming.

I went out with the lads one night and got pissed up. On the way home, I went to the Chinese takeaway in High Street, got myself a curry and stuck it inside my coat. As I rode along Finlay Road, I heard a siren, looked behind and saw the blue light flashing. I thought, Oh bollocks! I took off as fast as the A10 would go, but this was no Lightning, I went round the roundabout at St Barnabas and opened up along Southern Avenue, with the police car right up close behind me. It was obvious I wasn't going to outrun him on this old tub, so when I got to Firwood Drive, I braked as hard as I could and swerved to the left into it. The police car did the same and within a few yards, he swerved in front of me like the Highway Patrol in the American movies. The copper jumped out of the car with a look of fury on his face. I knew I was in the shit this time but I wasn't going to let them see that I was worried. He started the usual crap about, do you know what speed you were doing? I didn't care about the speeding ticket, it was the fact that I was over the drink drive limit that was worrying me.
I decided to go on the offensive and said, 'yeah I know how fast I was going, I've got a curry under my coat and I'm trying to get home before it gets cold, so cut the speeches, give me the ticket and fuck off.'

The copper seemed to go into shock and couldn't write the ticket out fast enough. He ripped it off the pad and gave it to me. I took it, stuffed it in my coat pocket and started the bike up. He fired a parting shot, telling me to be more careful in future. I said, 'yeah, cheers mate' and roared off into the night. I was sweating with relief as I rode the last mile home, I had got away without having to take a breathalyser. I knew how lucky I had been and never again drove after I had been drinking.

As the year wore on, I started to make more use of the little van, one weekend I took Angel (Christine) and her brother to a motorcycle scramble at Fostons Ash. To get to the event we had to bump our way down a long track, through a field. The track was bumpy in the extreme, with a big hump in the middle which kept scraping the underside of the van. On the way home, we went down Birdlip Hill. As we picked up speed, I pressed the brake pedal and realised all was not as it should be. The pedal was decidedly spongy and the more I pressed it, the worse it got. Soon there was no braking effect at all and we were gathering speed at an alarming rate. I started to haul on the handbrake but that had never been very effective and made no difference at all. I tried to change gear but with only a three speed gearbox, the ratios were so wide, I couldn't change down at the speed we had already reached. All I got was a lot of crunching and grating noises. We just kept going faster and faster. Faster I think, than that little van had ever been before. Fortunately, nothing came in the opposite direction, because I was using all of the road, trying to get round the bends, travelling at tremendous velocity. When we reached the main road, at the Twelve Bells, I was praying that nothing would be coming past the junction at the same time as we were going to shoot out of the side road. Again we were lucky, I looked to my right and saw a car coming, but it was far enough away that we could get out in front of it easily. From there, going up the hill towards the Cross Hands, we managed to slow down and drive gently, using the gears and the handbrake, making it the rest of the way home. Angel and I had known each other for years, she was good fun to be with and we went out together a few times.

I met with the Scorpions, in the Dirty Duck, to find them engaged in a council of war. One of us had been to a gig in Cheltenham and had been threatened with a knife and made to leave, by some of the 'Wolves', an outlaw gang. It was decided that this could not go unchallenged. About twenty of us made our way to Cheltenham to find the ones responsible. We went to a few of their known haunts, without success, but eventually we heard that they were at a dance at the Tithe barn in Bishops Cleeve. We made our way there looking for a showdown, but unknown to us, word had reached the Wolves that we were coming. I was driving my van and had a few of the lad's with me. There was a small convoy of cars and vans, no bikes on this raid. I drove into the front entrance of the Tithe Barn and instantly realised that if I got caught in here, I wouldn't be able to get out, so I kept right on going, back out of the drive, onto the road, where I parked a little way away. I saw the other vehicles parking all around. We got out of the van and started to walk towards the entrance. As we reached it, I saw that the fighting had already started. Johnny Myatt was laying into some big hairy assed biker, but what was worrying was the amount of the enemy, pouring out of the door of the Tithe Barn. There were only about twenty of us and I think we must have been outnumbered by at least five to one, but the Wolves were about to learn what a mean fighting machine, the Scorpions were. We stood together, not getting split up and moved through the opposition, knocking down anyone in the way. We weren't having it easy though and it soon became obvious that weight of numbers was going to wear us down before long. Suddenly we came across a big man, wielding a crash helmet, to great effect. As anybody went for him he lashed out with the helmet, knocking a couple of our number down. I went to jump him from the side, but as I moved, he saw me and went to go for me. I backed off as fast as I could, without taking my eyes off him. One of the others went for him and took his attention just long enough for me to jump him and get my arms round him, preventing him from swinging the helmet. That was all the rest of the gang needed, he was knocked down and stomped into the ground. Then we moved on. By this time, the police had arrived. At one point, they came into the grounds of the Tithe barn and tried to mediate, but that didn't last long. The fighting started again, right in front of them, with such ferocity that they withdrew, deciding to wait at a safe distance until it blew itself out. We were getting the upper hand, despite the odds, because we had stuck together, but as the fight started to spread out and some of the Scorpions started to pursue some of the runners, it started to get more dangerous. A few of us went back to my van and piled in. We drove a short way down the road and waited for the rest to arrive. When some of them didn't come, I decided to go back to see what had happened. As I drove past the Tithe Barn, the police tried to stop me, but I kept going as far as the memorial, passing casualties all along the road. We passed the missing van and saw that it was surrounded by a large number of Wolves. I turned the van round, to go back the way we had come, intending to launch an attack on the men surrounding our friends. As I stopped, we were immediately surrounded by a large baying mob. They started throwing bricks which were bouncing off the van, including the windscreen, which mercifully didn't break. I knew we couldn't do any more so I sped off, with a Wolf hanging on to one of my wing mirrors. He soon dropped off as I built up speed. We had done well, but had had to withdraw due to weight of numbers and we had lost some of our men. It wouldn't go down as one of our best victories. The boys left behind hadn't given up though, things were getting bad so one of them opened a door and fired off a shotgun, scattering the mob. At this, the police moved rapidly in and arrested all the occupants of the van.

That was the last battle I ever fought alongside the Scorpions. It was part of an age of badass bikers that was coming to an end. The Wolves went on for a few years, eventually giving way to other outlaw clubs. The Scorpions just faded away. Thankfully, even the outlaw clubs have a much more respectable outlook these days. Bikers tend to come in all ages and from all walks of life now and the influence of the more mature men probably leads to a better attitude, whereas all bikers tended to be young men when I rode with the Scorpions in the late sixties, early seventies.

Chapter 16
Heart Beat

I was living life in the fast lane, I was young free and single but was missing Cath almost all of the time. I was making the best of it until one night, my cousin Hugh I were in the Tabard pub in Northgate Street. It was the 'in place' for a while and was very busy. Suddenly I saw Cath across the room. I immediately became agitated and was on the point of leaving. Hugh thought it was because I didn't want to see Cath, but nothing could have been further from the truth, my heart was beating so fast I had that buzzing feeling in my chest. The problem was, I wanted her but I knew the split had been my fault and I was scared she would reject me. Eventually I had to do something, so I went to her and said that I needed to talk to her. She agreed and that was the start of us getting back together, we were friends again.

Things were different though, Cath was living with her parents and we were back to being an engaged couple, but living apart. It worked okay, but sometimes I hated taking her home, I wanted us to be together all the time, so one night when I was taking her home in the little van, I said, 'I'm getting fed up with this, I think we'd better get married.' Not very romantic but Cath agreed and we went as soon as we could, to the Register Office to get our wedding day booked.

They told us we would have to wait for weeks before we could get a date, which I wasn't very happy about. Then they told us we could have a special licence, allowing us to be married in ten days time. We said, that's the one for us, there's nothing to arrange, we'll take it. The special license cost more than an ordinary one but it was the best seven pounds I've ever spent.

We invited a few friends and family and on the bright blue morning of the sixth of October 1973 we arrived at the Gloucester Register Office, to be married. Cath looked lovely and I was as proud as a peacock. I had asked my brother Gordon to be my Best Man but when we were called into the room where the ceremony was to be performed, Gordon and his girlfriend Wendy, were still not here. We waited for a while, getting a little concerned. The registrar mentioned that we might have to choose someone else, then there was a screech of tyres outside and I knew Gordon had arrived. There was a thunderous noise as he came bounding up the stairs, bursting red faced into the room, saying breathlessly, 'I'm not too late am I?'

From then on, the ceremony went as planned and a few minutes later, we were husband and wife.

We had decided not to have a reception, mainly because we had no money, but Aunty Ina wouldn't hear of it and laid on a reception at her house. We all went there and had as good a time as anybody could wish for, with just a few people but all very important.

We had very little money to spend on a honeymoon either, but we were ardent speedway fans and as it was the last match of the season, we decided to go to Swindon to watch it and the big firework display, which was always held on the last night. We had a good evening at the match, then made our way into Swindon, where we sought out an Indian restaurant that was owned by an old friend of Hughie MacPherson. We had promised Hughie that we would look him up and tell him that Hughie was emigrating to Australia. After the meal, we booked into The Goddard Arms Hotel and spent our first night as husband and wife. It was my first experience of staying in an hotel. I was initially horrified at the price of what I saw as just a bed for the night but in the end I didn't begrudge the £7.96 it cost for the room and breakfast for the two of us. Next morning after breakfast, we set out in the little Ford Thames van, for London. We had a day walking around the sights of London, then went to Aylesbury to visit Cath's nan and granddad and finally made our way back home. Not much of a wedding and honeymoon by today's standards, but it was what we could afford and we were happy just to be together.

Two weeks after our wedding, Hughie, his second wife June and their new-born son Michael, left for their new life in Australia. It was a time of very mixed emotions for me. Hughie was a very important person in my life and I knew that I would miss him forever, but I wished him the best of luck for his great adventure.

Fortunately, the fact that Hughie and Diana divorced made no difference to my relationship with either family. I am still close to all of them, whether near or far.

Cath and I were still having trouble with the council over the tenancy of the prefab, but now they were saying we would have to accept a one-bedroom flat or face eviction. I went to the council office and put my case to them that it was only a two bedroom prefab, which had been my home for twelve years and was unlikely to last much longer before demolition. They were unsympathetic to that argument so I made a deal with them that if they offered me a reasonable flat in a nice area then I would take it, but if they continued with the sort of offers and threats they had so far tried, I would continue to fight my case. I pointed out that they had been trying to get me to move for three years and I was sure I could hang on another three years, one way or another. That worked, the next place they offered was a nice flat, in Prescott Avenue, Matson, overlooking Robinswood Hill. Prescott Avenue was a quiet little road with fields directly opposite, ideal for Wimpy to run around, Tina had died some time ago. It was a nice flat, but so small. I wasn't used to living in such cramped conditions. It was much warmer than the prefab, but I knew where I would rather have been.

I had gradually got fed up with my job at Dowty's. I was still a restless young man looking for something new. I got a job that was totally different, delivering bread to shops, for Sunblest bakery in Lower Tuffley Lane. For two weeks, I went with an experienced man, on a run around the Witney area to learn the job. Right from the start, I knew I had made a big mistake, this job was a nightmare. Everybody stole from everybody else, it was a way of life. The system was, that each deliveryman had to pay for whatever was loaded on his van. At the end of the week, we had to collect the money for the deliveries we had made, then pay the bill for the goods that had been invoiced to our van. If there was a shortfall, it had to be made up out of our wages. If there was a surplus, it was ours to keep. This led to a system of wholesale fiddling throughout the whole depot. People stole from all of their customers, in many different ways. They also stole from their colleague's vans if they could. Anything to increase the amount of bread and cakes they could sell. The fiddling was so rife that each delivery man kept a book detailing how much he fiddled from each of his customers, in case he was off sick or on holiday. Then whoever took over the round could continue the thefts without causing suspicion. I saw a driver who had been sacked from FMC for theft, doing a round and thought how apt a job it was for him. Then I heard of a driver getting caught, but instead of sacking him, they moved him to another round. After the two week training period, I only lasted a week on my own, then packed it in without working any notice.

As luck would have it, a few days later, I was parking my car in Weddel's company car park in Longsmith Street, when I bumped into Neville Wilkins, the manager of British Beef Co. I told him the bread story and he immediately said, I've got a driving job you can have if you want it. I jumped at the chance and started back to work with my old friends.

I drove all over the country delivering meat, but mainly I travelled the south of England, only venturing north occasionally. I started driving a three tonner, the only small lorry in the fleet. It was nice, having my own lorry, as all the others had to take any vehicle they were given. There was no such thing as a tacograph then, so if I could make up time anywhere on the journey, I could use it as I pleased. With the early morning starts of around two or three o clock, I often needed a nap during the day, in order to keep going. Sometimes driving was extremely dangerous due to nodding off at the wheel. One morning while driving down the M5 towards Taunton I heard a knocking sound, tap, tap, tap, then I awoke with a start and realised I was knocking down a row of cones covering some road works.

On Saturday mornings, I had a regular run, delivering to shops within a sixty mile radius of Gloucester, west into Wales. When delivering to shops, it was traditional that if we helped the shopkeeper by carrying the meat into the shop, we were rewarded with a small tip, usually in the form of a piece of meat or a chicken or a couple of tins of something. Some weeks, I was given so much food I didn't know what to do with it all. I would put it in boxes and have to make two trips to the car, to carry it all into the house. Very soon we realised that we would have to buy a freezer to keep the meat in. We bought the biggest freezer we could get into the flat and had great difficulty getting it up the stairs, but it was worth its weight in gold. We soon started to fill it and were eating better than we had in years.

One day, one of the drivers was accused of stealing a lorry load of meat. The police arrested him and went to his house for a search. They found a terrific haul of tinned food and a freezer full of meat, similar to what they would have found in any of the driver's houses. The police thought they had hit the jackpot and loaded all the food into a police van and took it away as evidence. When the police told Neville of their find, he told them that it was probably all legitimate, as the accused had tried to tell them. They couldn't believe that so much stuff could be accrued honestly, but that's how it was, so they had to take it all back with an apology. No one was ever caught for that robbery.

The depot was in St Oswalds Road, where the new Tesco supermarket is now. They never lit it at night and it was a very dark place, ideal for thieving, which happened on a regular basis. I went in one morning, opened the door of my lorry and thought, what a nuisance, the interior light has gone out. It was a bit inconvenient without an interior light, because I was never sure where I would be going until I looked at my delivery notes. The lorry was often loaded after I had gone home for the day. I put the key into the ignition and turned it. Nothing happened, so I realised that it wasn't the light at all, perhaps the battery had gone flat. I got out of the lorry and went to have a look at the battery, but there wasn't one. Somebody had taken it, cutting the cables and the battery carrier in the process.

Eventually they decided to put me through my Heavy Goods Vehicle test, so that I would be able to drive any of the lorries on the fleet. I had been driving long enough to be pretty good at it already and passed the test easily. Now my horizons opened up and I was on an equal footing to all the other drivers.

It meant that I would no longer have my own lorry, but it had more advantages than disadvantages. Some of the big trucks were really nice. The system they had was to tell us, before we went home, what lorry we would take the next day and roughly where we would be going. There was a strongbox bolted to the wall, which contained all the keys. When we came in at our starting time, say three o clock in the morning, there would be no one about and the place would be in total darkness. We clocked in, then went to the strongbox and took out the keys we required. We opened the door to the lorry, checked the delivery notes to make sure we had the right one, then drove off. I came in one morning and saw that the lorry I had been told to take was empty. I thought, well that's handy, now I've got to go through them all, one by one, until I find which one they've loaded for me. I went through them but didn't find my load. Then I went to the driver's door of the empty one and saw the broken glass. I opened the door and found the delivery notes inside. The load had been stolen, the whole lot was gone without trace.

Some Saturday mornings, I went to work at about one o clock to help load for the shop run. At about three, we were sitting in the canteen looking out at the ATS tyre depot across the road. There was an articulated lorry backed into the building and we remarked that it was very unusual for them to be taking a delivery this early. We could see the men walking around, wearing the ATS uniforms and stopping for cups of tea and thought little of it. A few hours later with the arrival of an army of police, it dawned on us that the lorry we had seen wasn't being unloaded, it was being loaded. Thieves had taken a forty foot trailer load of tyres out of there and we hadn't even realised.

With all the thieving going on, it wasn't unusual to come to work in the middle of the night and spot an unusual car in the car park. It was quite funny at times because we could see the detectives sliding down in their seats, trying to keep out of sight as our headlights came to bear on them.

One Saturday morning I set out for Monmouth, arriving at six o clock. I made the delivery, then made for my next call in Abergavenny. A few minutes before seven, I was only about a hundred yards from the shop, in the main street, when I heard a terrific bang. There was a shower of glass and the lorry bucked high into the air, careering across the road almost going into a shop front. I managed to turn the wheel away from the shop and stop the lorry at an angle of about forty five degrees across the road. I jumped out and ran back towards the car that had run into me. It was an amazing sight, an elderly couple were sitting in what was left of their Morris Marina. I later found out that they had been driving through the night from the ferry at Haverford West and probably through tiredness, they hadn't realised they had come to a junction and they thought they were still on the main road. They hit the side of my lorry at full speed of about fifty miles an hour without braking. Shops surrounded the junction on both sides and there was a small road opposite which was a service road for a hotel. They hadn't seen anything coming and the first thing they knew was when they hit me. They were very fortunate that they hit my front wheel, because a few feet back and they would have gone underneath the lorry taking their heads off. As it was, they had just caught my front wheel stopping them dead, my back wheels running over the front of the car. That was what had launched me into the air.

When I reached them, I could hardly believe my eyes. They were sitting in what was left of a car, with no front on it. The wheels had been flattened and the engine was some yards away. There was nothing left in front of the bulkhead, but they were relatively uninjured, just a few cuts and bruises. After making a statement at the police station, I was able to continue with my round, albeit a couple of hours late. It was a horrible, cold wet morning and with the window broken, I was perished all the rest of the journey, but at least I had come out unscathed. I felt quite sorry for the old couple, I heard later that he had been prosecuted for driving without due care and attention.

I started doing a regular delivery in Woolwich, South London. On one of these runs, I managed to fit in a visit to my old mate from the marines, Alfie Hammond. I had found out that he had married and bought a house in Woolwich, so early one morning I knocked on his door. It was a lovely reunion, I was so impressed with Alfie's house and what he had achieved. While we talked, Alfie told me that the house had cost £13,000 and although it was difficult paying the mortgage, it was well worth it.

Houses were much more expensive in London than they were in Gloucester and all the way home I was thinking, 'if Alfie can do it at that price, I'm sure Cath and I can do it.' I was very excited by the idea of owning my own home, it was something we had talked about, due to the harassment we had endured from the Council. I wanted never to be in the position of being told where to live ever again. Talking to Alfie made up my mind that it didn't need to be just a dream, I resolved to get on and do something about it. That very weekend, we went looking at houses.

We looked at lots of small houses at Matson, Podsmead and Quedgeley, all over the place, but none compared with the houses along Brionne Way for value for money at around £9,000. The only problem was that there weren't any left on the first phase of development, but if we waited a year, we could have our pick of the second phase, so we chose a plot from the map and put a deposit of fifty pounds to secure our new house. Now we had a year to save the ten per cent required by the building society in order to obtain the mortgage. We were almost there.

Prescott Avenue was undergoing a period of change. The Council had made it into a cul de sac and put a new road through from Matson Avenue to Reservoir Road. They were going to build a new housing estate on the fields in front of our flat, but for the time being all they did was lay the roads. At night it was pitch dark across the new site. When it had been a green field it seemed all right, but now it seemed sort of dangerous, with people moving around in the darkness.

Late one night there was a tremendous loud banging and shouting. As we went to the door, we could hear girls voices shouting, 'HELP! HELP! PLEASE HELP!'
I opened the door to two very distressed girls who quickly told me that they thought there was a rape in progress, in a car parked in the darkness in the middle of the building site. I told them to take me quietly to where it was happening. As we approached the car, there was indeed something badly wrong. A girl was screaming and the car was rocking about as if a fight was in progress. I stole quietly to the driver's door of the Ford Anglia crouching low so that I wouldn't be seen. My heart was beating so hard I thought they might hear it. I waited for a few seconds trying to be sure of what was going on, then I heard a slap followed by another scream. At that moment, I yanked open the car door, grabbed the man by the collar of his jacket and pulled him out of the car onto the road. I had him down so that he had difficulty moving and was about to make sure he wasn't going to escape, when I heard the girl in the car saying, please don't hurt him.
I said, 'What?'
She repeated, 'please don't hurt him, we were having a row.'

She had been having a fight with her boyfriend, I could hardly believe it. It had sounded like she was being murdered. I was so angry at the distress I and the two girls had been caused, I felt like still belting him, but I just told them to clear off.

Some time after that incident, we were sitting watching the television one wild and wet evening when there was a blinding flash outside and all the lights went out. I went out and had a look around and soon realised that along with the flat downstairs, we were the only ones with a power cut. I went to the phone box and reported the fault. Cath got the candles out and placed them around the room. After a while, an engineer arrived to find out what had happened. Apparently there had been some underground damage done when they had dug up the road while making it into a cul de sac. With the storm we were having, the water must have got into the area of damage and caused the small explosion we had witnessed. The engineer told us it would be a considerable job and it would be some time before power would be restored. I told him we could manage all right but it was really cold and I had tropical fish that would all die if I couldn't keep the water warm. He said, don't worry I'll get you a gas fire. Keep the room as hot as you like, then the water won't cool. Off he went, returning a short while later with a portable gas fire and a couple of bottles of gas. I lit it and the temperature soon rose to an acceptable level.
We went to bed unconcerned over the welfare of the fish. That MEB man was the first official in my experience who had ever done what he said he would do. It got so warm in that room that when we got up in the morning, the candles had all bent double from the heat. Next day, the power was restored and the MEB collected their fire, for which we were very grateful.

I decided that I was going to do a real custom job on the Lightning. I had no room to work on it here though, not like the spare bedroom at the prefab. My friend Roger Haines was the manager of Bell Fruit Machines in Cheltenham. They had a warehouse with plenty of spare room, which Roger let me use. I started on the most ambitious project to date. I was going to use a different frame to turn it into a real chopper. I welded the tank to the frame, then moulded it in, so that it looked all one piece, then I loaded it into the back of my British Beef lorry and took it to a top class custom painter in Bournemouth. A few weeks later I picked up a magnificent transformation and delivered it to my workshop in Cheltenham ready for assembly.

That wasn't the first bike I had carried in a meat lorry. Some time earlier, Neville the manager, had asked me if I would take a moped to his sister in Exmouth. I told him that it was dodgy for me to have a moped in the back of a food wagon. If an inspector saw it, I would be in big trouble, but I said I would do it for him. I just wanted him to know that it was a big favour. I also took a plank so that I would be able to roll the moped off when I got there. Neville's sister thanked me for the delivery and offered me some money. She said, 'I know how tight Neville is, I don't suppose he'll give you anything.' I didn't want it but she insisted. Neville did have a bit of a reputation for tight fistedness, she knew him well. When I got back to the depot, I told Neville I had made the delivery with no problems. He took me aside and thanked me, giving me a couple of quid. I laughed like hell when I got outside. I had never known Neville part with any money that he didn't have to.

There had always been lots of fun, working at British Beef. It was often very hard work but there were lots of good times and practical jokes. Cath and I went regularly to Swindon speedway and while driving there one Saturday evening, Cath started accusing me of farting. I protested my innocence but as the smell got worse, Cath got angrier and wouldn't believe that it wasn't me. On the way home, the smell came into the car again and I realised that something was wrong. I got out of the car and looked under the bonnet but couldn't see anything. The next day, I got under the car and had a look around, but again I found nothing. I knew they had done something but I couldn't find out what. My suspicions were confirmed by the sniggering when I said anything about it. It took me another week to find the cause of the offensive odour. Someone had got under the car and wired an Ox spleen to an almost inaccessible piece of exhaust pipe. Not only was the spleen rotting, every time the exhaust got hot, it got cooked as well.

Another favourite was to carry a large rubber bin up the stairs, which led to the mess room. When at the top of the stairs, it was balanced on the edge of the top step, then filled with about fifty gallons of cold water. The stairs had a turn in them, halfway up, so when the unsuspecting victim turned the corner, he was met with a wall of water, which often sent him sprawling back to the bottom.

Many an apprentice was stuffed into the wicker laundry basket and thrown down those stairs.

More serious, but just as funny. A slaughterman shot a large bullock then released the body from the shooting box onto the floor of the abattoir. This time, he hadn't got it right and the bullock got up and started rampaging round the hall. Understandably, it was far from happy and was intent on making its escape. As it went towards the way out, someone came out of the office. The bullock charged straight through the doorway into the small office and started bellowing with rage, crashing around knocking everything flying. There was more action in that office than had ever been seen, before or after. There was only one door and no one could get to that, but the office staff came flying out of the windows, in a blind panic. Eventually a slaughterman went into the office and shot the beast again, but then they had the problem of getting it back out. There was no chance of getting back through that small door, so they had to cut it up and take it out in pieces. The mess was terrible.

I bought a Vauxhall Cresta from Ken Artus, one of my colleagues. It was the biggest car I had had to date. I had arranged for Ken to leave the car in the car park at work, ready for me to collect, after I finished my deliveries on Saturday. That day, I was the last lorry back, so the Cresta was the only car there. I got in and started the engine, I immediately noticed that the fuel gauge was on empty, so I made straight for the Blue Star Garage which was only about 150 yards away. I didn't make it, I only got half way there before it ran out of petrol. This was only the beginning of my short relationship with this car.

We decided to go on holiday to Scotland. My cousin Jenny was on holiday here in Gloucester with her husband so we took them with us. They lived in Wallyford, just outside Edinburgh.

I checked the oil and water prior to setting off and our spirits were high. About fifty miles up the road, just passing Birmingham, there was a terrific knocking noise coming from the engine. I pulled onto the hard shoulder and got the bonnet up. I pulled the dipstick out of its tube and found it to be dry as a bone. Fortunately I had half of a gallon can of oil in the boot, so I poured it all in. It hardly registered on the dipstick. This was a bit worrying so I decided to stop at the earliest opportunity to get another gallon of oil so I could top it right up. Fifty or so miles further on, the same thing happened again. I couldn't see any smoke coming out of the back and I couldn't see any oil leaking, but it was going somewhere. We used five gallons oil on the way there, but when we got off the motorway and slowed down a bit, the consumption seemed to drop. As we went through Edinburgh, the car started lurching to a halt then starting again with the lights on the panel flashing on and off. I got out again and lifted the bonnet. This time the battery had fallen off and was rattling around the engine compartment, shorting out whenever the terminals touched metal. I put it right and we travelled the last few miles to Jenny's house.

We stayed for a few days, then drove to Fauldhouse, between Edinburgh and Glasgow, to stay with Cath's Aunty Mary and Uncle Pat. They came with us for a drive around Loch Lomond, taking a circular route, coming back through Callander and Stirling. The car ran well and I was beginning to think our troubles were over.

At the end of the week we set off for home but hadn't gone very far when there was a terrific vibration coming through the car. It was so bad, I had to find a garage to take a look at it. The mechanic told me that all the engine bolts had fallen out, allowing the engine to move around, causing the universal joint to fail. He replaced the bolts and the joint and we set off again. I had had enough of this car by now and told Cath that I was going to go for home as fast as I could and if the car blew up we would leave it and get the train. I gunned it down the motorway and got all the way home without it missing a beat. I checked the oil when we got home and it hadn't used a drop. If this car thought it was going to get round me now after the last two weeks, it had another think coming. I sold it within a week and good riddance.

I came home from work one evening to find Cath in a distressed state. She had our little cat in her arms and told me that there was something wrong with him. As soon as I saw his poor little face, I knew what had happened. He had been shot with an air gun and the pellet had penetrated his nose, so that all that could be seen was the hollow base of the pellet. With his face so swollen, it was an awful sight, but we took him straight to the local vet in Stroud Road. When we arrived, the waiting room was full of people. I thought that as it was an emergency, they would see him immediately, but I was mistaken. The receptionist told us we would have to wait our turn. I remonstrated with her, but she was adamant that we would not be seen out of turn. I told Cath to go across the road to the phone box and find any vet who would see him immediately. She came back a few minutes later, telling me that a vet at Stewart's surgery in Painswick Road would see him as soon as we got there. When we arrived, Bill Stewart took him straight into a consulting room and started to attend to Tibbles. Bill Stewart reassured us that we had been right to seek emergency treatment. He made a full recovery and lived a long and happy life. This was the start of a good relationship with the veterinary practice belonging to Bill Stewart which has lasted twenty four years so far and I'm sure will last a lot longer yet.

A few weeks later, Cath was in the bedroom overlooking the back garden and the flats beyond. She called me over to the window to look at two cats squaring up to each other, in one of the neighbour's gardens. Suddenly, they leapt in the air and ran off across the gardens at breakneck speed. I had a feeling about what had happened and looked along the windows of the flats opposite.

219

I said to Cath, 'look! There he is, there's the cat shooter.'
We could see the barrel of a rifle poking out of a window. I had him caught. I knew who it was, it wasn't a youth, it was a grown man who had a reputation as a generally unpleasant character.

I wanted to go round there and give the bloke a good hiding but we decided to let the police deal with it in the proper manner. A policeman came to see us and told us that he had had a word with the person concerned and had told him that if he did it again he would be in trouble, but there was very little the police could do as it wasn't illegal to discharge an air weapon on private property. We were very disappointed at this outcome but had to accept what the policeman had said. in the light of my past experiences with the police, I should have known better. The policeman had given us a complete load of nonsense, not only was it illegal to discharge an airweapon across other people's property, it was also an offence to cause or intend to cause injury to a domestic animal. What a surprise, I had just come across another lying copper, too lazy to do his job properly. We had been fobbed off, but I was learning.

A few weeks later, I came home from work again, to find Cath hugging our dog Wimpy and crying her eyes out. I asked her what was wrong, but she didn't want to tell me. I insisted that something must have caused her to be so upset and eventually she told me that she had been in the garden with Wimpy when the cat shooter had come to the fence and told her that he would cause trouble for us and that he would hurt Wimpy in retaliation for us setting the police on him.

I was outraged, there was nothing that could stop me sorting this out, my way. I stomped into the back garden and saw him standing on his balcony. As I crashed through the fence between our gardens, I pointed up at him and shouted 'I'm coming for you, you bastard.' I went through the door and up the stairs to the door of his flat. I banged on the door, shouting for this so called hard man to come out. It soon became obvious that he wasn't going to open the door so I proceeded to bash it down. The door flew open and I went into the flat, I couldn't find him initially, until I got to the bathroom and found the door locked from the inside. I started to attempt to break down this door but it was more difficult with his weight against it from the other side. By this time I has started to calm down and thought that if he was this scared I had made my point. I shouted through the door that seeing as he was a coward, I was going, but if he ever gave me cause to return I wouldn't leave until the job was finished.

As I came out of the door of the flat, his immediate neighbours were standing there waiting for me. The man came towards me and pressed a large bunch of bananas into my hands. They thanked me profusely for giving them the best day they had had for ages. They said that this man made their lives a misery and it had been wonderful to see someone stand up to him. I asked them, why they had given me a bunch of bananas and it turned out that he drove a lorry for Fyffes and always had a supply. They told me to come as often as I liked if I wanted any more. I thanked them, but I never did. I was glad that some good had come out of a nasty incident.

Chapter 17
A New Dawn

Our new house in Brionne Way was beginning to take shape. From the plot we had originally chosen, a new house began to emerge. We were managing to save the deposit required and the excitement of the big day when we would move in was beginning to mount.

We knew things would be hard financially, but it meant everything to me to get into my own house. We wouldn't be able to afford new furniture but what we had would do for now. The only thing we would have liked was a new carpet, but that would have to wait.

One thing we did need was a washing machine, so we decided to take the plunge and go for an Indesit automatic at £80 in the sale at Comet. We could store it for a while until it was time to move in. I was starting to get domesticated. Things really were changing, I might have become housetrained but I would always be an individual with a wildness that would sometimes come to the surface.

When the big day came, I borrowed a lorry from British Beef Co and with a little help from some friends, managed to move all of our belongings in one load. Our new house had three bedrooms, two of which would remain empty for the time being. Everything was bigger and more spacious than we were used to. I felt like I had when as a boy I had moved from Clapham to Matson. Only this time the feeling was even more intense. The house was brand new and so light and it was ours. One of the greatest feelings I can think of. For the first time in my life I had a house with a garage and wonder of wonders, central heating.

We thought we were going to be able to live without any floor covering, but it was awful and we went out and bought the cheapest carpet we could find to lay in the lounge. It lasted us until we could afford a better one.

All along Brionne Way, people were moving in at around the same time. That summer we met with our new neighbours while we were all laying our new lawns and getting our gardens sorted out. A few years ago, no one would ever have believed it. We got to know more of our neighbours here than I had ever known anywhere else.

I did a good job on the garden, mainly due to the peat and manure I put on it. If the health inspectors had seen some of the things I carried in that meat lorry, I would have been locked up. I took bins of manure home from the piles that were kept in the fields behind the abattoir. When I was on the Taunton run, I started calling in to the peat farms around Sedgemoor. At first I only brought a few bags to spread on the garden, but when I realised how cheap it was, compared to the prices at the garden centres, I started bringing back tons at a time and selling it.

During the next couple of years, Cath and I prospered, not due to the peat sales, which only lasted a short time. Cath was working and earning good money. I was still driving lorries but left British Beef co and went to work for Goodrem and Nicholson, Export Agents.

While working for Goodrem and Nicholson, I regularly went to France and had some good experiences there. I often went to "Airospaciale Francais" a company on the outskirts of Paris. One weekend I was able to take Cath with me, allowing us to have a weekend in Paris. They seemed to treat me with much more respect than I was used to in England. They always made sure that while the lorry was being unloaded, I had a really good meal at their expense. When I arrived on Friday with Cath, I asked if I could leave the lorry in their compound while we went into Paris. They said, of course I could. The manager sent a secretary to take Cath and me for a meal, telling us to come back to see him before we were ready to travel the twenty miles into Paris. After the meal, we went to see the manager who told us that he had arranged a car to take us to Paris. We looked outside and there was a big black chauffeur driven car, the chauffeur wearing a grey suit and hat, it looked very grand. Then he gave me an envelope, which he said contained a small map and enough money to pay for a taxi from Paris, back to the plant. The chauffeur took us to Paris and drove around the city, showing us the sights, before dropping us on the Champs Elysees. The only problem we had was trying to get a taxi driver to take us the twenty miles back to the plant. They didn't seem to want to go outside the city, but eventually we found one who agreed to take us. On the journey we had a little conversation with the driver, as much as his little bit of English allowed. When we got near to the plant, the driver stopped to ask a soldier if he was on the right road. While talking to the soldier, the taxi driver said that he was carrying two wealthy English people. I only speak schoolboy French, but I picked up what he had said. He was astonished when suddenly, I told him that we weren't rich, I was just a lorry driver. I told him the story of how we happened to be taking a taxi all this way, he was flabbergasted. We had a real good weekend away.

On one of these trips to France, I went to an agency at Orly Airport to pick up a small consignment of springs for Dowty Rotol. When I collected these few boxes, I had no idea what would be in store when I got Southampton. When I went out, I was carrying missile guidance systems. The documents I carried, allowed me to go through Customs on both sides of the Channel, without inspection or delay. When I arrived at Southampton, off the overnight ferry from Le Havre, I had to get in the queue along with everyone else. When it came to my turn to be inspected, the Customs Officer took one look at the paperwork, gave a sharp intake of breath and said, 'I can't let this in, it's military equipment.'

I said, 'military equipment? It's a few boxes of springs.'

He said, 'No, it says military equipment here, we're not allowed to inspect it, you'll have to wait until we can get further instructions.'

He put a seal on the lorry and told me to make sure I didn't allow that seal to be broken. Six hours later, after lots of phone calls and arguing, I was told that I would have to go to Bath.

I thought, Oh well, at least that's in the right direction, maybe I'll get home tonight after all. When I got to Bath, they told me I was in the wrong place. The only Customs office that could handle military equipment was in Portishead, so off I went again. I arrived at Portishead at quarter to five, after landing in Southampton at seven thirty in the morning. I reported at the office, only to be told that they would be closing in fifteen minutes and there would not be time for an inspection today, the lorry would have to be impounded for the night.

I said, 'come on mate, I'm only half an hour from home. Can't I come back in the morning?'

He said, it would be all right as long as I was back, bright and early at nine-o-clock, with the seal unbroken.

So I was on the road again, this time for home, but still not clear of Customs. After spending the night at home, I arrived back in Portishead at the specified time. About half an hour later, an Officer arrived and said, 'okay let's have a look at what you've got here.'

He broke the seal, pulled the doors open and looked inside. He said, it's only springs.

I said, 'I've been trying to tell everybody that since yesterday morning.' He just closed the doors back up, stamped my papers and said, you can go now. It took about thirty seconds for him to clear the load, but about twenty-six hours to find anyone with the authority to do it. What a situation? It turned out that these springs that everybody had been so concerned about, were valve springs for an engine that would end up in a military vehicle. Very frightening.

My friends often said that they thought a job driving abroad must be really good, but it wasn't so glamorous. They never thought of the rough crossings where everybody was sick all night. The boat banging and crashing through the waves making so much noise and vibrating so badly that I couldn't get a wink of sleep. The cold nights spent on the dockside waiting for the ferries to load, having to wait for hours on end due to cancellations due to bad weather or strikes. Like anything it had its good side and it's bad side.

I also regularly went into a number of extrusion die factories, collecting dies for export. After a while I realised how high the wages were compared to mine. My old friend Chris Rogers, worked at one of them and I asked him what were the chances of getting a job. He said he would find out for me. The next time I went there, the boss came over and said that Chris had told him I would like a job. I replied that I would. He said okay, you can start as soon as you like. So a week later I started in the extrusion die industry and have since spent most of my working life in it.

We spent most of our time and money on things for the house and improving our lifestyle. I managed to finish the last reincarnation of my BSA Lightning. I completely transformed it into a chopper with long forks and beautiful custom paint job. I also bought my first Jaguar for the princely sum of £500, it was a 1967 240 saloon in Old English White. I liked it so much that as time went on, I hinted to Cath that we should look for an E Type. After a lot of searching, we bought a 1967 4.2 litre 2+2 fixed head coupe in blue, costing £2750. It was absolutely magnificent, like driving a guided missile. We hurtled about at speeds up to 150 miles an hour.

We drove to Llangrove to see my old friends Phil and Ruth Large. Phil was working for Rockfield Recording studio so we decided to take the E type for a quick run down to Monmouth to see "Rush" the Canadian heavy rock band, who were recording a new album. One of the band fell in love with the car and offered to buy it, but it wasn't for sale at that time.

After about three years at Brionne Way, we decided to look for something bigger. We decided to look for an older house, finally deciding to move to Tuffley Crescent, where we chose one with four bedrooms and a large attic room. This house would give us plenty of room to move around in. It was a long way from the small council houses I had been brought up in. A long way in terms of satisfaction and a long way in terms of size but not so far in distance. I was still a Gloucester boy and didn't want to go far from my roots. The best thing about owning our own house was the very fact that we could live where we wanted, in the kind of house we wanted, rather than be told by the council where to live and what to live in.

In order to raise some extra money to enable us to afford to buy our new house, we decided to sell the E Type and buy something small and cheap. So the E Type was sold, realising £3000. To get me to work, I bought an old 850cc Mini for fifty quid, it was quite a come down but I've never been much of a car person. As long as a car doesn't give too much trouble, I'm happy. It's when they go wrong I get annoyed with them. This old Mini didn't have much going for it though. It was a rough old banger, full of rust. I drove it to work one morning, as I opened the car door to get out, it fell off with a resounding clatter. The hinges on those Mini's were bolted to a thin steel "A" shaped panel which had rotted through causing the door to just drop off when it was ready. I bought a new panel quite cheaply and the problem of welding it on was solved by an offer by Steve Craven, one of my workmates. After work, we got the car into the factory and started the job. We had to cut off the old panel, position the new on and weld it on. We only had oxy acetylene gas welding equipment available to us, not the best option, but better than nothing. Steve did a good job on it and in no time the door was back in position. My friend Hughie MacPherson was here on holiday from Australia and I had asked the boss, 'Brian Boon', if I could borrow the firm's Land Rover so that Hughie could use my Mini. After the repair, Hughie was to drive the Mini home and I was to follow him in the Land Rover. As I followed him, I kept wondering what he was playing at. The lights kept flashing and every time he used the indicators he turned the wrong way, though sometimes all four of them flashed at the same time. The brake lights kept going on and off for no reason, there were lights flashing on and off all over the place, it was like a mobile Christmas tree complete with twinkling lights. By the time we got home, Hughie and I were laughing our heads off, we had both realised that something had gone seriously wrong with the wiring. I took off the panel behind where we had been welding and found that all the wires ran down the windscreen pillar and down behind the door where they had melted from the heat of the welding, fusing the plastic of the wiring into a solid block so they could short out at random. By heaving on the mass of wires until my eyeballs bulged, I managed to drag enough of the wiring loom down so that I could cut out the melted bit and join then together with those little white electrical connector blocks. There were so many of them that by the time I had finished, the repair was so large that I couldn't get the panel back on properly. But what the hell, It worked.

Shortly after this, we made the move to Tuffley Crescent. Again I managed to borrow a lorry. My old friend 'Andy Richards' was still working for Goodrem and

Nicholson and he borrowed the lorry for me, so with a little help from some friends we managed to do the move with very little expense.

We were also very lucky in Tuffley Crescent that we had P.J. and Nora Wade as our neighbours. Good neighbours make a big difference to a happy existence. We have never been in each other's pockets but have been good friends.

Very soon after moving into Tuffley Crescent, the Mini failed the MOT and wasn't worth spending the money to repair it. The rear sub-frame had rotted and would have been expensive to renew, but the whole car was a rust bucket. I had also got fed up of having to wear wellingtons to keep my feet dry every time it rained. I had drilled holes in the floor to let the water out but even these kept getting blocked. It was just too bad. It had to go.

Our next car, a BMW 2002, we bought from a garage in Longsmith Street. It was my first experience with a dodgy car dealer masquerading under a guise of respectability. From the beginning there were problems that had to be addressed. I had spotted the problems before I took the car but was foolish enough to believe the dealer when he said he would put them right at my convenience. Once he had my money I could never get hold of him even when I visited the garage. After trying for weeks to get satisfaction, I had to resort to what I knew best. I went to the garage only to be told once again that the owner was unavailable. I went into the workshop where I knew the mechanic working there, we had been at school together. I asked him to pass a message to Peter, the owner. The message was that I would not contact him again. He was to come to my house, take the car away and get everything done to my satisfaction within a week or I would find him and beat the crap out of him. I told Lennie to be sure that he made Peter understand who I was and that the threat would be carried out. He obviously got the message because he soon turned up on my doorstep with a completely different attitude. Once sorted out, that car lasted me for years.

Not long after this, Cath passed her driving test, so we went looking for a second car. We looked at lots of old Mini's and Austin/Morris 1100's. We saw some terrible sights until finally we saw an ad in the Citizen for a choice of two Volkswagen Beetles at a part time dealer in Churchdown. One was £400 and the other was £500. When we arrived I looked at the two Beetles, parked side by side. The one for £400 was in a terrible state, it had the rust in and where it had been welded, part of the interior had been damaged by fire. The one for £500 was a beauty, there was no comparison. The dealer came over and asked if we were

227

interested. I said we had come with £400, hoping to buy a Beetle but we weren't interested in the one for that price. We liked the more expensive one and would buy it for £400. He laughed and said, be sensible, make me a near offer and it's yours. I told him that we only had £400 and had no way of raising any more, in fact if I paid him the full amount, we would struggle to eat for the rest of the week. He said no, he wouldn't sell at that price. I said it was a pity as it was just what we were looking for, then thanked him for his time, turned and started to walk away. We were almost back to the car, when he came running up to us and said, just give me the £400 and a few quid for the tax and you can take it. I replied that I was really sorry, when I said I couldn't raise another penny, I meant it. It's £400 or nothing. He started bleating that he wouldn't make a penny on it but we could have it. I said I would take the car if he put a new MOT on it. I thought he was going to burst into tears, but he agreed. We got up the road and started laughing, we knew we had got a bargain. The next day we collected what was undoubtedly the best buy we ever made. That car gave us great service for fifteen years before we sold it for a more modern Volkswagen that couldn't hold a candle to that old Beetle.

One evening I got a phone call from Suresh Karadia who was by now a successful photographer, living in a fashionable part of London. He told me he had two invitations to the British Film Awards to be held in a Drury Lane theatre. He couldn't go himself due to another engagement so he thought of Cath and me. We arranged to meet at a MacDonalds burger bar in Marble Arch, it was the first fast food outlet we had ever seen. There were two in London but none that I knew of anywhere else. Suresh said to me that it was a new thing in this country and if I had any money I should buy a MacDonalds franchise and set up in the Gloucester area because it was a thing of the future, sadly I didn't have the kind of money required. We thanked him for thinking of us with the tickets and the trouble he was going to to meet us and show us where to go. In his usual modest way he said it was no problem, he was glad to do it for us. He is truly a gentleman. From MacDonalds, Suresh led us through London to the Theatre, showed us where to park, wished us a good evening and left us to it. He had told us to go in through the side entrance to avoid the crowds, but when we got inside we found ourselves crossing a glass corridor. There was a crowd outside and it was obvious they were trying to see who it was crossing the corridor, then all of a sudden we were in the auditorium. It was then that I realised that we were not in the public gallery, which was upstairs, separate from the area we found ourselves in. I saw film and television stars all around us and thought we must have taken a wrong turn. I walked up to a security man and showed him our invitations, I asked him if we were in the right place not thinking for one minute that we were.

The guard answered, 'yes sir your seats are there', pointing towards a seat next to Joanna Lumley. We were surrounded by people we had seen on our screens for years. John Ford, the film producer was also seated near us, as was Toyah, Judy Geeson, Barbara Windsor and her husband Ronnie Knight, George Cole and Dennis Waterman. There were so many stars there, I can only remember a small number of them. Michael Aspel was the host for the evening. Denholm Elliot picked up an award for his part in Zulu Dawn. Seated at the front was Princess Grace of Monaco, as well as two of our greatest comedians, Eric Morecambe and Ernie Wise. After the ceremony, everyone went into a private bar for a drink but we knew that we had nothing in common with any of them, so we just looked around, then left. It was a great evening out though, one we could never forget. It was televised live, but it was in the days before we had a video recorder so we never got to see it.

What a change from a few years earlier when I couldn't afford to eat without stealing vegetables from my neighbours garden. Driving to London in my BMW for a flashy event then coming home to the comfort of my own house. Very soon we had that video recorder and goodness knows what else that my parents couldn't even have dreamt of.

In 1980 Aunty Ethel died, bringing to an end the link with my childhood in Clapham. The loss of my Great Aunt was probably a greater emotional wrench than the loss of my parents. I can't explain the reason for that except that somehow I expected her to go on forever. At the age of 94 she had outlived two generations of her family, then suddenly she slipped away.

Although the loss was great, this time I didn't feel that I was being left alone. This time I had Cath to share my feelings with and to help me through it.

Epilogue

I hope you have enjoyed reading about this part of my life. Gloucester has changed beyond recognition in the thirty years covered in this book. I have also changed a lot during this time and am reasonably happy with my circumstances. I have come to realise that I am never going to be completely satisfied with my lot and even though I have a wonderful wife, a nice house and a comfortable standard of living, I will always be dogged by a deep sense of failure.

In the years following the end of this book, I went on to become a shooting champion, competing in this country and in America. I learnt to play the harmonica and have played the blues on stage with some great artists. I have also learned to play the guitar, something I wish I had done when I was young enough to make more of it, but now I play just for the pleasure of it. I still ride a motorcycle, though my trusty BSA is only a memory. I ride a Harley Davidson now.

I am a reasonably accomplished photographer and have a portfolio spanning such diverse subjects as sporting events, fashion modelling and musical events. I have sold many of these photographs over the years; Bella Freud, the fashion designer, purchased one of Kate Moss. I took a picture at the Gloucester Guildhall of Kent Duchaine, an American National Steel Guitar virtuoso. Kent has used this picture for the cover of one of his compact discs and for his promotional material, such as posters and on T-shirts. Many of my sporting pictures have been used in publications as diverse as The Irish Post and The Target Gun Magazine.

When I think about my achievements and my standard of living, one thing that saddens me is that my parents are not here to see it. My mums illness and subsequent death was a great blow to our family. She represented the softer side of life. Once she was gone there was only masculine hardness left. The balance was all wrong. It might have sounded as if I didn't think much of my dad, but nothing could be further from the truth. He was his own man and I respected him for that and in our own way, we loved each other. Sometimes I do things and think to myself how like him I am. I think that's what life after death means. If you have children, you live on through them. I chose not to have any children so when I die that will be the end of me.

It may seem that I have blamed others for my failures at school. I do not mean to do so, just to explain things as I remember them. I talk to young people now and find that they are so positive in their goals. The encouragement that they get at school is so different to what it was in my experience. Their aspirations are so much greater. When I left school, I didn't know anyone who went to university or had a degree. Now the children of many of my friends go to university and have a clear plan of what they intend to do with their lives. Whether such a positive environment would have helped me I will never know. I was very headstrong so I have the feeling I may still have rejected any help that might have been offered. I blame no one for my lack of education but myself.

Even though I am essentially an insular person, I am lucky enough to have some good friends, most have been mentioned somewhere in this book. Without them I would not have the rich experience of life that I have had. These friends sometimes say to me that they envy some of my talent at one thing or another, but to me my talent is very limited. I admit to a modest amount of success in certain endeavours but can never get away from that overwhelming sense of failure, which sometimes bears down on me like a ton weight.

Gloucester, my hometown. I staked a claim to a very small part of it when I bought the house in which I live, but my memories of Gloucester are far more valuable than any material possessions. Those memories are a source of comfort to me. When I feel down, I can go into town and just walk around. Maybe I'll bump into a friend, maybe not, but everything is so familiar it doesn't matter. I feel good just being there among my own people.

It is a great source of pride to me to be a Gloucester Boy